The New Q

the NEW Q

A Fresh Translation with Commentary

richard **valantasis**

t&t clark

NEW YORK • LONDON

T & T Clark International, Madison Square Park, 15 East 26th Street, New York, NY 10010

T & T Clark International, The Tower Building, 11 York Road, London SE1 7NX

T & T Clark International is a Continuum imprint.

Cover design: Lee Singer

Library of Congress Cataloging-in-Publication Data

Valantasis, Richard, 1946-
    The new Q : a fresh translation with commentary / Richard Valantasis.
        p. cm.
    Includes index.
    ISBN 0-567-02571-3 (hardcover) — ISBN 0-567-02561-6 (pbk.)
1. Q hypothesis (Synoptics criticism) 2.   Bible. N.T. Gospels—Criticism, interpretation, etc.   I. Title.
    BS2555.3.V35 2005
    226'.066—dc22

                                                                2005012892

Printed in the United States of America

05 06 07 08 09 10   10 9 8 7 6 5 4 3 2 1

For Will and Allie,
Janet and Chris,
Del and Nancy
—Readers Extraordinary

Contents

Acknowledgments

I completed the final draft and revisions of this book with the help of EKEMEL, The European Center for Translation and the Human Sciences, at its House for Writers in Lefkes, Paros, Kyklades, Greece. EKEMEL's facilities, under the able supervision of Kyrio Niko, provided quiet, comfortable surroundings in which to write and to revise. The other translators and authors who passed through the house during our stay provided intellectual stimulation and social camaraderie during the often frustrating writing process.

My dean at Iliff School of Theology, Thomas Troeger, encouraged me to take a quarter's research leave to finish writing this book. His encouragement for my scholarship and writing helped me complete this book in the months I was released from all other academic administrative and teaching duties. I deeply appreciate Iliff School of Theology's emphasis on scholarship and publication, which a realistic and generous research leave policy makes achievable.

Štelios Ghikas, Monique Mailloux, Mouschoula Kontostavrou, Demetri Stavrakis, Maria and Aristides Varrias, our friends on Paros, have spent hours hearing me talk about these sayings and their interpretations. The wine, the food, the view of Paroikia's harbor, and especially their enthusiastic engagement with the intellectual life probably helped the book along more than they know.

The summer I finished the first draft, my grandnephew Will, then in kindergarten, sat with me and read from real books for the first time. Reading opens new worlds, and I was amazed at the speed at which his imagination took flight. His sister Alexandra has of course already achieved expert status in reading, but the imaginative process continues in the narratives that they create to fill an afternoon on the hammock at our summer home at the shore, telling endless stories "like in the chapter books." They learned to value reading, imagination, books, and the things of the spirit from their parents, Janet and Chris Maurillo, whose house is replete with many, many books to stir the imagination and delight the mind and the eye. Del and Nancy Brown, first colleagues and now dear friends, spend hours with my wife Janet and me, talking about what we have read and, of course, reading each other's writings. The progression—Will, Allie, Janet, Chris, Nancy, and Del—constitute a noble sequence of generations of people who will read Jesus with imagination, joy, curiosity, enthusiasm, critical skepticism, and sheer astonishment at the words themselves. I dedicate this book to them and to their intense delight in reading.

Introduction

I have always wanted to hear the voice of Jesus unmediated and directly. That probably explains why I love the hymn that begins, "I heard the voice of Jesus say, 'Come unto me, and rest.'" That hymn, as do many hymns and writings, indicates that a living person may hear the words of Jesus directly, in the ear, in the mind, without the filters of other people's interpretations and without the intrusion of other people's understanding. That desire to hear the unmediated voice of Jesus led me to study the sayings traditions translated and analyzed here.

In antiquity, people collected the sayings of certain respected wise philosophers and religious figures because the sayings seemed to encapsulate their teachings and their lives. "Encapsulate" sounds too distant. These sayings made the revered teacher present again through the intellectual effort to study and interpret the sayings after their contemporary followers no longer lived or studied with them. Sayings were a kind of telepathic presence.

Followers of Jesus, treating him in the same way as they would any revered philosopher, gathered his sayings to retain and honor the words, beliefs, emotions, values, thought patterns, bon mots, humor, wit, and character of their beloved teacher. The collection of the sayings, however, did not represent merely an attempt to keep the memory of Jesus' actual words or deeds alive for them. Followers collected his sayings in order to help themselves became part of the empire of God that Jesus proclaimed. They did not wish merely to preserve memory, because Jesus as a living presence in the life of both individuals and communities was always accessible through prayer, or revelation, or the promulgation of a saying likely to have been spoken by Jesus if he were ever in a particular circumstance. So the sayings do not provide history as we know it, nor even biography as we know it. The sayings provided a means of formation for early followers of Jesus and their successors, you and me, to engage in a process of formation of self and community. Those engaged in hearing Jesus' sayings and reading his words and deeds sought to transform themselves, their society, and the world in which they lived. The collection of Jesus' sayings presented Jesus' words to his hearers, his seekers, his listeners in such a way that they were empowered to interpret, to understand, to confront the meaning for their own lives, and to enact the empire of God that Jesus proclaimed. By engaging the sayings of Jesus, participants in the Jesus movements transformed themselves and their world as well as learned about the character of their beloved teacher. I wrote this book to hear, or in this case to read, Jesus' words.

I began my own quest by turning to the only extant manuscript of a collection of Jesus' sayings, the *Gospel of Thomas.* Thomas's gospel does not have a biblical narrative to tell me how to interpret the sayings of Jesus, no biographical frame to give context to the sayings, and no history of biblical exegesis to direct my attention to the traditional meaning of words and phrases in the Christian context. There is only Jesus' voice, narratively connected with the phrase, "Jesus said." Repeated over and over, this phrase gave me direct, unmediated, and imaginatively challenging contact with the voice of Jesus preserved on the page. I wrote a commentary on the *Gospel of Thomas* not to explicate the problems of early Christian literary history or to discover the original words that Jesus might have spoken, but to hear the voice of Jesus. In my commentary I read the gospel as a seeker engaging with the words of a living person.

The recent publication of the critical edition of the Sayings Gospel Q enabled me to engage in this exercise of hearing Jesus again. Q is actually not a real document. It does not exist on its own. Rather, Q is a scholarly reconstruction of a supposed source used by Matthew and Luke to supplement their revisions of the Gospel of Mark. Scholars, including myself, have long been fascinated by the literal similarities between the sayings material in Matthew and Luke; for over a hundred years, they have posited a single sayings source that would account for those linguistic and grammatical similarities. A dedicated group of scholars, among them the editors of the reconstructed source, James M. Robinson and John S. Kloppenborg, began over a decade ago to create a text that could have been the text that both Matthew and Luke had before them as they wrote their gospels. It was a painstaking and difficult task, requiring not only knowledge of the theological and linguistic tendencies of the writers of Luke and Matthew, but also knowledge of the *Gospel of Thomas*, Mark, and other early Christian writings. They succeeded in producing a text that allows me again to hear the voice of Jesus, to read Jesus directly and without mediation. I am deeply indebted to their work.

This commentary begins with a fresh translation of the work intended to make the reading of the sayings of Jesus accessible to a wider public. I have tried to avoid "Bible-speak" wherever I could (there are not many of us today who say "Woe to you!" or "Behold!" in our common speech!). I have also tried to hear the voice of Jesus as it might have been heard by a seeker, not necessarily a believer, but someone interested in hearing the voice, in getting the information for him- or herself, in encountering that presence and deciding what it means and how to incorporate it into his or her own thinking and living.

The Formative Function of Sayings Collections

Sayings collections present information in a very interesting way. Obviously, the sayings themselves were at some point spoken to a group of people—that original performance of the oral text cannot be recovered. The original speaking voice of Jesus has been lost forever. But a collection of sayings presents itself as the collected recordings of these initially oral performances: they purport to present in written form what the speaker originally performed orally. As a written source, a collection of sayings permits others to perform them either orally before others or silently in their minds. Sayings carry forth the original speaker's presence in different circumstances and at different times. So in hearing a saying, each hearer or each reader enacts the same saying in his or her own context and in his or her own times so that the voice of the teacher transcends the original oral performance and interjects itself into new times, new circumstances, new ears, new minds, new communities, and new cultures. In a sense, the voice can be heard long after the speaker's speech has disappeared. In fact, in antiquity readers always spoke the words, so the readers also both performed the text and became its hearers. So the voice persists—not quite *the* original voice, but a voice refracted through others' voices. Hearers and readers connect with that voice through their engagement with the sayings collection.

So why would anyone want to enact a saying? Why would a community continue, long after the death of the philosopher, to keep the sayings alive by rehearsing them alone and together? Why collect sayings and make them available to other individuals and communities? As I said earlier, historical memory or biographical information did not impel the collection and promulgation of sayings. Those historical and biographical impulses fascinate modern and postmodern people more. Ancients used sayings as a means of personal and corporate formation. The sayings functioned as a way to engage with the mind and voice of the speaker so that the hearer and reader could experience the presence of the speaker instantiated in the saying. That presence experienced through the hearing and interpreting of sayings promoted different understandings among the hearers and readers. By thinking through each saying, meditatively and intellectually, pursuing the various strands of meaning woven into the saying, the saying gradually changed the readers' and the hearers' perception of themselves, their social relationships, and their world. That new perception, those new avenues of understanding, moved each participant slowly, incrementally, and almost imperceptibly toward becoming a different sort of person, which the sayings themselves promulgated. The sayings made a difference, a profound difference, to the lives of the hearers and readers and to the way that they lived in the world; they had a transformative function, and people engaged with them precisely to be transformed.

An Ascetical Approach to the Sayings of Jesus

Another way of articulating this concept is to say that the engagement with the sayings had an ascetical function. Asceticism describes the way I read these sayings. I define asceticism as performances within a dominant society intended to inaugurate a new subjectivity, different social relations, and an alternative symbolic universe. The point of asceticism and of ascetical formation revolves around doing things (performances, actions, deeds, including thinking and analyzing) intended to create a new identity subversive of the identity promulgated by the dominant culture in which the ascetic lives. Asceticism, as opposed to formation *for* living in the dominant culture, creates a subversive alternative. Since social relationships inherently enable and support particular identities, this subversive alternative identity demands new social relationships to sustain its viability in a hostile context. And since the symbolic universe authorizes the sustainable patterns of a culture by providing the often submerged intellectual, scientific, and theoretical underpinnings necessary for such patterns to exist, the new subjectivity demands changes in the symbolic universe that will authorize the subversive subjectivity. In other words, asceticism creates a whole package for a new, subversive identity, social relationships, and intellectual foundation.

Engagement with the sayings accomplishes this ascetical transformation. The sayings, both individually and certainly as a whole collection, alter the parameters of self, social relationships, and the symbolic universe by continually forcing readers and hearers to consider something different. By thinking through the sayings, the readers and hearers allow themselves to be nudged into a new understanding of themselves. The interpretive process forces the readers and hearers to think in different ways, to consider new ideas, to envision different economic relationships, to engage in different political and religious activities, and alternatively to reconceptualize the divinity and the divinity's relationship with self, community, and cosmos. Gradually, over the course of reading and hearing the sayings, a new subjectivity emerges, along with new concepts of social relationship and responsibility as well as new ways of understanding the world. While each sayings collection holds an implicit understanding of self, social relationships, and intellectual universe so that it develops the subversive identity in a particular direction, it is unable to stipulate the exact parameters of the readers' and hearers' emergent subjectivity. The collection, that is, promulgates certain aspects of the alternative lifestyle without having the capacity to define the identity specifically. Varieties of subjectivities emerge from interpretation of the sayings, all of them fostered by the sayings within a certain range of possibilities that the sayings collection promulgates. Readers of this book will see how these three categories (subjectivity, social relationships, and symbolic universe) function within these particular sayings of Jesus.

I think that Jesus' followers engaged with his sayings not so much to learn about Jesus and his personality, but to train themselves for the empire that Jesus proclaimed. Jesus did come proclaiming an empire alternative to the Roman and Jewish imperial structures existent or envisioned in his time. Usually that empire is translated "kingdom of God," a phrase that has become so spiritualized and devoid of significant meaning that I have avoided it altogether in my translations. An "empire" (Greek, *basileia*) organized the political, social, economic, and religious realities of a given society, sometimes ruled by a king (as in a local authority in the Roman Empire) or by the emperor of Rome. The same word describes both small local and large global political structures. I cannot imagine Jesus' empire being of the local and regional variety. His use of the term seems more global, more universal, and so I translate his *basileia tou theou* as the empire of God, correlating it directly to the universal power and authority of the Roman imperial structure. Jesus did not proclaim a mere tweaking of authority and power in the Roman context, he advocated a complete over-throw and revision of all structures of power and authority under the divine and imperial authority of God, who alone rules both the heavens and the earth. This revision constitutes a radical imperial policy that I wanted to emphasize in my translation.

Doors to the Empire of God

The sayings of Jesus provided one door to the empire of God in the early church. There were other doors as well. Paul relates that he came to know Jesus through a revelation of Jesus that sent him on a mission to the Gentiles, non-Jews in the lands outside Palestine (see Galatians 1:11–15). He does not seem to know the sayings of Jesus, although he speaks at times of having received a "word from the Lord," which may have functioned in the same way (see 1 Corinthians 7:10 and 25). Although the content of his preaching and the issues he discusses in his letters diverge significantly from the subjects found in the sayings collections, Paul still proclaims the empire of God enthusiastically and energetically. So revelations became another door to the divine empire.

Apocalypticism also provided a door to the empire of God. Apocalyptic scenarios of the end of the age and the end of time when God will judge the deeds of the living and the dead pervade the various early writings of the Jesus movements. These followers of Jesus envisioned a cataclysmic end that would fully inaugurate the empire of God. An image of the magnificent destruction of worldly empires and the simultaneous establishment of the divine empire spurred these believers on, both to warn others of the impending doom and to prepare themselves for their own judgment. Jesus functions as the heavenly figure who will bring about the end, so these apocalyptic followers tended not to interest themselves in the earthly sayings or the revelations of Jesus, but to orient themselves completely toward the impending doom. We find such apocalyptic scenarios in Mark 13, in the letters of Paul (see, for example, 1 Thessalonians 4:13–18 and 5:1–11), and even, as we will see, in some of the sayings of Jesus.

Yet another door to the empire of God was a kind of biblical meditation on Jesus' actions, particularly on his miracles. We know that some followers of Jesus collected his sayings and promulgated them as a kind of biblical meditation on the significance of the empire of God as a reformulation and renewal of the religion of Israel. The miracles show Jesus as replicating the great events of Israel's mythic epic as a new Moses, a new Elijah, or a new Elisha. This worked in two ways: Jesus' Mosaic miracles evoke critical incidents in Israel's epic, such as the parting of the sea (see Mark 4:35–41; 6:45–51) and the feeding of the multitude in the desert (Mark 6:34–44, 52), while his healing miracles and his raising of the dead invoke the deeds of the great prophets of Israel, Elijah and Elisha. Followers reflected on these miracles as indicators of a new era, a new stage in Israel's sacred history inaugurated by Jesus and manifest in his miraculous deeds.

Other doors to the divine empire certainly existed and could be listed here, but these suffice to make the point that multiple avenues for entrance into the empire of God existed in the earliest period of the development and expansion of the divine empire inaugurated by Jesus. These multiple ways of entering the divine empire speak of multiple movements among the followers of Jesus. The gospel narratives portray one simple (and, I might add, simplistic) narrative of Jesus and the inauguration of the empire of God: Jesus begins in Galilee with his baptism, gathers a dedicated cadre of uneducated male disciples, meanders among the predominately (and, some would think, exclusively) Jewish communities of the region, and ultimately dies by crucifixion while on the only trip he ever took to the capital city, Jerusalem. The

evidence provided by early Christian writing does not support this explanation of Christian origins. Paul was no simple fisherman—he traveled, had
messengers at his disposal, wrote with the aid of secretaries, sent literarily
and rhetorically sophisticated letters of substance and of some length to
communities dispersed throughout the Mediterranean world. Paul's writings in fact constitute the earliest window on a Jesus movement that we have
available, and they show a very different image of Christian origins than do
the narrative gospels. In addition to Paul, other indicators point to multiple,
divergent, and complex origins for the early Christian movements announcing the empire of God. The various doors (sayings, revelations, apocalypticism, miracles) provide some inkling of those diverse avenues toward the
proclamation and entrance into the divine empire. It is proper, therefore, to
speak not of *a* Jesus movement, but of *many* Jesus movements, which probably preached and conducted missions simultaneously among various social
groups and in various settings throughout the Near East and the
Mediterranean basin. Throughout this book I refer to Jesus movements in
the plural in order to underscore these multiple and coeval missionary
efforts.

In commenting upon the sayings of Jesus in this book, I am developing
and concentrating on only one of the strands of early Jesus movements. This
is an important delimitation of my project. I do not wish to portray the Jesus
movements arising in the interpretation of Jesus' sayings as the primary, or
as the original, or even as the most important means of accessing the true
meaning of the empire of God that Jesus proclaimed. I want simply to
explore one of the many options and follow it to its logical conclusion. Many
New Testament scholars consider the sayings as the core material for understanding the (singular) original Jesus message and thus essential to understanding the historical Jesus. I am not among those scholars. As I stated
above, I think there were multiple avenues and multiple directions for both
Jesus and his various followers from the very beginning. Perhaps it would be
best to explain to you my own theory of Christian origins.

Diversity, Universality, and Christian Origins

For my construction of Christian origins, I begin not with Jesus in the New
Testament, but with Paul. What enabled and who authorized Paul to begin

a mission in the name of Jesus Christ and to travel the Mediterranean world announcing the empire of God that Jesus inaugurated? I respond that it was, of course, Jesus who empowered and authorized Paul to do this. But Paul did not know Jesus in his earthly life; Paul encountered Jesus in a different way (Galatians 1:11–24) and yet understood his mission as extending and promoting the very same divine empire that Jesus proclaimed and promoted. Paul's message and concerns differ significantly from those found in the sayings of Jesus, and yet the church recognized Paul as a valid promoter of the empire of God, even if his message differed from and contradicted the perspectives and teaching of other apostles numbered among those who knew Jesus during his earthly life (James, John, Peter, and the others mentioned in Galatians 2:1–14).

The diversity found in Christian literature results from just this process of empowering people who have had an experience of Jesus to proclaim the empire of God in their own contexts, taking up their own concerns, engaging with the people immediately around them and in their own cultures and languages. This empowering impulse explains the very diverse and often conflicting strands in early Christian literature (gospels, epistles, and acts, for example). The narrative gospels for unknown reasons chose to portray the Jesus movements as singular and all directly related to Jesus, but the New Testament canon argues a very different concept of diverse, localized, fully empowered people who never had any contact with the earthly Jesus but who had an experience of Jesus that drove them into itinerant mission. Some followers like James, Peter, and John seemed to have aligned themselves with the Jerusalem temple and with established Judaism, while others like Paul engaged entirely with non-Jews and foreigners. But the possibilities for different understandings and articulations of the empire of God were as diverse and rich as the many people who experienced Jesus and began to proclaim it.

So Jesus, whether in person or by some revelation, empowered people everywhere to establish the divine empire. That part of Jesus' message, the sayings, come down to us only in Greek (without a sense that they have been translated) indicates that Jesus intended a universal mission to everyone—Jew, Roman, Greek, Samaritan, Syrian, Phoenician. In short, Jesus attempted to communicate with anyone who knew the common language of the Greek and Roman world of his time. The gospel narratives, again for unknown reasons, find such a blatant creation of the empire of God sufficiently problematic that they later developed an alternative view of Christian origins, but the larger biblical witness itself moves in the opposite direction. The proclamations are diverse in subject, orientation, and application because of the varied contexts in which they were proclaimed and lived.

So the wisdom sayings in Q, the heart of the message regarding the new wisdom in the empire of God, attest to that universal mission: they were originally spoken and preserved in a Greek that would be readily accessible to the general population. A wide variety of Jesus movements existed because a wide assortment of people empowered by Jesus proclaimed the empire of God in diverse contexts to diverse people. Christian origins evolved from just such a combination of empowerment and diversity.

Q, A Collection of the Sayings of Jesus

A number of ancient texts preserve sayings of Jesus. The most accessible example is the *Gospel of Thomas*, which has been discovered in a variety of different texts, both Greek and Coptic, from the ancient world. The ancient Christians collected and published collections of the sayings of Jesus for use by Christians and perhaps even by Jews and Romans. Q is one of those early collections of Jesus' sayings.

But Q, unlike Thomas, does not really exist. As I explained earlier, scholars have created Q out of overlapping material in Matthew and Luke that is not found in Mark. Long before the discovery of the *Gospel of Thomas*, which consists entirely of sayings of Jesus strung together, scholars theorized that just such collections of Jesus' sayings must have existed. The scholarly consensus attempted to make sense of the fact that many verbal correlations exist between some sayings in Matthew and Luke, sayings each of them used as the basis of their gospels. Matthew and Luke used a collection of Jesus' sayings to revise and renew the Gospel of Mark, which both of them used as the outline for their own gospels. New Testament scholars call this the solution to the literary problem of the gospels: Matthew and Luke both use Mark in their gospels; they both use what appears to be a common source of sayings (Q); and they also use other material peculiar to themselves (referred to as M for Matthew; L for Luke). When scholars placed the common sayings material of Matthew and Luke side by side (synoptically), they realized that they seemed to be using much of the same language and, therefore, that they must have used the same text for writing their revision of Mark's gospel. In recent years, scholars have begun to reconstruct what they imagine to be the text that Matthew and Luke had before them.

Scholars define Q as that which Matthew and Luke have in common that does not come from Mark. Scholars assume that Mark did not know, or did not use, the collected sayings of Jesus as part of his gospel, even though Mark 4 contains a number of parables that properly come from some collection of Jesus' sayings. As a result of this way of thinking about the content of Q, material other than sayings have found their way into the reconstructed text of Q. This expanded material includes such accounts as the speech of John the Baptist (Sayings 1 and 2) and a miracle story (Saying 18), which the scholars have included in Q because of the way that they have defined what constitutes Q.

I do not believe that Matthew and Luke used *the same* collection of sayings of Jesus, but I think they each had a very similar collection of sayings that they used for their revisions of Mark in the writing of their own gospels. The same way that the *Gospel of Thomas* bears many verbal similarities with the sayings in Matthew and Luke without having a direct literary dependence upon them, so do the words of Matthew and Luke have close correspondence and verbal similarities without necessarily deriving from the same text. But having said that I doubt the same source was used by Matthew and Luke, I find it an interesting exercise to look at this collection of Jesus' sayings nonetheless. The vast majority of the sayings common to Matthew and Luke, derived as they probably are from a similar but not the same text, have sufficient agreement to treat them as a common, single source. I believe firmly that such collections of sayings existed, that the sayings indeed had a common form, and that many of them were sufficiently well known and widely read that they would be found in similar if not *exactly* the same language in many different parts of the Mediterranean and Near Eastern worlds.

In this book, however, I follow the editors of the critical edition of Q. These editors have painstakingly constructed a text that essentially captures the voice of Jesus as it was heard by both Matthew and Luke. Their resultant text provides a rich basis for hearing a Jesus unmediated by Mark or Matthew or Luke. Their pursuit of one common text does not in any way inhibit the process of reading the texts or attempting to hear the voice of Jesus in them, regardless of whether they came from one or from two or more different collections of sayings. These sayings present the voice of Jesus in written words, and they command our attention as important witnesses to what the early followers of Jesus heard either from Jesus directly or through visions and revelations of Jesus.

Reading Jesus

The critical edition of this reconstructed and theoretical text still serves my purposes well. I have two objectives: first, to model by my literary analysis, commentary, and interpretation how collections of sayings serve an ascetical function; second, to create a mode of reading Jesus' sayings and hearing his voice that instructs twenty-first-century readers in understanding how to work, to interpret, to puzzle over, to engage, and finally to come to their own understanding of the meaning of Jesus' words and to have in their own minds a sense of the timbre of his voice. As a historian, I find the process of trying to read through ancient eyes and to hear through ancient ears fascinating. So I tried to understand the sayings from within the context of the earliest readers and hearers. In the end, I also know as a historian that such a task remains beyond my capability. Not only have the performative voices of Jesus and his followers been lost, they cannot be recovered by someone living in a totally different culture in a totally different historical context. But the sayings are worth the effort, and I hope you find it as challenging and as fascinating as I do.

For the second purpose, I have tried for years to train students *not* to read the Bible as a flat, mono-signified text. Students and church people alike seem to think that scripture has *one* meaning, one single direct communication from the text to any historical context it encounters. I counter this mono-logical or monothematic way of reading with a revelatory reading: a reading of scripture intended to reveal a mysterious and ultimately incomprehensible God in inadequate and ultimately insufficient human language. Readers of the Bible in antiquity and through the Middle Ages sought revelation, knowledge, and suggestive meditative meanings that leapt from the literal meaning of the words into the moral/ethical meaning and finally rested on the bedrock of the spiritual or mystical meaning of the text.

Ancient readers read the biblical text as polysemic, complex, intentionally opaque so that they, of necessity, had to work hard to get to the meaning and significance for themselves and their times. This book tries to do the same.

The use of a text established by others who did not have the same purposes as I provided a kind of corrective. The incredible work of James M. Robinson, Paul Hoffmann, and John S. Kloppenborg in their critical edition *The Sayings Gospel Q in Greek and English; with Parallels from the Gospels of Mark and Thomas* (Minneapolis: Fortress Press, 2002) has provided the basis for my work here. If I both chose the text and commented on it, I could (and would) have omitted those difficult sayings or those sayings inconsistent with my method or theory of Christian origins. By using their text, I was forced to consider alternatives even to my own thinking and goals. Their text, I hope, kept me honest. The fact that we disagree about whether there was one collection (Q) used by both Matthew and Luke, or whether multiple editions of collections of Jesus' sayings circulating at the same time, does not impinge on the final product. I am confident that this reconstructed text of the Sayings Gospel Q probably circulated in one form or another with very similar words and phraseology. I have tried on the whole to be faithful to their text and to translate it carefully as the basis for my analysis and commentary, although in a very few instances I have altered their texts slightly to make more sense in English or to fill out the range of meanings implicit in the Greek language.

I have retained the critical edition's symbols for describing the texts in Matthew and Luke: square brackets ([ ]) around verses indicate the editors' uncertainty about whether the text was found in Q; question marks (? ?) also indicate uncertainty about a verse; and square brackets within the text indicate words added to fill in the Greek to make sense of a saying. In many cases, I have divided a saying into discrete enumerated sections such as (1) and (2) to aid in discussing what I believe to be the distinct parts of the saying. In the case of Saying 68, I have added material from both Matthew and Luke in order to provide some substance to the parable.

So I invite you now to engage with the sayings of Jesus. Perform them in your mind. Hear the voice of the speaker in your mind as you read and accept the instantiated voice of Jesus far removed from the historical Jesus but linked to him by his words. Shift perspectives often from Jesus to his historical audience, then to the early Christians reading, then to the people around you, then to your own circumstances. This playfulness enhances the many levels at which the sayings operate and enables readers to increase both their pleasure and the challenge of the words. For they were always challenging and confrontational, intended to inaugurate an empire of God that would confound all other empires to establish a transformative divine reign to remake the face of creation. These words were dangerous—dangerous enough for the Roman government to crucify their speaker as an imperial threat. To begin to understand their radical messages, people must begin simply by reading Jesus.

The Translation
of the Text

Saying 1
Q 3:7–9
Matthew 3:7–10 and Luke 3:7–9

(1) He said to the mobs coming to be baptized: "Snakes' kids! Who directed you to flee from the coming wrath?

(2) Produce fruit worthy of repentance

(3) and do not pretend to speak among yourselves, 'We have a father in Abraham,' for I say to you, 'God is able to raise up offspring for Abraham out of these rocks.'

(4) But already the axe is laid against the root of the trees. Every tree that does not produce good fruit is to be cut down and thrown into the fire."

Saying 2
Q 3:16b–17
Matthew 3:11–12 and Luke 3:16b–17

(1) While I baptize you in water, the one coming behind me is more severe than I, whose sandals I am not competent to carry. He will baptize you in a holy wind and fire.

(2) His winnowing shovel is in his hand and he will thoroughly cleanse his threshing floor and he will gather the wheat into his storage bin, but the chaff he will completely burn in an inextinguishable fire.

Saying 3
Q 4:1–4, 9–12, 5–8, 13
Matthew 4:1–11 and Luke 4:1–13

(1) Jesus was led up into the desert by the spirit to be put to the test by the devil. And since he was there for forty days, he was hungry.

(2) And the devil said to him, "If you are a son of God (and I know you are), speak [a word] that [will cause] these stones to turn into bread."

And Jesus answered, "It is written, 'human[s] will not live only on bread.'"

(3) And [the devil] invited [Jesus] to Jerusalem and stood on the eaves of the temple and said to him, "Since you are a son of God, plunge yourself down, for it is written, 'he will order his angels to act for you: they will catch you with their hands so that you will not strike your foot against a stone.'"

And Jesus answering said to him, "It is written, 'Do not test the Lord your God.'"

(4) And the devil invited him to an extremely high mountain and displayed to him all the empires of the universe and their glory and he said to him, "All these [empires] I will bestow upon you, if you bow down [and worship] me."

And Jesus answering said to him, "It is written, 'You will bow down [and worship] before the Lord your God, and you will give service to God alone.'"

(5) And the devil went away from him.

Saying 4
Q 6:20–21
Matthew 5:1–4, 6 and Luke 6:20–21

And setting his eyes upon his students, he said: "Blessed are the poor, because the empire of God is yours. Blessed are those who hunger, because you will be well fed. Blessed are those who grieve, because you will be comforted."

Saying 5
Q 6:22–23
Matthew 5:11–12 and Luke 6:22–23

You are blessed whenever they reproach you and persecute [you] and say every injurious thing against you because of the son of humanity. Rejoice, be exceptionally happy! Your restitution will be great in heaven, for in this way they persecuted the prophets who preceded you.

Saying 6
Q 6:27–28, 35c–d
Matthew 5:44–45 and Luke 6:27–28, 35c–d

Love your enemies and pray on behalf of those who persecute you, in this way you will become sons of your Father, because he makes his sun to rise over useless and capable, and he rains down upon just and unjust.

Saying 7
Q 6:29, [29–30/Matthew 5:41], 30
Matthew 5:39b–42 and Luke 6:29–30

Whoever strikes your cheek with a stick, turn the other to him as well. And to the one who wants to sue you in order to seize your underwear, hand over your clothes as well. And whoever presses you into service for one mile, go with him two. Give to the one who asks you; and from the one to whom you have lent, do not demand back what is yours.

Saying 8
Q 6:31
Matthew 7:12 and Luke 6:31

Precisely as you wish that folks do to you, that [is what] to do to them.

Saying 9
Q 6:32, 34
Matthew 5:46, 47 and Luke 6:32, 34

(1) If you love those who love you, what have you gained? Even the tax collectors do the same, don't they?

(2) And if you lend to those from whom you hope to receive, what have you gained? Even the Gentiles achieve the same, haven't they?

Saying 10
Q 6:36
Matthew 5:48 and Luke 6:36

Become a merciful person just as your Father is a merciful person.

Saying 11
Q6:37–38
Matthew 7:1–2 and Luke 6:37–38

Do not judge, [for fear that] you would be judged. For in that judgment you judge, you will be judged. And in that measure that you measure, it will be measured for you.

Saying 12
Q 6:39
Matthew 15:14 and Luke 6:39

Is it possible (and I know it is not) for a blind person to guide a blind person? Will not (and I know it to be true that) both fall into a ditch?

Saying 13
Q 6:40
Matthew 10:24–25a and Luke 6:40

A student is not greater than the teacher. It is sufficient for the student that he become just like his teacher.

Saying 14
Q 6:41–42
Matthew 7:3–5 and Luke 6:41–42

Why do you see clearly the bit of straw that is in your associate's eye, but do not observe closely the bearing-beam in your own eye? How [can you say] to your associate, "Let me cast out the bit of straw from your eye" and [not] look at the bearing-beam in your own eye? Hypocrite, first cast out the bearing-beam in your own eye, and only then [will you] see clearly [enough] to remove the bit of straw from your associate's eye.

Saying 15
Q 6:43–45
Matthew 7:16b, 18; 12:33b–35 and Luke 6:43–45

(1) There is no good tree that produces rotten fruit, nor again is there a rotten tree that produces good fruit.

(2) The tree is known by its fruit. Are figs gathered from an acanthus bush, or grapes from a prickly plant?

(3) The good person produces good things out of the good treasure and the evil person produces evil out of the evil treasure, for the mouth speaks from the abundance of a heart.

Saying 16
Q 6:46
Matthew 7:21 and Luke 6:46

Why do you invoke me [saying] "Lord, Lord," and not do that which I tell you?

Saying 17
Q 6:47–49
Matthew 7:24–27 and Luke 6:47–49

(1) Everyone who hears my oracles and performs them is similar to a person who constructed his house upon the rock. The rain came down, and the arroyos [literally: rivers] flowed, and the winds blew and fell upon that house, and it did not fall, for it was well established upon the rock.

(2) And everyone who hears my oracles and does not perform them is similar to a person who built his house upon sand. The rain came down, and the arroyos [literally: rivers] flowed, and the winds blew and struck that house, and immediately it fell, and its fall was great.

Saying 18
Q 7:1, 3, 6b–9, ?10?
Matthew 7:28a; 8:5–10, 13 and Luke 7:1, 3, 6b–10

And it happened that, when he had completed these oracles, he went to Capernaum. A ranking military officer came to him and implored him, saying, "My child is doing badly."

And he said to him, "Since I am coming, shall I heal him?"

And in answering, the military officer said, "Sir, I am not [sufficiently] acceptable for you to come under my roof, but [simply] say a word, and my child will be healed. For I myself am a person under authority, and I say to one person, 'Go!' and he goes, and to another person 'Come!' and he comes, and to my servant, 'Do this!' and he does it."

And when Jesus heard this, he was astonished and said to those following him, "I tell you, not even in Israel have I found such trust!"

Saying 19
Q 7:18–19, 22–23
Matthew 11:2–6 and Luke 7:18–19, 22-23

When he heard about all these things, John, sending [a message] through his disciples, said to him, "Are you the one who is coming, or should we look for another?"

And answering, he said to them, "Go announce to John that which you hear and see: the blind see again and the lame walk about, those with scaly skin are cleansed and the deaf hear, the dead are raised, and the poor receive good news, and blessed is the person who is not offended by me."

Saying 20
Q 7:24–28
Matthew 11:7–11 and Luke 7:24–28

(1) After they left, he began to speak to the mobs concerning John: "What did you go out into the desert to view [as spectators]? A wind-tossed reed?

(2) So what did you go out to see? A finely dressed person? Don't you get it that those who wear refined clothing live in kingly palaces!

(3) What, then, did you go out to see? A prophet? Yes, I tell you! Even more extravagant than a prophet.

(4) This one is he about whom it is written: 'Behold I myself send my angel into your presence; he will prepare your road ahead of you.'

(5) I say to you, there has not been raised up among those born of women one greater than John, but the one who is the smaller in the empire of God is greater than he is."

Saying 21
Q 7:[29–30]
Matthew 21:32 and Luke 7:29–30

For John came into your presence, and the [sinners and] tax collectors received him, but [the mobs did not].

Saying 22
Q 7:31–35
Matthew 11:16–19 and Luke 7:31–35

(1) To what shall I compare this age and to what is it similar?

(2) It is comparable to children sitting in the market streets calling out to

the others saying, "We played the flute for you, and you did not dance; we sang a dirge, and you did not cry."

(3) For John came neither eating nor drinking, and you were saying, "He's demonic!"

(4) The human one came, eating and drinking, and you were saying, "Here is an eating and wine-drinking person, an associate of tax collectors and sinners."

(5) Wisdom is determined by her children.

Saying 23
Q 9:57–60
Matthew 8:19–22 and Luke 9:57–60

(1) And a certain person said to him, "I will follow you wherever you might go!"

And Jesus said to him, "Foxes have dens and the birds of the heavens have protective covering, but the human one does not have anyplace to lay his head."

(2) Another person said to him, "Allow me first to return and to bury my father."

And he said to him, "Follow me and let the dead bury their own dead."

Saying 24
Q 10:2
Matthew 9:37–38 and Luke 10:2

He said to his students: "While the harvest is great, the laborers are few! So beg the master of the harvest to send out laborers into his harvest!"

Saying 25
Q 10:3
Matthew 10:16 and Luke 10:3

Go! Look, I send you as sheep among wolves!

Saying 26
Q 10:4
Matthew 10:9–10a and Luke 10:4

Don't carry a pouch, nor lunch bag, nor shoes, not even a walking stick; and salute no one on the road.

Saying 27
Q 10:5–9
Matthew 10:7–8, 10b–13 and Luke 10:5–9

(1) If you should enter into a house, say first, "[May] peace be upon this house." Then, if a child of peace is there, let your peace be upon him; but if not, let your peace be turned back upon yourself.

(2) In that house remain eating and drinking their [food], for the laborer is worthy of his salary.

(3) Do not travel from house to house.

(4) And if you should enter a city and they receive you, eat the things placed before you, and heal those who are sick in the city, and say to them, "The empire of God is close to you."

Saying 28
Q 10:10–12
Matthew 10:14–15 and Luke 10:10–12

But if you were to enter a city and they do not receive you, on leaving that city, shake the stirred-up dust from your feet. I say to you that it will be more tolerable for those living in Sodom than for that city.

Saying 29
Q 10:13–15
Matthew 11:21–24 and Luke 10:13–15

(1) Curses on you, Chorazin! Curses on you, Bethsaida!

(2) If the powerful deeds that were done in you were produced in Tyre and Sidon, they would have changed course in sackcloth and ashes. To be sure, it will be more tolerable for Tyre and Sidon at the end of the trial than for you.

(3) As for you, Capernaum, will you be exalted up to heaven? [No] you will fall into Hades!

Saying 30
Q 10:16
Matthew 10:40 and Luke 10:16

The one who receives you receives me, and the one who receives me receives the one who sent me.

Saying 31
Q 10:21
Matthew 11:25–26 and Luke 10:21

In [that hour] he said, "I give thanks to you, Father, Lord of the heaven and of the earth, because you concealed these things from the wise and intelligent, and revealed them to infants. Yes [I praise you], O Father, because in this way it became well-pleasing before you."

Saying 32
Q 10:22
Matthew 11:27 and Luke 10:22

All things have been transmitted to me by my Father, and no one knows the son except the Father, nor [does anyone know] the Father except the son, and the one to whom the son wishes to reveal (him).

Saying 33
Q 10:23b–24
Matthew 13:16–17 and Luke 10:23b–24

Happy are the eyes that see what you see, for I say to you, that there were many prophets and emperors [who desired] to see what you see, but they did not see [it], and to hear what you hear, and they did not hear [it].

Saying 34
Q 11:2b–4
Matthew 6:9–13a and Luke 11:2b–4

Whenever you pray, say, "Father, may your name be holy; may your imperium come. Give us today our daily bread, and forgive us our debts just as even we have forgiven those indebted to us. And do not lead us into [mere] experimentation."

Saying 35
Q 11:9–13
Matthew 7:7–11 and Luke 11:9–13

(1) I say to you: "Demand and it will be given to you, examine closely and you will discover, knock and it will be opened to you. For the one who demands, receives; the one who investigates, finds; for the person knocking, it will be opened.

(2) What person among you, of whom his son demands bread, would rather give him a stone? Or even if he were to ask for a fish, would give him a snake?

(3) If you, then, being worthless, know how to give good gifts to your children, by how much more will the Father in heaven give to those who demand of him?"

Saying 36
Q 11:14–15, 17–20
Matthew 9:32–34; 12:25–28 and Luke 11:14–15, 17–20

(1) And he exorcized a demon of muteness, and when the demon was cast out, the mute person spoke, and the crowds were astonished.

(2) And some said, "He exorcizes in [the name of] Beelzebul, the commander of the demons."

(3) Knowing their thinking, he said to them, "Every empire split into factions against itself is laid waste, and every household split into factions against itself will not survive.

(4) And if I myself exorcize demons in the name of Beelzebul, in whose [name] will your sons exorcize? For this reason they themselves will be judges over you.

(5) If then by the finger of God, I myself exorcize demons, then indeed upon you has come the empire of God."

Saying 37
Q 11:[21–22]
Matthew 12:29 and Luke 11:21–22

No one is capable of entering a strong person's house to steal from it without first tying up the strong person. Only then can the house be robbed.

Saying 38
Q 11:23
Matthew 12:30 and Luke 11:23

The one not with me opposes me, and the one who does not gather [people] together with me drives [them] away.

Saying 39
Q 11:24–26
Matthew 12:43–45 and Luke 11:24–26

Whenever the foul spirit has been exorcized from the person, it passes through arid places seeking rest, and it does not find it. It says: "I will return to my house from which I was exorcized." And returning, it finds [the house] swept clean and beautified. Then it goes out and it associates with itself seven other spirits more useless than itself and they come together to set up house there, and [so] it is that the last state of that person [is] worst than the first.

Saying 40
Q 11:?27–28?
Gospel of Thomas 79:1–2 and Luke 11:27–28

And a woman cried out: "Blessed is the womb that bore you and the breasts that fed you."

He said to her: "Blessed are the ones who heard the oracle of the Father and cherished it."

Saying 41
Q 11:16, 29–30
Matthew 12:38–40 and Luke 11:16, 29–30

Some desired a sign from him. He answered, "This generation is a worthless generation. It seeks for a sign, and a sign will not be provided it except the sign of Jonah. For just as Jonah became a sign to the Ninevites, thus even the son of the human one will be to this generation."

Saying 42
Q 11:31–32
Matthew 12:41–42 and Luke 11:31–32

(1) The Queen of the South will arise at the judgment with this generation and give sentence for it, because she came from the boundary of the

earth to hear Solomon's wisdom, and behold, here is something more than Solomon.

(2) The Ninevite men will arise at the judgment with this generation and give sentence for it, because at the preaching of Jonah they repented, and behold, here is something more than Jonah.

Saying 43
Q 11:33
Matthew 5:15 and Luke 11:33

No one lights a lamp and places it in a hidden place but instead places it on a lamp stand, and it provides light to all those in the house.

Saying 44
Q 11:34–35
Matthew 6:22–23 and Luke 11:34–35

(1) The eye is the lamp of the body.

(2) If your eye is clear, all of your body is luminous, but if your eye is useless, your whole body is dark.

(3) So, if the light that is within you is dark, how great is the darkness!

Saying 45
Q 11:?39a?, 42, 39b, 41, 43–44
Matthew 23:1–2a, 6–7, 23, 25, 26b–27 and Luke 11:30, 41–44

(1) Damn you, Pharisees, because you tithe mint and dill and cumin and you chuck justice and mercy and trust. It was necessary to do these, not to chuck them.

(2) Damn you, Pharisees, because you cleaned the outward parts of the cup and the plate, but the inward parts are full of greediness and incontinent living. Clean the inside of the cup and the outside will also become clean.

(3) Damn you, Pharisees, because you love the prime seats at dinner parties, and the front seats in the synagogues, and greetings in the marketplaces.

(4) Damn you, Pharisees, for you are like invisible tombs, and people who are walking upon them do not know it.

Saying 46
Q 11:46b, 52, 47–48
Matthew 23:4, 13, 29–32 and Luke 11:46b–48, 52

(1) And damn you, legal scholars! You bind up loads and place them upon human shoulders, but you yourselves do not want to move them with your finger.

(2) Damn you, legal scholars! You lock up the empire of God in front of people. You did not enter nor did you permit those who were coming to enter.

(3) Damn you! You constructed tombs for the prophets, but [it was] your fathers [who] killed them. You yourselves acknowledge that you are sons of your fathers.

Saying 47
Q 11:49–51
Matthew 23:34–36 and Luke 11:49–51

For this reason also Wisdom said, "I will send prophets and sages to them, and they will [choose to] kill and to banish from among them, so that an account of the blood of all the prophets that was spilled from the creation of the world may be demanded from this generation, from the blood of Abel to the blood of Zechariah who was killed between the altar and the house. Yes, I say to you, an account will be demanded from this generation!"

Saying 48
Q 12:2–3
Matthew 10:26–27 and Luke 12:2–3

(1) Nothing is veiled that will not be unveiled and hidden that will not be made known.

(2) That which I say to you in the dark, tell in the light and that which you hear in your ear, preach upon the housetops.

Saying 49
Q 12:4–5
Matthew 10:28 and Luke 12:4–5

And do not be fearful of those who kill the body, but are not able to kill the soul. Rather fear the one capable of destroying the soul and body in Gehenna.

Saying 50
Q 12:6–7
Matthew 10:29–31 and Luke 12:6–7

(1) Are not five sparrows sold for two coins? And one from among them will not fall down to the ground without your father.

(2) And even all the hairs of your head are numbered.

(3) Do not fear: you yourselves excel over many sparrows.

Saying 51
Q 12:8–9
Matthew 10:32–33 and Luke 12:8–9

(1) Whoever would agree with me before people, the son of humanity will agree with that person before the angels.

(2) Whoever would deny me before people will be denied before the angels.

Saying 52
Q 12:10
Matthew 12:32a–b and Luke 12:10

And whoever would speak a word against the son of humanity, it will be forgiven that person, but whoever would speak against the holy spirit, that person will not be forgiven.

Saying 53
Q 12:11–12
Matthew 10:19 and Luke 12:11–12

When they bring you into synagogues, do not have an anxious mind about how or what you might say, for the holy spirit will teach you at that time what you should say.

Saying 54
Q 12:33–34
Matthew 6:19–21 and Luke 12:33–34

Do not hoard for yourselves treasures on earth, where moth and corrosion destroy and where thieves dig through and steal, but hoard for yourselves treasures in heaven, where neither moth nor corrosion destroy and where thieves do not dig through nor do they steal.

Saying 55
Q 12:22b–31
Matthew 6:25–33 and Luke 12:22b–31

(1) So I say to you, "Do not worry about your life, what you might eat, nor about your body, what you will wear. Is not life more than food and the body [more than] clothing?

(2) Consider the crows, they neither plant nor reap, nor gather into storage bins, and God feeds them. Are you not more excellent than birds?

(3) And who among you through worrying is able to add an arm's length to his height?

(4) And why are you worrying about clothing? Acquire knowledge from the lilies, how they grow: they don't work hard nor do they spin, but I say to you, even Solomon in all of his glory is not clothed as one of these.

(5) Then if God so dresses the grass in the field, present today and tomorrow thrown into a cooking pan, will [God not dress] you much more, O small-minded believers?

(6) So do not worry, saying, 'What shall we eat?' or 'What shall we drink?' or 'How will we be dressed?' Search first for his empire, and all these things will be delivered to you."

Saying 56
Q 12:39–40
Matthew 24:43–44 and Luke 12:39–40

(1) Understand this: If the master of the house knew in which night watch the thief was coming, he would not have permitted his house to be breached.

(2) And you yourselves must be made ready, because the son of humanity comes at an hour you do not imagine.

Saying 57
Q 12:42–46
Matthew 24:45–51 and Luke 12:42–46

(1) Who indeed is the trustworthy and sensible slave whom the master appointed over his household slaves so that he would serve them food at the right time?

(2) Happy is that slave whom, when the master comes, he finds [the chief slave] so doing. I am sure that he would appoint him over all his possessions.

(3) But if that slave should say in his heart, "My master takes a long time [to return]," and he will begin to hit his fellow slaves, [while he himself] eats

and drinks with the drunkards, that slave's master will come on a day that he does not expect and in an hour that he does not know, and he will punish him severely and set his destiny with the untrustworthy.

Saying 58
Q 12:[49], 51, 53
Matthew 10:34–35 and Luke 12:49, 51, 53

(1) Fire! [That's what] I have come to cast upon the earth, and how I wish it had already burst into flame.

(2) Do you imagine that I came to cast peace upon the earth? I did not come to cast peace, but a dagger.

(3) I came to divide into two: son against father, and daughter against her mother, and [new] bride against her mother-in-law.

Saying 59
Q 12:[54–56]
Matthew 16:2–3 and Luke 12:54–56

When it is evening, you say, "Fair weather, for the sky shines fiery red." And in the morning: "Today is winter, for the lowering sky shines fiery red." You know how to discern the appearance of the sky, but are you not able [to discern] the fullness of time?

Saying 60
Q 12:58–59
Matthew 5:25–26 and Luke 12:58–59

When you meet your adversary in a lawsuit on the way, make it your business to free yourself from him, lest [the legal adversary] hand you over to the judge, and the judge [hand you over] to his underling, and the underling throw you into jail. I tell you: you will not escape from there, until you pay the last penny.

Saying 61
Q 13:18–19
Matthew 13:31–32 and Luke 13:18–19

To what is the empire of God similar and to what shall I compare it? It is similar to a mustard seed, which a person, taking it in hand, threw into his garden. And it matured and became a tree, and the birds of the sky found covering in its branches.

Saying 62
Q 13:20–21
Matthew 13:33 and Luke 13:20–21

To what shall I compare the empire of God? It is like yeast, which a woman, taking it, hid in three pounds of flour until it leavened it completely.

Saying 63
Q 13:24–27
Matthew 7:13–14, 22–23; 25:10–12 and Luke 13:24–27

(1) Come in through the narrow door, because many will demand to enter and those who enter through it are few.

(2) Whenever the housemaster gets up and locks the door, and you begin to stand outside and to strike the door, saying, "Master, open for us!" and giving you an answer, he will say, "I do not know you!"

Then you will begin to say: "We ate and drank together, and you taught us on the main streets [of our town]!"

And he will speak to you saying, "I do not know you! Get away from me, you workers of iniquity!"

Saying 64
Q 13:29, 28
Matthew 8:11–12 and Luke 13:28–29

And many will come from the east and the west and will recline [to eat] with Abraham and Isaac and Jacob in the empire of God. But you will be cast into the outer darkness. [That is] where [there is] weeping and grinding of teeth.

Saying 65
Q 13:[30]
Matthew 20:16 and Luke 13:30

The lowest [person] will be [the] first [citizen of the city], and the first [citizen of the city will become the] lowest.

Saying 66
Q 13:34–35
Matthew 23:37–39 and Luke 13:34–35

(1) Jerusalem! Jerusalem! She who murders the prophets and stones the ones sent to her!

(2) How often I desired to collect your children, in the way that a bird collects her chicks under her wings, and you did not want it.

(3) Your house is abandoned!

(4) I say to you: you will not see me until it comes [to the point] that you say, "Blessed is the one who comes in the Lord's Name!"

Saying 67
Q 14:[11]
Matthew 23:12 and Luke 14:11

Everyone who exalts himself will be humiliated, and everyone who is humiliated will exalt herself.

Saying 68
Q 14:16–18, ?19–20?, 21, 23
Matthew 22:2–10 and Luke 14:16–21, 23

A certain person made a great dinner, and invited many [to it]. At the dinner hour, he sent his slave to tell those who had been invited, "Come, because [the dinner is] now prepared." [One excused himself, citing the necessity of his] farm. [Another excused himself, citing the necessities of his business. And another excused himself because he was newly married.] [And the slave returned to his master and told him these things.]

Then the infuriated master of the house said to the slave, "Go out on the highways! As many as you find there, invite them to fill my house [with dinner guests]."

Saying 69
Q 14:26
Matthew 10:37 and Luke 14:26

Whoever does not hate father and mother is not capable of being my student, and whoever does not hate son and daughter is not capable of being my student.

Saying 70
Q 14:27
Matthew 10:38 and Luke 14:27

Whoever does not seize his cross and follow me is not able to be my student.

Saying 71
Q 17:33
Matthew 10:39 and Luke 17:33

Whoever finds his life will destroy it, and the one who destroys his life on my account will find it.

Saying 72
Q 14:34–35
Matthew 5:13 and Luke 14:34–35

Salt is good. But if salt becomes tasteless, in what will it serve as seasoning? Neither for the earth nor for the manure [used for fertilizing it] is it ready for use—they throw it out.

Saying 73
Q 16:13
Matthew 6:24 and Luke 16:13

No one is capable of serving two masters, for either she will hate the one and love the other, or he will cling to one and hold the other in contempt. You are incapable of serving God and Mammon.

Saying 74
Q 16:16
Matthew 11:12–13 and Luke 16:16

The law and the prophets [existed] until John. From that time, the empire of God is overpowered by force and the violent seize it hastily.

Saying 75
Q 16:17
Matthew 5:18 and Luke 16:17

It is easier to disregard heaven and the earth than for one iota or one letter-marking of the law to pass [without notice].

Saying 76
Q 16:18
Matthew 5:32 and Luke 16:18

Everyone who puts aside his wife and marries another woman commits adultery, and the one who marries the woman who is put aside [also] commits adultery.

Saying 77
Q 17:1–2
Matthew 18:7, 6 and Luke 17:1–2

It is necessary that the offenses come, but [damn the one] through whom it comes. It is more advantageous for that one if a millstone were placed around his throat and he were hurled into the sea than that he would offend one of these little ones.

Saying 78
Q 15:4–5a, 7
Matthew 18:12–13 and Luke 15:4–5a, 7

What person among you, having a hundred sheep and losing one from among them, does not leave behind the ninety-nine on the mountains and going forth searches for the lost one? And should it happen that he find it, I say to you that he rejoices over it more than over the ninety-nine who had not wandered away.

Saying 79
Q 15:[8–10]
Luke 15:8–10

(1) Or what woman having ten drachmas, if she were to lose one drachma, does not light a lamp and sweep the house clean and search until she finds [it]? And finding it, she invites her girlfriends and neighbors, saying, "Be happy with me, because I found the drachma that I had lost."

(2) Thus I say to you, a joy occurs before the angels for one person who fails of his purpose and who then changes course.

Saying 80
Q 17:3–4
Matthew 18:15, 21 and Luke 17:3–4

If your brother wrongs you, upbraid him, and if he changes course, forgive him. And if seven times in a day he should wrong you, also seven times you will forgive him.

Saying 81
Q 17:6
Matthew 17:20b and Luke 17:6

If you have trust just as a mustard seed [has trust], you could say to this mulberry tree, "Be uprooted and be planted in the sea!" And it would obey you.

Saying 82
Q 17:[20–21]
Matthew 24:23 and Luke 17:20–21

But being questioned about when the empire of God is coming, he responded to them and said, "The empire of God is not coming with close observation. Nor will someone say, 'Look, here it is!' For the empire of God is within you."

Saying 83
Q 17:23–24
Matthew 24:26–27 and Luke 17:23–24

If they say to you: "See, he is in the deserted places," do not withdraw [there]; "See he is in the storeroom," do not pursue [him there]. For just as lightning exceeds all bounds from east and appears as far as the west, so will the son of humanity be on his day.

Saying 84
Q 17:37
Matthew 24:28 and Luke 17:37

Wherever the corpse is, there the eagles will gather around.

Saying 85
Q 17:26–27, ?28–29?, 30
Matthew 24:37–39 and Luke 17:26–30

The day of the son of humanity will be just the same as things that took place in the days of Noah. For in those days, [people] were eating and drinking, marrying and giving in marriage, until the day that Noah entered into the ark and up came the flood and carried them off; so will it also be on the day when the son of humanity is disclosed.

Saying 86
Q 17:34–35
Matthew 24:40–41 and Luke 17:34–35

I tell you: there will be two men in the field; one is taken up and one passed by; two women will be grinding [wheat] in the mill; one is taken up and one passed by.

Saying 87
Q 19:12–13, 15–24, 26
Matthew 25:14–15b, 19–29 and Luke 19:12–13, 15–24, 26

(1) A certain person about to travel away summoned ten of his slaves and gave to each one of them ten minas, and said to them, "Engage in business

until I return." After a great period of time, the slaves' master returns and makes an accounting with them.

(2) The first one came saying, "Master, your one mina earned ten minas in addition."

And [the master] said to him, "Excellent, good slave, you were trustworthy in little things, I will place you over many [more things]."

(3) And the second [slave] came saying, "Master, your mina made five minas."

[The master] said to him: "Excellent, good slave, you were trustworthy in little things, I will place you over many [more things]."

(4) And the other [slave] came saying, "Master, knowing that you are a harsh person, reaping where you did not sow and gathering from where you did not winnow, and being fearful, I went out and hid your mina in the ground. Here! Take what is yours."

The master said to him, "You good-for-nothing slave! You knew that I reap where I did not sow and gather where I did not winnow! You should have put my silver pieces into the banks, and returning I would acquire what is mine with interest."

(5) So snatch the mina from him and give it to the one who has ten minas, for all things will be given to the one who has, but even what he has will be taken from the one who does not have.

Saying 88
Q 22:28, 30
Matthew 19:28 and Luke 22:28, 30

You who have followed me will sit upon thrones passing sentence upon the twelve tribes of Israel.

The
Commentary

Saying 1
Q 3:7–9
Matthew 3:7–10 and Luke 3:7–9

(1) He said to the mobs coming to be baptized: "Snakes' kids! Who directed you to flee from the coming wrath?

(2) Produce fruit worthy of repentance

(3) and do not pretend to speak among yourselves, 'We have a father in Abraham,' for I say to you, 'God is able to raise up offspring for Abraham out of these rocks.'

(4) But already the axe is laid against the root of the trees. Every tree that does not produce good fruit is to be cut down and thrown into the fire."

The saying has two elements: the saying itself communicates important information and it is ascribed to someone who is considered an authority by the community. Wisdom sayings are notorious for their tendency to drift from one authority figure to another. A saying attributed to Pythagoras (a pagan philosopher) is later ascribed to Sextus (a later pagan philosopher) and even later included among the sayings of Anthony the Great (a Christian ascetic) by Athanasius in his *Life of Anthony*. Given the nature of the sayings, this common occurrence makes sense. The combination of saying and attribution results in a definitive statement about some aspect of practical living that bears some authority within a community.

First, let's look at the content of the saying. This saying begins (1) with a narrative frame: "he said to the mobs coming to be baptized." The narrative establishes the nature of this collection as a series of sayings. It begins simply with "he said," and what will follow is not only this saying, but a whole collection of sayings. The "mobs" indicate that this and subsequent sayings do not consist of esoteric teaching. The narrator tells the reader that the speaker addresses ordinary people in a most impersonal and generalized way. But among that large group of generic persons, the speaker specifies that this saying refers only to those who have distinguished themselves by coming forward for baptism. The narrative introduction, then, provides a number of important clues about the collection of sayings that follows as well as the context for this specific saying.

Those who have distinguished themselves among the crowd have come forward to be baptized. The Greek verb "to be baptized" means simply to dip or plunge, with the connotation that the dipping and plunging takes place in water. These common folk come forward to be dipped or plunged in water. The action may signify, at its least suggestive level, a process of washing the body in water. At its most suggestive level, the action signifies the Jewish covenant renewal, a kind of metaphoric reenactment of the Israelite crossing of the sea into the promised land. This latter understanding suggests that the Jewish rite of baptism constituted a kind of personal appropriation of the sanctification produced by leaving Israel and coming back wholly oriented and faithful to the God of Israel. Whether one adopts the least or the most metaphoric signification, baptism indicates a new beginning for a person who has cleansed him- or herself of moral or physical dirt, or for a person involved in a community preparing itself for a new beginning, or the inauguration of a new era of human existence.

The narrative begins with a vituperative statement and message. The accusatory "snakes' kids," which negatively characterizes the hearers and those coming to be baptized, poses a question: "Who directed you to flee from the coming wrath?" The wrath here seems to imply a kind of apocalyptic view of the world, suggesting that God would soon release a cosmic wrath in order to separate the good from the bad as a preparation for establishing God's permanent reign on earth. We find this same perspective in Paul, who argued that the function of Jesus Christ was to hold back the just wrath of God until the Gentiles become part of Israel and enter into the newly established reign of God (1 Thessalonians and Romans). The wrath comes as a prelude to the establishment of God's reign, and someone has warned a group of people that they should flee before the wrath. We learn who those people are in the next part of the saying.

The next section (2) introduces the main theme of this saying: that all should produce fruit worthy of repentance. The general statement applies to everyone, not just the people addressed in the next part of the verse. I say this because the conclusion to the saying states the general principle that every tree that does not bear fruit will be cut down and destroyed. Repentance designates a shift in an understanding of the world, and "fruit worthy of repentance" is a metaphor for the process of manifesting in day-to-day life the reality of a change of thinking and living. Within this general group of people, however, the speaker singles out the Israelites who claim Abraham as their progenitor for particular attention (3). These people cannot claim election by virtue of their religious genealogy, because election comes from God, who may elect anyone whom God pleases. The same God who can give the Israelites water to drink from a rock in the desert can use the same power to produce Israelite offspring. God's miraculous power and authority to elect stands strong. So the necessity to manifest the reality of a new understanding of God's activity cannot be circumvented by reference to religious genealogy or tradition. Human reaction to God's activity must be articulate, manifest, and visible.

The point made at the end of the saying (4) summarizes the teaching. God begins to separate the productive from the unproductive agents of the divine plan. God will preserve the productive agents but destroy the unproductive. This judgment inaugurates a time of choice, of change, of reflection, of self-justification concerning one's own capacity to "produce fruit worthy of repentance." This sayings collection, then, begins with a call to choose, to start anew, to begin afresh, leaving aside the old conceptions and privileges and starting again from a decidedly different perspective.

Now we can turn to the ascription. This saying, reconstructed out of Matthew and Luke, has been attributed to John the Baptist. On the lips of John the Baptist, this saying becomes a propaedeutic, a preliminary educational introduction to a lesson presented more fully later. For John the

Baptist and his presumed coterie of Jewish followers, the message is apocalyptic, threatening, and points forward to the work of Jesus.

As in sayings collections generally, however, this saying may also be placed on the lips of Jesus (note how a similar speech of John the Baptist in John's gospel melds into a generalized discourse by Jesus, John 3:22–36, with the discourse beginning at verse 31). Here Jesus himself begins to speak in heavily judgmental and seriously apocalyptic terms to call his hearers to a change of orientation no longer dependent on religious tradition or genealogy and to manifest that change in concrete ways.

On the lips of either Jesus or John, this saying reaches back to an apocalyptic orientation in the earliest Jesus movements. The apocalypticism calls for a choice, a change, a reorientation, an integration of thought and action, which the impending judgment intensifies significantly. There is no time for leisure or for resting on the externals of status or genealogy, because the judgment has already begun.

Readers of the saying may locate themselves at two different points—they may be either part of the mob or one of the Israelites. The subject of the saying is the same for both groups, as is the injunction to bear fruit or bear the consequences. These sayings, then, have a universal significance in speaking both to Jews and to Gentiles, to Romans and to Greeks. The saying reaches beyond the narrative and speaks to any reader throughout the ages who is capable of hearing and responding to Jesus' words. So the universality of the message exists not only at the time of Jesus, but also to anyone at any time who picks up the collection of sayings to read them. The message applies to postmodern as well as to ancient people, to religious as well as to secular people, and to any seeker with a modicum of desire to hear the voice of Jesus at any time or any place. That universality makes sayings collections perpetually relevant.

Saying 2
Q 3:16b–17
Matthew 3:11–12 and Luke 3:16b–17

(1) While I baptize you in water, the one coming behind me is more severe than I, whose sandals I am not competent to carry. He will baptize you in a holy wind and fire.

(2) His winnowing shovel is in his hand and he will thoroughly cleanse his threshing floor and he will gather the wheat into his storage bin, but the chaff he will completely burn in an inextinguishable fire.

The judgment continues. The first part of this saying contrasts the present one with the coming one, which in turn juxtaposes the one who baptizes with water and the more severe and more powerful one who will baptize with holy wind (or holy spirit) and fire.

The saying also describes the relationship of the present one and the coming one by characterizing their associated power, authority, and stature. The present one cannot act as a servant, cannot even carry the sandals of the coming one, because the coming one (by implication) has greater status and stature than the one who is present. The coming one comes to distinguish the useful from the unproductive, the beneficial from the useless. In comparison to the first saying in this collection, the subject shifts from the nature of baptism to the nature of the separation of good from bad. The one who comes in power and authority will process those who have borne fruit (the wheat), gathering for safety and preservation those parts that are useful and burning the parts that are useless. Notice that this is not a separation of wheat and weeds from one another, but a separation of the parts of one plant: the seed from the chaff, the edible from the inedible, the useful from the useless. It is a separation of one unit into its constituent parts based upon their usefulness to human beings. The good, the morally upright and useful aspects of human life, will be separated from the bad. The fate of the good is to be preserved; the fate of the bad is to be burned so that the threshing floor will be clean.

The threshing floor (2) stands at the center of the saying, both thematically and narratively. The coming one separates wheat from chaff precisely in order to "thoroughly cleanse" the threshing floor. The emphasis is on the creation of a pure space, a clean place for harvesting the fruitful production of the grain. The separation does not in that sense constitute simply a judgment, but also a discerning and evaluative cleansing either of the individual or of the place where individuals meet. The thresher must clean the space used for processing the production of fruitful produce of the earth, either from an individual's or from the community's perspective. The point of the separation, then, seems to be the preparation and sanctification through cleansing of both the individual and the community. The community becomes holy by gathering in the useful and burning the useless, just as the individual person becomes holy by destroying the detrimental parts of his or her personality and by preserving that which is ethical and good.

The inextinguishable fire has cosmic connotations. This makes the point of the comparison significantly more intense. It is not simply a fire but an inextinguishable fire, suggesting eternal hellfire, an apocalyptic rain of fire, that destroys quickly, permanently, and perpetually.

Readers of this saying and hearers of the voice of Jesus cannot ignore the evaluation of personal and corporate growth and development. The powerful one yet to come will ultimately make the judgment to destroy the useless and to preserve the good, not so much to punish as to cleanse. The person and the community must be made sacred by purification, a purification not gentle but severe in its effects. The severity of the wind/spirit/fire baptism indicates an incremental but complete transformation, a ruthless evaluation and critical discernment of people and communities that none may avoid. This saying dramatizes the call to repentance and to renewal that the first saying introduces.

Saying 3
Q 4:1–4, 9–12, 5–8, 13
Matthew 4:1–11 and Luke 4:1–13

(1) Jesus was led up into the desert by the spirit to be put to the test by the devil. And since he was there for forty days, he was hungry.

(2) And the devil said to him, "If you are a son of God (and I know you are), speak [a word] that [will cause] these stones to turn into bread."

And Jesus answered, "It is written, 'human[s] will not live only on bread.'"

(3) And [the devil] invited [Jesus] to Jerusalem and stood on the eaves of the temple and said to him, "Since you are a son of God, plunge yourself down, for it is written, 'he will order his angels to act for you: they will catch you with their hands so that you will not strike your foot against a stone.'"

And Jesus answering said to him, "It is written, 'Do not test the Lord your God.'"

(4) And the devil invited him to an extremely high mountain and displayed to him all the empires of the universe and their glory and he said to him, "All these [empires] I will bestow upon you, if you bow down [and worship] me."

And Jesus answering said to him, "It is written, 'You will bow down [and worship] before the Lord your God, and you will give service to God alone.'"

(5) And the devil went away from him.

Musonius Rufus, a Roman philosopher contemporary with the collection of the sayings of Jesus, advocated a system of education based on memorizing texts or formulas that summarized a whole process of analysis so that students would be able to apply the old analysis to new problems. The proofs, as he called them, were then "ready at hand," memorized and ready to be applied to any new circumstance. In this narrative, we find the devil and Jesus engaging in the kind of argument through scriptural proofs about which Musonius wrote. They both have their arguments, summaries of entire ways of thinking, ready to be used in the intellectual contest between two students of God. The devil, as intellectual and spiritual adversary, puts Jesus to the philosophical test to discover who will win in the war of ready-at-hand proofs. In the end, the devil simply leaves Jesus, and the contest remains largely inconclusive: both have produced their scriptural proofs and countered one another, but there is no mention of a decisive win for either one.

In an academic environment, this kind of debate would have been common. It was a way of learning and of demonstrating and practicing what was being learned. At any time, a student could be called upon to recite proofs, to engage in debate with others, and to engage in an intellectual contest with other students of the same teacher. Such a contest could also help to establish the reputation of a new teacher.

But there is another way of reading this argument between the devil and Jesus, and that is as a scriptural "talking back" or a "speaking against," in Greek, an *antirhetikos*. In ancient ascetical literature, the writings of mostly Christian ascetics of the first four centuries CE, writers developed a series of "talking back to" or "speaking against" responses to temptations. Often organized by kind and degree of temptation, the *antirhetikos* provided a scriptural phrase to use in the contest with a particular temptation. The almost magical power of the scriptural verse overpowered and subdued the temptation and became a weapon in the monk's arsenal against the tempting demons. The genre grew out of this encounter between Jesus and the devil. Here Jesus offers scriptural counter-texts to the tempting texts quoted by the devil. Jesus is literally "talking back" through the scriptures. His ability to make the devil leave indicates his success. His quoting scripture helped him conquer the satanic attack and set him on the proper course; he passed the test. This was the function of the *antirhetikoi* (plural of *antirhetikos*).

The combination of the ready-at-hand Musonian proofs and the *antirhetikoi* makes this narrative about Jesus a model for the proper training of a follower. It says less about Jesus and more about those who follow Jesus: it provides an example of a way of living for ardent and true followers of Jesus' social, political, and religious movement. It is meant to communicate not simply the content of the test; it also provides ways to respond to tests/temptations as Jesus' followers encounter them. Two modes are presented: (a) a student/follower must study the scriptures to the point that he or she can use them as ready-made arguments available for any circumstance, and (b) the student/follower must learn the proper scriptural passage to talk back to temptations when they come. Such an orientation toward the modes of argumentation in the saying deflects from the intensely christological interpretations about the person of Jesus and the nature of his ministry found in most of the academic and pastoral commentary on this passage.

Having said this, we can now turn to an analysis of the content of the saying. Teaching/learning methods (proofs and *antirhetikoi)* are set within a narrative context of the testing of a student by a fellow student. Both Jesus and the devil have a relationship with God, who is implicitly their mutual teacher, and both have learned from their study, although clearly they have arrived at significantly different understandings of themselves and their importance. The Israelites learned about their God, having received the revelation at Sinai and the ordinances that bound them to God while they wandered in the desert. The desert also provided the place where later ascetic movements established their strongholds. The desert, therefore, functions as a place of learning and testing. The narrator presents this testing as part of the divine plan, since the spirit leads Jesus into the desert to this test.

Through scriptural quotations, the devil presents Jesus with three scenarios: to use his power to change stones into bread to satisfy his hunger (2), to perform powerful deeds to display his election (3), and to gain authority over every empire of the earth (4). Food, faithfulness, and authority—these are the three testing points.

Food is an important topic in these sayings. Followers are warned not to worry about food—or clothing, for that matter (Saying 55), and in fact those hungry participants in the movement that Jesus spearheaded are considered blessed (Saying 4). The sayings portray Jesus himself as an eater and a drinker (Saying 22). Jesus instructs his messengers not to take a lunch bag with them when they travel (Saying 26) and to eat whatever is put before them without any concern about it (Saying 27). So it is not surprising that one test involves food. While food and eating remain issues for those involved in the various Jesus movements, this saying says nothing definitive about food. The talking back rebuts the need for food with the acknowledgment that there is more to life than eating. The talking back then fulfills the expectation set up in Saying 55—that a believer should not worry about food because God will provide sufficient, if not abundant, food for those who remain trusting.

It is also not surprising that faithfulness that does not rely on powerful deeds is included here. Works of power, repudiated even by Paul in his argument with his Corinthian opponents, became an issue in the Jesus movements. Both participants and observers of the movements found these powerful deeds attractive, demonstrative of divine authority, and indicative of divine agency and presence. This connection between religious authority and personal performance finds a number of expressions in the sayings: the tree is known by its fruit (Saying 15); communities are judged by their ability to respond to religious authorities (Saying 29); and Jesus even performs a miracle of healing (the healing of the military official's boy in Saying 18). These powerful deeds, however, do not reflect the person performing them, but, as Jesus points out in his response, the faithfulness and power of God. A messenger does not test God by these deeds, but rather manifests the personal power bestowed upon the messenger by God. The powerful deeds function as agents of renewal and restoration, not as a self-justification for the messenger's power and authority.

Many of these sayings are about the divine imperium, the empire of God, frequently translated simply as the "kingdom of God." When the devil tempts Jesus with imperial power, he strikes at the heart of Jesus' words and sayings. The concept of a divine empire, ruled by God, inaugurated on the earth by Jesus, extended and advanced by those who have entered the divine empire through their trust in God, pervades these sayings and describes their central theme. This divine empire defines a participant's trust, actions, and state of being. Jesus attributes the glory and the dignity of the empire not to himself, but to the God who established it and who alone deserves service and worship. The talking back aptly describes the parameters of the empire organized by Jesus but serving God.

The school exercise, then, with its attendant modeling of the *antirhetikoi* responses to temptation, focuses on three central issues of the sayings of Jesus: food, powerful deeds, and the divine empire. The reader learns about these subjects; they are central and important themes, but the sayings contain so much more material to master. I conclude that what is important about this saying is not the specific content alone: the saying demonstrates how to use scriptural knowledge in discussion as well as the practice of talking back to temptations. In other words, readers of the sayings and hearers of the voice of Jesus refracted through them learn not only from the content of the saying, they also learn a model of discourse. The instruction operates at various levels. The saying provides a surplus of knowledge and understanding that thrusts its readers compellingly into the center of an ancient school of discourse, covering timeless issues and questions that continue to resonate with modern readers.

Saying 4
Q 6:20–21
Matthew 5:1–4, 6 and Luke 6:20–21

And setting his eyes upon his students, he said: "Blessed are the poor, because the empire of God is yours. Blessed are those who hunger, because you will be well fed. Blessed are those who grieve, because you will be comforted."

Ascetical teaching and the wisdom tradition relish irony and reversal. The fool actually turns out to be the wise or holy person; the prostitute turns out to be a secret ascetic and to have attained great holiness despite her supposed profession; the pure and holy person associates with the lowest members of society and lives among the least pure and the most sinful. Irony and reversal are important resources to promote growth in the religious life. We find such reversals here and in many of the sayings that follow in this collection of the sayings of Jesus.

For Jesus and for the Jesus movements, this process of reversal with its attendant irony was very important. So, in this saying, Jesus looks at his disciples as a collective of poor, hungry, and grieving people whose dedication to the movement has become central to their lives. They follow him, and that has not brought them riches and social status, or food, or perhaps even solace. And Jesus speaks three sayings to them. Each of the sayings associates the word "blessed" with something that on the surface is not blessed at all: poverty, lack of food, and grief. One would not normally associate the word "blessed" with these states; in fact, they appear to be the opposite. That is precisely the point! Those who experience these denigrating and debilitating states will find their fortunes and their status reversed: the poor will be welcomed into the imperial presence, the hungry will be fed, and the grieving will receive solace and comfort.

Such a theology of reversal, if you will, strengthens followers to interpret and to endure the debased status of poverty, hunger, and grief. The bad experiences open the way, by reversal, to the very best experiences. The poor will find a place in the divine society, the hungry will be thoroughly fed with food abundant, and the grieving will find the solace and comfort that alleviates their sadness. The purpose of the reversal is not just to bolster the ego or status of the participant in the movement; it enables the participant to endure hardship, to find courage in difficulty, and to live patiently through grief.

By focusing his eyes upon the students who are his followers, Jesus gives them direct instruction. Even those reading rather than hearing these words understand the importance of being looked "straight in the eye" and told the harsh truth: "You will be poor. You will be hungry. You will suffer loss and grieve." That truth, however, sets the stage for followers then and readers now to hear the reversal as well, addressed to each: "You will enter the imperial society, be fed well, and receive consolation no matter how much you have suffered." The narrative voice describes Jesus' action of looking intently at his then-disciples, but his voice now reaches beyond the historical context to speak directly to readers and hearers of his words at any time.

One final issue deserves brief mention. The word "disciple" has lost its educational associations in modern English because it has been used to designate an early follower of Jesus, one of those in Jesus' inner circle during his ministry. But the word in Greek emphasizes student status. Disciples were learners, mastering a new philosophy that inaugurated a different way of life. Jesus portrays himself as the gracious teacher instructing his students on the pain of their own education. Their learning will come at great cost—poverty, hunger, loss, and grief—and if they persevere in their debilitating state, Jesus guarantees them a reversal of their fortunes. It is precisely this kind of teaching that inspires students to persevere despite all odds.

Saying 5
Q 6:22–23
Matthew 5:11–12 and Luke 6:22–23

You are blessed whenever they reproach you and persecute [you] and say every injurious thing against you because of the son of humanity. Rejoice, be exceptionally happy! Your restitution will be great in heaven, for in this way they persecuted the prophets who preceded you.

The reference to the persecution of the prophets provides a starting point for understanding this saying. Here Jesus identifies the fate of his followers, emissaries, and other participants in the empire of God with the fate of the prophets. Just as their coreligionists and fellow Israelites, both elite and common, maltreated them, so will the participants in the movements Jesus inaugurated also be treated. They too will be reproached, persecuted, and verbally denigrated, just like the prophets.

The role of the prophet in the Israelite scriptures was to reveal the oracles of God. Prophets embodied a divine voice spoken to an often rebellious people whose lives and values had strayed from the divine path. They revealed the divine mind to kings, noble leaders, priests, religious leaders, and the ordinary Israelite. They often voiced bad news, decrying the sin and apostasy of the people and announcing divine punishment. The early Christian prophets functioned similarly: they carried the oracles of Jesus, the sayings and revelations of the divine one among them, from community to community. We can see this played out in the document known as the "Teaching of the Twelve Apostles," a second-century document that describes the ordering and rules for governance of early Christian communities. These prophets, then, functioned as revealers, but the revelation concerned not simply the judgment of God for a rebellious people, but now also a revelation of the establishment of a divine empire which anyone could enter. These missionary prophets carried these very sayings from place to place in order to shape and direct the communities of those who entered into God's reign.

Accepting this revelation, however, comes at a cost. Outsiders deem the revelation worthy of legal action (I have translated this saying from a decidedly legal perspective)—of pursuit, persecution, and slander. What seems to be good, wholesome, and intrinsically valuable to the prophets and emissaries of God's empire becomes the object of persecution and rejection. Here the saying guides readers and hearers to expect reversal and irony, and the saying does not disappoint us.

According to the saying, those who suffer persecution ought to account themselves blessed. It does not say "you will be blessed" in the future, but "you are blessed" in the present. There is something about the rejection and punishment that brings an immediate, present, ongoing blessedness. The very acts of revealing Jesus' truth and suffering the consequences bring a state of divine happiness, and this happiness is connected with the son of humanity, simultaneously on behalf of all human beings and on behalf of the special one called by God to represent all humanity in the divine plan. The witness and suffering of the missionary prophets and Jesus' followers connect them with the human one in their midst, bringing them great happiness and joy.

Two words with roughly the same meaning ("Rejoice, be exceptionally happy!" in English) emphasize the dramatic and intense quality of this joy. Not only do these emissaries of and participants in the empire of God experience happiness, but their current situation will also be reversed. They will find their recompense, their reward, their restitution in heaven. They may suffer in the human realm, a suffering that brings blessedness, on behalf of the one whose revelation they propagate and distribute. They may find happiness in being emissaries and revealers, and they will find a just reward for their labors in the heavenly imperial realm.

Heaven and earth are linked in this saying in a particularly interesting way. They do not represent separate realms. The effects of works performed on earth have a consequence in heaven. The two realms mutually reflect the influence of the other so that the effects of heaven (the revelation?) are made known on earth and the results of earth (the rewards) become operative in heaven. The empire of God, this saying seems to argue, encompasses both realms, both the work on earth with its attendant rejection and the work in heaven with its attendant rewards. Both realms, as part of the divine empire, contain blessedness and happiness. The prophets who carry the oracles of God may find themselves persecuted, rejected, and maligned, but they simultaneously experience happiness and joy, just as their ancient Israelite forebears did.

For readers and hearers of these sayings, the beginning seems ominous, filled with judgment, inextinguishable fires, hunger, poverty, grief, persecution, and the need to reverse all the negative effects of entering the divine empire through the interpretation of the sayings. Without any narrative by a gospel writer or a historical context in which the face and intonation of Jesus' voice is modulated, these sayings underscore the high cost of participating in one of the Jesus movements. They stand in stark juxtaposition to the gospels because they speak directly to the readers and hearers of these words without mediation, without the gentle guiding hand of a teacher or interpreter to apply them to new circumstances. Such interpretive contexts are built up in readers' minds as they meditate on the sayings.

Saying 6
Q 6:27–28, 35c–d
Matthew 5:44–45 and Luke 6:27–28, 35c–d

Love your enemies and pray on behalf of those persecute you, in this way you will become sons of your Father, because he makes his sun to rise over useless and capable, and he rains down upon just and unjust.

For modern people, the usual understanding of the relationship of a child to its parents is biological: parents and child have a genetic and biological bond that unites them. This becomes evident when we consider the time and money that childless couples invest in reproductive technology. Biology, however, did not form the basis of familial relationships in antiquity. Ancients normatively created and sustained their families by adoption. In adoption, the father made a decision, often in the ritual act of physically picking up a child, to accept the child into his household. This child, and often in the case of emperors they were actually adults, became a part of the family by choice of the paterfamilias, the head of the household. Even paternal biological offspring became children by adoption and choice rather than biological reproduction, so that a father could choose to expose (that is, *not* adopt) a child and condemn it thereby to death, slavery, or adoption by other people. Again, families did not constitute biological entities; they were constructed households.

This saying describes the criteria established by God, the paterfamilias of the Jesus movements, for the adoption of children into the divine household. The saying consists of three parts: first, the description of the criterion for adoption; second, the assurance of adoption; and third, a theological and moral principle that makes election into the family necessary.

The singular requirement for adoption into the divine household presented in this saying consists of one very simple instruction: "Love your enemies, and pray for those who persecute you." This startling statement flies in the face of the function of a household; namely, to protect and nurture its members. It instructs those who should find protection and security in the household to pray for those who would destroy or disturb its sanctity. Loving enemies expands the notion of household to include enemies. The saying inverts categories so that those who attack or are inimical to the household receive a gracious and hospitable response from its members. In a sense, this saying argues that the proper household includes both its members and its detractors and enemies, and the recognition of this reality provides the basis for adoption into the household. Seekers become sons of the Father as they love their enemies and pray for their persecutors.

Adoption into the household of God, then, requires potential members to respect, love, and pray for their enemies and persecutors as their means of entry, as the basis for their adoption in the divine household. This inverts the significance of adoption as well. One gains entrance not by the choice of the paterfamilias but by the actions of the potential adoptee. One gains entrance into the divine family by virtue of one's attitude toward one's enemies and the willingness to pray for one's persecutors. Not the Father's choice but the child's actions and reactions form the basis for adoption by the Father.

The third part of the saying explains this peculiar understanding of adoption. Why is it that one becomes adopted by one's actions and attitudes? Because the Father remains the father of the useless and the productive, the just and the unjust. God's fatherhood, if you will, encompasses the entire created universe both in its good and in its evil, its successes and its failures, and its justice and injustice. God does not differentiate; God offers everyone the opportunity of adoption into the household. Both the just and the unjust as well as the good and the bad, the useless and the capable, may find their way into the household of God if they love their enemies and pray for their persecutors. The sun does not discriminate on where it shines, nor does the rain distinguish upon whom it will fall—the moral categories remain irrelevant to both sun and cloud, because their function is to shine and to rain irrespective of those upon whom they operate. So it is with God, who provides the richness and the potential of adoption to all alike, holding out two simple criteria for adoption: love of enemies and prayer for persecutors. So simple, and yet so difficult a task to accomplish, then and now.

The voice of Jesus then and now challenges readers and hearers to reconsider the nature of their primary supportive community while questioning the biological basis of our concept of family. The divine empire demands new ways of forming and sustaining community, family, and all other relationships. Those who read these sayings and hear Jesus' voice in them cannot simply rely on the traditional relationships determined by their society and culture; they must seek instead to establish divine societies consisting of those who are loved and hated, friendly and inimical, and good and bad— over all of whom God reigns.

Saying 7
Q 6:29, [29–30/Matthew 5:41], 30
Matthew 5:39b–42 and Luke 6:29–30

Whoever strikes your cheek with a stick, turn the other to him as well. And to the one who wants to sue you in order to seize your underwear, hand over your clothes as well. And whoever presses you into service for one mile, go with him two. Give to the one who asks you; and from the one to whom you have lent, do not demand back what is yours.

The saying consists of four rather dramatic injunctions. Each one articulates a particular application of a general rule: that a member of the empire of God, or a participant in one of the Jesus movements, ought always to act generously, returning double of all that is asked or demanded. The rule seems rather innocuous in general, but the particular examples show the danger of such a simple rule of thumb. The examples play out the rule in the context of great personal harm and loss, and they show the harsh realities of daily living in the Roman Empire as well as the high expectations for those involved in this religious movement.

In the Roman context, the person striking another would always be a social and political superior. Generally, equals who valued dignity and social propriety would not put themselves in the position of striking one another and such punishment, especially administered to the face, would be reserved only for slaves. So this first example shows a socially powerful person striking one in a subservient relationship. The fact that the rule demands that the slave, the subservient person, turn the other cheek, offering it to be stricken as well, demonstrates the general rule of acting generously even at great personal cost. Although the action would seem ludicrous to the one doing the striking, turning the other cheek to be stricken would provide a participant in one of the Jesus movements the opportunity to bear witness to the depth of his or her commitment and faithfulness to the principles of the movement.

The same applies to suing others in court. Here we have a situation in which the litigants would be social equals and of sufficient standing to engage in the Roman legal system. One of them, however, wants to sue the other for his personal belongings, here signified by what I have called underwear (literally, the *chitōn*, the garment worn next to the skin) and clothes (literally, the *himation*, the outer garment often translated "coat"). When one person sues a member of a Jesus movement, demanding his or her undergarment, the person being sued is to offer his or her outer garment as well. In his advice to the Corinthians, Paul advised them not to take each other to court and not to allow one believer to defraud another. Courts were serious places and not the arena in which to air or resolve disputes. This saying agrees with that assessment and tells the one being sued, "Give more than what is asked; in fact, give it all!" But the saying provides no evidence that this injunction only concerns other members of the Jesus community. This saying indicates that avoiding court disputes and giving even more than is asked ought to be practiced with everyone without restriction and without distinction. Generosity is to be extended to everyone.

The saying provides early evidence for the conscription of local people by the Roman army. It appears that a military official, whose rank here is unspecified, could demand labor from a person for some limited amount of time or distance. This saying instructs the person to double the request: two miles instead of one. I suspect it represents a startling response to an intrusive and demeaning request.

The last part of this saying constitutes what is perhaps the most difficult of all the sayings for Christians today: "Give to the one who asks you; and from the one to whom you have lent, do not demand back what is yours." Most people lend money in order to make more money; the borrower pays back the principal plus interest for the use of the money. That defined lending both then and now. But here Jesus tells his followers to give whenever anyone asks and never to demand the money back. The issue here is not just about the interest; it includes the principal as well. This represents an amazing reversal of economic practice. It amounts to an injunction simply to give money away, whenever asked, with no thought of either getting it back or earning interest.

The generosity rule could be said to have two purposes: to draw attention to the adherents of the religion and to undermine normal social, economic, juridical, and cultural practices. There is no doubt that this rule of generosity would attract attention. Turning the other cheek, offering more than the law demands, doubling the length of a military conscription, and lending money without expectation of repayment—these constitute very dramatic practices for members of one of the Jesus movements, advertising their values in a dramatic way. At the same time, their actions provide a marked contrast to the culture in which they live, dramatizing and undermining its bankrupt, unacceptable cultural practices. The people devoted to living out these sayings live, think, respond, and react from a decidedly more generous position than the culture at large, and they are proud of it.

Saying 8
Q 6:31
Matthew 7:12 and Luke 6:31

Precisely as you wish that folks do to you, that [is what] to do to them.

This is probably the most universal and ancient of the wisdom sayings, found in Confucian, classical Greek and Roman, and Jewish texts, as well as here among the sayings of Jesus. That should not surprise anyone, because wisdom itself is a universal phenomenon: wisdom brings forth the learning from prior generations in such a form that it can be used by subsequent generations, and wisdom can migrate from one community to another, from one culture to another (always, of course, being contextualized and reinterpreted), and from one religious context to another. It would not properly be called wisdom if it could not migrate. So this saying, well known in a variety of ancient contexts, found its way into the sayings of Jesus because it correlated with the movements' understandings of the import of Jesus' message about the empire of God, and it encapsulated a value promulgated by Jesus and his followers in the early Jesus movements.

It is odd, though, to find this saying juxtaposed with Saying 7, which talks about generosity of response. The saying advocates reciprocity in an ethical sense: treat others as you wish to be treated; do to others as you would have others do to you. But Saying 7 spoke of doing more than what is demanded: its ethics is one of superfluity and excess, while this one is of reciprocity and mutuality. This juxtaposition of seemingly conflicting sayings within a collection of the sayings of Jesus indicates a number of things. First, it shows that there were divergent views on the way to live within the various communities of followers of Jesus, probably dating back to the earliest period of the foundation of the movements. We know, for example, from Paul's letter to the Galatians, that in Jerusalem there were two leading factions: those who saw themselves as functioning completely within the Torah of the Jews (like James), and those who were willing to make accommodation for Gentiles (like Peter). Add to this mix the perspective of Paul, and we have a very diverse set of opinions and ways of organizing life within the Jesus movements described at a very early point in their history. Therefore, conflicting sayings within the collection of sayings of Jesus show that the manner of living within the communities of Jesus remained diverse and varied.

Second, the conflicting sayings have an ascetical purpose. The juxtaposition of a saying about reciprocity with a saying on extreme generosity forces readers to create a place in their minds that will accommodate both perspectives. Readers cannot meld the two sayings into one, but must discover a way of holding both of them together in their conflicting diversity by creating some mental scheme or philosophical narrative that allows both perspectives to cohere within their religious experience and understanding. The juxtaposition of conflicting and opposing sayings is an intentional literary ploy inviting readers and hearers to do their own spiritual work and to find a way to hold together what seems to be incomprehensibly conflicting.

Third, the juxtaposition of opposing sayings within the collection also reflects how people collect wisdom sayings. If the saying does indeed reflect universal wisdom, there will be a time when it will be needed. Collectors of wisdom sayings preserve such sayings for the time when their message is the perfect one to be applied to a particular situation. So they do not discard old wisdom in favor of new, but add the new to the old in order to pass on to subsequent generations wisdom received from the past. In the same way that a grocery list continues to grow by simple addition of new items needed, the wisdom collections grow to preserve ancient advice for the time when it will again be relevant and necessary for survival.

Let me try to put these two conflicting sayings together. The saying on reciprocity, "Do to others as you would have them do to you," promulgates a uniformity and equality of experience in social relationships. It does not include any social restrictions (for example, do this only if you are the more powerful or have more resources than the "others"). Nor does it say to act this way only at certain times or in particular circumstances. The saying levels all the social and circumstantial elements to assert simply that you should treat others as you wish to be treated. On the other hand, the saying about generosity (turn the other cheek, walk two miles) provides readers with information about how to act when inappropriate demands are made on them. They can be made to cohere if it is understood that when others impose their will, members of the community must act with generosity, but when acting themselves, they must restrict their behavior to the way that they would want to be treated. Because of this saying, one of Jesus' followers would not strike anyone in the face, sue another person in a court, conscript another, or expect repayment of lent money, because that is not how Jesus' follower would want to be treated. When the participant has control or the ability to set the tone, the Golden Rule of mutuality and reciprocity takes precedence, but when the participant in the movement does not have control or such ability, then the rule of generosity takes precedence. I have created a scenario, or a narrative, that holds both of these conflicting sayings together without diluting their meaning and significance. This is how sayings collections train the reader in the diversity of wisdom that is being passed on from generation to generation.

Saying 9
Q 6:32, 34
Matthew 5:46, 47 and Luke 6:32, 34

(1) If you love those who love you, what have you gained? Even the tax collectors do the same, don't they?

(2) And if you lend to those from whom you hope to receive, what have you gained? Even the Gentiles achieve the same, haven't they?

Wisdom sayings challenge their readers or hearers to think. Questions such as these force the reader to consider subjects of importance to a community. The Greek grammatical construction anticipates either a negative or a positive response, challenging readers or hearers to turn inward, to examine their own lives, and to evaluate themselves regarding the topics presented.

Our topics here are themes we have already encountered: love and money. The first section of the saying (1) expands on the injunction of Saying 6 to love your enemies. Here, however, the rule is stated as a question about loving "those who love you." The message remains the same: the participants in the empire of God, or in the communities of the Jesus movements, must love not just reciprocally; they must also extend love to those who would wish them harm. The question asks how people benefit by loving only those who love them back. The question's grammatical structure posits the answer—for those involved in these movements, no benefit accrues from only loving those who love them in return.

To underscore the necessity of loving comprehensively and extravagantly, the saying compares those who love only those who love them back with tax (or it may be toll) collectors (2). In the Roman Empire, tax collectors were local people who collaborated with the Roman administration to collect the imperial taxes, or in the case of the toll collectors, the local, smaller fees imposed by the Rome. As a group, these collectors had a reputation for being dishonest and disreputable because they overcharged for taxes and pocketed the excess or because they collaborated with the Romans who imposed duties on their coreligionists. At any rate, the tax collector, then and now, was no popular figure. The only people who would associate with tax collectors were people who loved them; among them, of course, must be numbered Jesus, who had a reputation for associating with them. So what benefit, either to the collector or to the society at large, would loving a tax collector bring? None at all, and yet they love those who love them. The first part of this saying, then, emphasizes that love transgresses the social and political bonds that naturally exist in a society, as well as the boundary between friend and enemy, insider and outsider, good person and bad. The benefit, this saying implies, only accrues to those who love beyond, those who love their enemies, as Saying 6 enjoins.

The second part of the saying (2) talks about lending. Jesus says a lot about money, the value of things, poverty, and the need for food, that is, economic issues. This second part of the saying articulates the economic theory developed by Jesus and his followers. Again, the question intends to confront the reader and to challenge him or her to find new ways of understanding and living. Jesus' saying challenges the participant in the movement to think about whether it is appropriate to lend at interest. The grammar of the question again posits a negative response: "No, there is no benefit from lending with the expectation of making interest." This injunction would be difficult to follow in the postmodern world, and I suspect it was just as difficult in antiquity. After all, society valued (and still values) wealth and socially prominent people, including people who were prominent only because they had more money than people lower on the social scale, displayed their wealth by lending to others, and increased their wealth by earning interest on monies lent. Not so for the Jesus movements! This saying of Jesus expects followers to lend without hope of either receiving interest or having the principal returned. In essence, the saying calls for giving money away to anyone who needs it. That promulgates a radical economic perspective.

The saying presumes that all Gentiles will lend with the expectation of earning interest and having the principal returned to them. The saying also directs the members of the community to consider simply giving without expectation of return or gain. The disparity of views toward lending draws a clear distinction between a participant in the empire of God and a Gentile. So unless a participant wishes to be thought of as a complete outsider, a Gentile, he or she should lend without expectation of repayment.

The themes of love and money in these sayings point to the centrality of community for those who read or hear them. Community life—including enemies who have been defined as part of the community even if they do not know or appreciate it—is about love, and love demands no expectation, has no limits or boundaries, endures socially debilitating stigma (as in turning the other cheek), and expects no return for its investment. These sayings, preserving the voice of Jesus in such a simple and direct way, jump off the page and out of their historical context to raise the same questions for post-modern readers, challenging them to consider anew their attitudes toward love and money.

Saying 10
Q 6:36
Matthew 5:48 and Luke 6:36

Become a merciful person just as your Father is a merciful person.

This saying advocates the imitation of God. Members of the community should cultivate a virtue because God personifies that virtue. Since God is merciful, then participants in the movement should be merciful. The follower must embody the attributes of God by imitating them in daily living. Imitation involves the reproduction of divine attributes in a person's life; therefore, imitation creates a strong bond between divinity and person as well as between divinity and the community dedicated to God. Imitation of God is not a common theme in these sayings; they tend toward reciprocal treatment rather than imitation. So it is significant here that this saying directs readers toward imitation of God, because the saying envisions the sort of reciprocal relationship normally characterizing social relationships between Jesus' followers and other people as characterizing the relationship of God to human beings. In other words, imitation of God creates as strong a bond between God and humanity as the social bond promulgated between people by these sayings. This implies that the same reciprocity with respect to justice, mercy, the reversal of fortunes, rejection, to name just a few, applies not only to human relationships, but also to the relationship of people to God.

The imitation is about having mercy, having compassion for others, just as God has been merciful to the world and its inhabitants. Mercy, as a divine attribute to be imitated, defines one's relationships with people less fortunate, with those lower on the social scale or experiencing harshness and cruelty. The imitator of God responds to those who hurt not by gloating or condemning them for their harsh lives, but by expressing mercy and compassion. Mercy creates a bond between less fortunate and fortunate, as the imitation of God creates a bond between human mercy and divine mercy. That bond takes precedence in these sayings: the connection of one person to another, of human to God, of a member of the empire of God with all others, and of insider with outsider. These connections bind up the society into one cohesive whole, and connect the unified human society to the divine presence. Mercy, the divine attribute embodied in the human participant in the empire of God, binds all things in the universe together.

But mercy goes one step further. Because mercy is a divine attribute, the expression of mercy divinizes those who express mercy. This means that those who express mercy manifest and make present the divine life in the lives of other people, because mercy resides in God and those who manifest mercy present God in human form. Later Eastern Christian ascetics understood the process precisely in this way: the divine presence mysteriously appears in the actions of those who imitate God, who love God, and who have compassion on the world. God's friends incarnate and materialize the divine mercy through their actions. Their actions join the world to the divine presence, extending divine mercy into every arena of human life.

Saying 11
Q6:37–38
Matthew 7:1–2 and Luke 6:37–38

Do not judge, [for fear that] you would be judged. For in that judgment you judge, you will be judged. And in that measure that you measure, it will be measured for you.

I wish the churches of the twenty-first century would hear this saying in all its power so that the endless arguments based on judging who is evil and good, who is acceptable and not, and who is biblically justified or rejected would cease. The habit of judging may simply be too engrained in the twenty-first century; understanding this saying may simply be beyond our capacity. But clearly, our judging one another ignores this saying of Jesus.

Now, as to the saying itself, it exemplifies a way of thinking that is typi-cal of the sayings tradition. The saying consists of three parts: a simple imperative, followed by an explanation of a principle directly related to that imperative, followed by a general explanation of the principle articulated in its most generic form. The saying moves from the most specific to the most generic articulation of its wisdom.

The base of the Greek word I have translated here as "to judge" (*krinein*) means simply "to choose." The word implies that to choose one person over another, or one group over another, means to pass judgment on them. The judgment is good for those chosen, bad for those rejected. When a person rejects another person or group, most likely the rejection will be recipro-cated. To break the cycle, this saying advocates not making the choice or the distinction in the first place. By not judging, a person removes the possibil-ity of being judged him- or herself.

The saying articulates a principle that the criteria for judging used by one against another will become the same criteria by which the person judging is judged. This articulates in yet another way the principle of reciprocity, now applied specifically to the question of making judgments. One should act in the same way that one would like to be acted upon; one should treat others as one would like to be treated; one should not judge, because it makes one liable to judgment.

The saying then generalizes the principle beyond its application to the imperative not to judge. The third part of the saying presents the principle more generically: "And in that measure that you measure, it will be measured for you." The criteria by which one lives will become the criteria by which others will evaluate one's life. This does not posit a split worldview, one that says that one way of living exists for participants in the Jesus movements and another exists for those outside the Jesus movements. The same evaluation will take place for those within the movements and those outside; the same measurement instrument applies to everyone and will be used against the discriminating person.

The sayings of Jesus seem to have an overarching concern for establishing a level playing field for all people, both those within the empire of God and those outside it, for follower and for Gentile, for the gracious and the pernicious, for adherents and enemies alike. The principle not to judge stands at the heart of the impulse toward egalitarian and mutual relationship. Yes, the language of egalitarianism sounds very modern, but it is difficult not to see it in the ancient sayings of Jesus. Somehow, the right and privilege of standing in judgment over others has no place in the symbolic universe of these sayings. Enemy and supporter must be treated alike; enemies, in fact, are to be loved, to be considered part of one's inner circle of friends. The playing field is leveled by not making distinctions, not judging, by treating people with the expectation of reciprocal identical treatment, and by acting as one would like to be acted upon. The principle of reciprocity establishes a basis for a new way of living that provides an essential element of the empire of God.

Saying 12
Q 6:39
Matthew 15:14 and Luke 6:39

Is it possible (and I know it is not) for a blind person to guide a blind person? Will not (and I know it to be true that) both fall into a ditch?

Greek questions syntactically anticipate their answers as either negative or positive. The first question anticipates a negative answer, and thus I have included the phrase "and I know it is not" to indicate that. The second question anticipates a positive response, and therefore I have included the phrase "and I know it to be true" to indicate the expected positive response. The constellation of these two questions, anticipating initially a "no" response and then a "yes," intensifies their importance. They are not rhetorical questions, nor are they open-ended questions, because both questions have predetermined and specific responses. Restated as a declarative sentence, the saying would be: "It is impossible for a blind person to guide a blind person, because both will certainly fall into a ditch." The presentation of the argument in the form of a question, however, challenges the hearer/reader to think it through, to consider the proposition, even if the syntax itself determines the anticipated response. The question does not offer a fixed rule, but a proposition to be considered carefully.

At the literal level, this saying, though probably not true since many visually challenged people do indeed get around well and do indeed guide one another in travel without harm, presents a straightforward observation: unsighted people generally do not make good guides because they cannot see the obvious dangers around them and thus they will experience difficulty. This is the literal level of the saying, and it makes sense, even though it may not be accurate.

The fact that two questions form the saying suggests that the reader ought to take it at a more figurative or metaphoric level. Maybe the subject is not visual impairment, but spiritual or social or political or some other form of figurative blindness. This metaphorical approach shifts the meaning from blindness to the function of guiding other people. The figurative question, then, is "Who is capable of being a guide?" The answer is certainly someone who can see clearly and protect the reader from falling into pits. The true guide both leads well and protects others from danger by leading through or around dangerous places to safety. Jesus is asking an entirely different question—one about guidance.

Having read the earlier sayings about egalitarian and reciprocal orientation toward social relationships, here the reader or hearer must begin to make a distinction; this saying demands it. The saying asks readers or hearers to consider who are their guides, their leaders, and what is the relative safety toward which they lead them. It calls for distinguishing who constitutes a good guide and who does not. That seemingly contradictory stance enables hearers or readers to consider the qualities of their leaders while avoiding judging them, not lording over them, and being reciprocal. It introduces into the discourse a discernment that does not condemn but carefully considers the gifts and limitations of leaders. The saying calls on readers and hearers to examine the spiritual, social, and political insights of their leaders while acting on the other values articulated in the sayings. To be discerning and wise about our guides does not violate communal reciprocal values or a commitment to egalitarian social relationships: it simply protects us from getting into trouble, hurting ourselves, or falling into error. Through discernment we question and evaluate our life choices; these two conjoined questions highlight the process.

Saying 13
Q 6:40
Matthew 10:24–25a and Luke 6:40

A student is not greater than the teacher. It is sufficient for the student that he become just like his teacher.

So much of the language and orientation of the sayings of Jesus relate to education. Clearly, the early movement, with its talk of students (disciples) and teachers (rabbis), organized itself as a school, or a philosophical movement, around the wisdom of an adept master of wisdom. Secondary and higher education in antiquity came about through the association of a student to a master teacher of distinction. Education was personal and organized around an intimate bond between student and teacher. In the Greco-Roman period and later, teachers acted as what we would call spiritual directors—the knowledge they communicated was not just factual; it was more like an initiation into a way of thinking. In that sense, education was like a personality cult of the teacher.

In the third century, Porphyry, a student of the famous neoplatonist philosopher Plotinus, described Plotinus as teaching as an adept bringing to bear the mind of Ammonius, Plotinus's Alexandrian teacher. The way even a famous teacher related in turn to his teacher involved bringing the older teacher's mind to bear on new questions and issues that the older teacher may not have addressed directly in lectures or conversation. The way to honor a teacher, then, consisted of so mastering the teacher's way of thinking that the student could apply that thinking to new circumstances and situations. Education thus functioned as an orientation to both living and thinking, and philosophy became a way of life as well as a way of thinking.

With this background, the saying becomes a clear endorsement of Greco-Roman educational theory and practice. Indeed, the student is not greater than the teacher. This would be self-evident, or else the teacher would not have the stature or the knowledge to be a true guide, and we know from Saying 12 that the discernment of a true and good guide remains an important exercise. Just as in the saying about the blind leading the blind, the question of discernment does not displace the value of mutual relationship, so the fact that the student stands in an inferior position to the teacher does not denigrate the intensity and the depth of the relationship. It only makes sense that the spiritual guide and director have more experience, greater discernment, and incrementally more knowledge than does the person being directed. So this saying does not denigrate the student; rather, it recognizes the superior gifts of the teacher compared to those being taught.

The second part of the saying, that the student must become like the teacher, emphasizes the quality of the relationship. The goals of education are attained through the imitation of a teacher's life, including his or her manner of living, thinking, and processing information, not just through mastery of facts. Becoming like the teacher means that the educational process into which the teacher initiates the student must be internalized. Students assimilate the essence of their teachers' thinking so that they may bring the mind of their teachers to bear on new and different circumstances. The identification is intense.

The description by Gregory the Wonderworker of his teacher Origen of Alexandria described his encounter with his teacher as an encounter with a divine force. The teacher planted a spark of divine love in Gregory so that he yearned and longed for God alone as he experienced God in the person of his teacher. The teacher embodied and manifested the divine presence to the student because the teacher had been thoroughly assimilated to his teacher, God. A linking of relationship exists such that God teaches the teacher, who then embodies the divine in his teaching. Then students experience God in the teacher and thus connect with the source of the learning indirectly but immediately through the life of the teacher. The imitation of the teacher in this saying recalls the interconnected linking of student to teacher that ultimately leads to a direct link with God.

Much of ascetical learning involves this sort of imitation by internalizing processes of thinking and responding. These sayings of Jesus intend to model new ways of understanding the self, social relationships, and the symbolic universe. They present not so much a finished product but a work in progress that evolves and emerges as the student engages with the mind of the teacher, as the follower engages with the thinking of Jesus, as the reader or hearer internalizes the voice and message of Jesus in ever-new contexts and circumstances.

Saying 14
Q 6:41–42
Matthew 7:3–5 and Luke 6:41–42

Why do you see clearly the bit of straw that is in your associate's eye, but do not observe closely the bearing-beam in your own eye? How [can you say] to your associate, "Let me cast out the bit of straw from your eye" and [not] look at the bearing-beam in your own eye? Hypocrite, first cast out the bearing-beam in your own eye, and only then [will you] see clearly [enough] to remove the bit of straw from your associate's eye.

In a community of people closely related to one another by religious and personal commitments, it is often easier to see the faults of others than to tabulate one's own faults. This saying addresses that problem directly. The saying hinges on a number of elements: the close connection between helper and associate, the degree of the impediment (a bit of straw or a bearing-beam), the careful scrutiny of self and others, the facile and ill-conceived impulse to help others, and the careful preparation of the self that is necessary to be of assistance to others. Each element will be taken up in order.

The saying addresses help among members of a close community. The Greek word, which I translate "associate," is literally "brother," the filial metaphor emphasizing the degree of closeness. That filial relationship (brothers and sisters) describes those who are part of the Jesus movements, not just biological relationships, even though there may have existed a sense in which these members and associates were part of the body of Christ in the world, as we find described in the letters of Paul. Both at the literal and the metaphoric level, however, the saying describes the relationship of helper to associate as close, familial, and intimate. This saying is not about helping those outside the movement or attending to the needs of the general public; rather, it describes the internal workings of a close community.

The saying juxtaposes a bit of straw and a bearing-beam as a way of describing the degree of impediment. The person being helped has a smaller degree of impediment than the person helping, that is, the bit of straw versus the beam. The inverse ability to see relates to this disjunction. Someone with a large beam in his or her eye thinks he or she is capable of helping someone with a small bit of straw. The disjunction shows the relative lack of self-awareness of the helper: without self-awareness about one's own impediments and problems, one is not likely to be able to help heal another. We hear echoes here of the discernment of a proper spiritual guide, but in the context of the discernment of the relative status of one's own life and being.

The saying describes the impulse to jump in and help an associate before gaining or developing self-awareness. The saying illustrates the impulse conversationally, "Let me cast out the bit of straw from your eye!" The statement is an eager and enthusiastic desire to help. The problem is the difficulty of helping another, even eagerly and enthusiastically, while one suffers from an even larger impediment than the person to be helped. Without self-awareness, the impulse to help remains futile.

So the crux of the saying argues that in order to help others, the active members of the community of the empire of God must prepare themselves through introspection and self-examination. Properly assisting others starts with being aware of one's own impediments. With knowledge of the seriousness of one's own impediments, the helper becomes capable of seeing clearly, of understanding, and of relating to the person needing help from a perspective of humility and self-knowledge. Without such clarity of vision, the helper remains too debilitated to be of real assistance, and the person needing help receives no real assistance. Clarity of sight, both spiritual and physical, comes only through the awareness of one's own debilitations.

This saying begins to reveal the inner workings of the community envisioned (or projected) in these sayings of Jesus. This community not only looks outward toward the needs of others, it looks outward only after a careful assessment of itself. The healing of the self takes priority over the healing of others; the awareness of the limitations of one's own life precedes the engagement with others' lives. Then, armed with self-knowledge and self-understanding, community member may turn to others. And the reciprocal self-knowledge enhances mutual assistance within the community.

Saying 15
Q 6:43–45
Matthew 7:16b, 18; 12:33b–35 and Luke 6:43–45

(1) There is no good tree that produces rotten fruit, nor again is there a rotten tree that produces good fruit.

(2) The tree is known by its fruit. Are figs gathered from an acanthus bush, or grapes from a prickly plant?

(3) The good person produces good things out of the good treasure and the evil person produces evil out of the evil treasure, for the mouth speaks from the abundance of a heart.

This saying starts with a statement about fruit, moves to a more general statement about the sort of tree that produces the fruit, and concludes with a statement about the human condition that explains the sequence. Such sayings teach the reader and hearer to think in a particular way, from the analysis of the most concrete experiences of daily living to a general theory or a principle of living. In other words, this saying, as with many sayings in wisdom collections, not only transmits information about the best way of living, but also trains the reader/hearer in a method of analysis that makes him or her able to apply the knowledge in other contexts. So the reader/hearer must look both to the content of the saying and to its under-lying method of thinking in order to really learn the lesson.

The initial observation consists of a simple statement that good fruit comes from good trees and rotten fruit comes from rotten trees. The health of the tree determines the quality of its production of fruit. It tells the read-ers/hearers that if they see good, healthy, and delicious fruit, they know that the tree from which it came must be healthy and productive. Likewise, if they see bad, rotten, and inedible fruit, they know that the tree from which it came also must be bad and rotten, with inedible fruit. The agricultural reflection continues in the next part of the saying and is articulated straight-forwardly: "The tree is known by its fruit." The general observation about life that follows will be based on this agricultural principle.

Here the saying moves beyond fruit production to the nature of the tree and its fruit. It argues, through the connection of figs to acanthus bushes and grapes to prickly plants, that a plant can only produce the fruit appropriate to it. Something rooted in the nature of the plant itself determines its fruit, and, therefore, not only does the quality of the plant determine the quality of the fruit, the nature of the plant determines whether it is capable of producing the expected fruit. One goes to a fig tree to gather figs and to a grapevine to gather grapes; one will not be successful looking for figs from an acanthus plant or grapes from a prickly bush. This is somewhat at odds with the statement that good trees produce good fruit, but I will address this later. For the time being, the saying moves from an agricultural observation about fruit to a reflection on the trees that produce them.

The general principle (3) explains the saying, comparing people to kinds of fruit. There are three parts to this general statement: good people produce good things, bad people produce bad things, because each person operates out of the stuff of which he or she is made. The reference to the treasure suggests that people naturally store up their moral and spiritual goods within them, and when the time comes to act or to respond, they pull these moral goods out of their interior treasury and manifest them in daily living. The same applies to evil or morally bad goods—they, too, are stored within and made manifest in daily life. The concluding statement summarizes the process: "the mouth speaks from the abundance of a heart." The saying locates the center of this stored-up treasure in the heart, considered the seat of understanding in antiquity. The saying argues that, within him- or herself, a person produces the good or the evil fruit that later will become manifest in his or her speech and actions. It cannot be otherwise, because good comes from good understanding and bad from bad understanding as surely as good fruit comes from good trees and bad fruit comes from bad trees. A person's own nature creates the "tree" that reveals itself in the quality of its fruit.

Now we can discuss the statement about looking for figs on acanthus bushes or grapes from prickly plants. It suggests that by nature some people will never understand, nor will they be capable of manifesting good deeds and thoughts, precisely because nature limits their potential. One would guess that in a wisdom environment anyone could learn wisdom and be able to manifest it in daily life. Wisdom and understanding are learnable, so everyone has the potential to learn wisdom's precepts and acting accordingly—assuming that by nature wisdom attracts everyone. The statement about looking for figs on an acanthus bush or grapes on a prickly plant suggests the opposite: by nature, some people will never produce the proper fruit because they are unable to do so. Acanthus bushes cannot produce figs, no matter how hard they try (and how understanding they become!). It is impossible. This deterministic strand is unusual in wisdom sayings.

At least two explanations for inclusion of this deterministic statement work here: first, it startles readers and hearers and forces more careful thinking; second, it explains why some people seem to never understand or manifest the goodness that is within them. The sayings intend to challenge and confront the reader/hearer to think things through on his or her own and to come to a different understanding of self, society, and the world, then to live according to that understanding. The discordant note at the end of this saying encourages readers to think about whether there are indeed some naturally bad fruit and naturally bad trees and naturally bad people who only treasure evil in their understanding and manifest evil in their speech. The last part of the saying raises the question of nature versus nurture.

Saying 16
Q 6:46
Matthew 7:21 and Luke 6:46

Why do you invoke me [saying] "Lord, Lord," and not do that which I tell you?

Again, the saying presents readers with a question designed to compel them to consider its content in relationship to their own lives. It is an effective strategy for engaging readers in the process of developing communal understanding. The second person plural "you" puts the question directly to the entire community, not to an individual. So this statement is not about personal commitment but about communal commitment, and it challenges community members to consider their relationship with the master.

The Greek word *kyrios*, translated here as "Lord," has a broad range of meanings: a title of the God of Israel in the Septuagint, the Hellenistic Greek translation of the Israelite scriptures; the head of a household; the supreme authority in society or government; or the guardian of dependent people. Each meaning implies a person who has authority and power over others. Because of its use in the LXX (this is the abbreviation for the Septuagint), "Lord" implies the divine name or a divine attribution of power. But here, I think, the term bears a more generic and less specific meaning, because Jesus, the speaker of the saying, attributes it to himself. Jesus speaks in his role as the head of the household, the supreme authority, the protector of the community; he addresses this statement to the members of his household.

The saying states a problem: community members call Jesus "Lord," but they do not live as if Jesus is their Lord. They refuse to act as though Jesus has authority and power over them. The Lord has told the community to do things that it has not done, yet its members still invoke him as Lord.

These wisdom sayings repeatedly emphasize the correlation between speech and action, between interior commitment and life choices, between understanding and acting wisely. The sayings do not admit a disjunction between being and doing; they are not only related: they are mutually revealing. A community's commitments will be known by its actions, and a community's deeds reveal its interior spiritual state.

That this reality is posed as a question forces community members to stop and think. Are they naming Jesus as their Lord and not acting upon his requests? The question expects reflection on the interior dynamics of the community and its corporate life. What has the master asked that the community has not done? The question drives the community to recall the revelations of the Lord and the specific injunctions and instructions that the community has received from him. It demands that the community reassess the Lord's spoken instruction and evaluate whether members have indeed followed them or acted upon them. The question form does not condemn the community; instead, it encourages all members to reflect on and to evaluate their own communal response to the revelations and teachings of the Lord.

Among those who would engage with the sayings and the voice of Jesus, this question raises important issues about the depth and seriousness of their commitment to unity of thought and action, belief and lifestyle, and interior and exterior dynamics. Because the question is not set in a specific historical, social, or religious context, it challenges equally both ancient and postmodern participants in the Jesus movements. The voice of Jesus preserved in this saying operates outside a chronological or narrative framework, so there are no limits to the saying's applicability. All readers and listeners must take it seriously. And that is precisely the point.

Saying 17
Q 6:47–49
Matthew 7:24–27 and Luke 6:47–49

(1) Everyone who hears my oracles and performs them is similar to a person who constructed his house upon the rock. The rain came down, and the arroyos [literally: rivers] flowed, and the winds blew and fell upon that house, and it did not fall, for it was well established upon the rock.

(2) And everyone who hears my oracles and does not perform them is similar to a person who built his house upon sand. The rain came down, and the arroyos [literally: rivers] flowed, and the winds blew and struck that house, and immediately it fell, and its fall was great.

I have chosen to translate the Greek word *logoi,* usually translated "words," with an alternative meaning, "oracles," for a very specific reason. Both meanings are possible, as are several others, because the Greek word has many varied and interesting connotations. But here I have chosen oracle, because I think Jesus considers his words to be a divine utterance, a divine mandate that requires a response from those hearing them. These words function as oracles precisely because they reveal the mind and will of the divine so that those devoted to God might respond to them, embody them, and put them into practice.

This oracular dimension to the sayings of Jesus has important implications for understanding the role of Jesus in the collection of these sayings. Jesus presents himself as an oracle giver, a revealer of the divine dictates. This implies, of course, that Jesus points beyond himself either to a more divine figure or to another divine figure, since normally only those transparent to the divinity deliver the divine oracle to others. That transparency marks the giver of oracles as a holy person, a venerable medium, or even a holy prophet of God, and thus the giver of the oracles takes on a divine attribute and function. So Jesus portrays himself as the giver of oracles of God, and he emphasizes his intermediary position between those who should perform the deeds mandated in the oracle and the God who sends both the messenger and the revelation in the oracle.

Jesus then sets up two scenarios to compare those who hear the oracles and act appropriately on them. The comparison, again, functions as a challenge to those hearing the oracles. Jesus does not say, "Those who hear the oracle and perform them are good, and those who do not hear them and perform them are bad." Such a simplistic statement would not challenge the thinking or the actions of the listener or reader. Instead, Jesus presents the proposition in the form of two short narratives, which by virtue of their parallel elements force a comparison by the readers or hearers.

Both narratives talk about the effect of a storm on a house. A storm causes water to rush down the mountainsides in great gushes, filling the arroyos that lead the water and making them a potentially destructive river. The construction of the house becomes a metaphor for what results when an individual or a community hears and follows the oracles of God. This metaphor has a history in early Christianity: in the apocryphal *Acts of Thomas*, the apostle Thomas takes money from the king and gives it to the poor under the guise of building a mansion for the king. Then Thomas shows the king the real mansion built in heaven, a mansion he constructed for the king by using his money for acts of mercy. In a sense, the saying also talks about the inner treasure that is the source of both good and evil deeds of Saying 15. The house, then, symbolizes what results from the active and intentional hearing and performing the oracles of God.

Both houses in this saying face pummeling from the natural forces of the environment: "The rain came down, and the arroyos flowed, and the winds blew and fell upon that house." Their foundations are tested in the natural course of living; they are and will be assaulted by any number of destructive forces around them. These forces cannot easily be described—they have an important function in the narrative, but the narrative does not give them specific meaning. One might simply say that the houses will be severely tested by life as will be the fruits of a person's or a community's labor.

One house stands upon rock; the other, upon sand. The well-established house, built upon the rock, will withstand the trials, while the poor foundation of the other house will fail because it lacks suitable grounding. Hearing and responding to the oracles of God establishes a kind of foundation for living, so that a good foundation involves both active hearing and performing, while a bad foundation involves neither hearing nor acting on the revealed mind of God. The type of foundation of a house, a person, or a community determines the outcome. Foundations may be built on both kinds of ground, but only those firmly rooted in hearing and responding to the oracles of God will be able to sustain themselves in the trials that will certainly come.

The two stories in this saying inspire readers/hearers to think about what kind of foundation they construct through their engagement with the sayings of Jesus. The saying forces them to look inward to examine their own foundations and to consider how well they have withstood the trials and tests of life. The dual narrative structure points toward a way of thinking and analyzing, with a clear preference for the solid foundation of hearing and responding appropriately to God's oracles, and it simply describes the possible fate of both kinds of foundations. The saying opens the door to reflection and gives direction to it, but does not mandate a conclusion or condemn those who appear to have built their houses on sand. All options are open.

Saying 18
Q 7:1, 3, 6b–9, ?10?
Matthew 7:28a; 8:5–10, 13 and Luke 7:1, 3, 6b–10

And it happened that, when he had completed these oracles, he went to Capernaum. A ranking military officer came to him and implored him saying, "My child is doing badly."

And he said to him, "Since I am coming, shall I heal him?"

And in answering, the military officer said, "Sir, I am not [sufficiently] acceptable for you to come under my roof, but [simply] say a word, and my child will be healed. For I myself am a person under authority, and I say to one person, 'Go!' and he goes, and to another person 'Come!' and he comes, and to my servant, 'Do this!' and he does it."

And when Jesus heard this, he was astonished and said to those following him, "I tell you, not even in Israel have I found such trust!"

The narrative in this saying sets the stage for Jesus' final comment: "Not even in Israel have I found such trust!" This climactic comment indicates that Jesus spoke these words both to Israelites and to Gentiles, and he compares their response to his message. The Israelites, according to this saying, have not responded in trust to the words and deeds of Jesus, whereas this Roman military official has responded favorably. To a certain degree, Jesus expresses some surprise at the trust demonstrated by the Roman official without condemning the Israelites. He simply comments that the Roman official understands his message to a greater degree than Jesus has experienced among the Israelites. This narrative provides an important window into the early Jesus movements, because it indicates that Jesus performed his powerful deeds among both Jews and Gentiles; it also provides evidence that Jesus engaged in a universal mission to both Jew and Gentile from the beginning. The canonical gospels, written later, suggest that Jesus began his mission with Jews first and only reluctantly spoke with Gentiles. But here, in the collection of sayings that precede the narrative gospels, it seems that Jesus both spoke to and performed powerful deeds for Gentiles.

This saying also raises the issue of class. The narrative is about a lower-ranking Roman military official, a centurion who supervised a large contingent of soldiers at the base of the Roman military system, speaking to a social equal or superior. This becomes evident in the term I translate "sir," which could also mean "master" or "lord." The term itself implies social disparity, with Jesus receiving either the honorific title or the recognition of social and political superiority. In other words, we have here a Roman military official, arguably part of the ruling Roman class in the region, addressing a Jewish teacher with honor and respect. They engage as social equals. The situation indicates that Jesus did not simply associate with or engage with the poor, uneducated, or socially marginalized people of his society. This story questions the view that Jesus oriented his message and deeds to peasants only, because here we have middle-class people relating to one another and engaging in mutual conversation and in patronage. So this saying opens windows on both the universal nature of the early mission of Jesus and the social class of those engaged in the various Jesus movements.

A third issue needs to be addressed before I explain the narrative. The problem involves the translation of the Greek word *pais*, which I translate here as "child." The dictionary meaning of *pais* denotes child (either son or daughter), an adopted child (either male or female), or a slave child or servant. It has a broad set of meanings. Early Christian literature often calls Jesus God's *pais*, the holy and favored child of God, and the term implies that Jesus is a chosen, beloved child of God in language suggestive of intimacy and close relationship. In other Greco-Roman literature, however, this intimacy and connection also connotes a homoerotic meaning, because authors employ the term to describe the favorite boy of an adult male in a sexual relationship. Sexuality in antiquity remains a very complex and complicated issue. I doubt that the ancient relationship between adult male and young boy could be called a homosexual relationship, because homosexuality now implies a singular orientation toward a person of the same sex, and Romans and Greeks did not have such a category. Relationships between adult men and prepubescent boys, including sexual relations, formed part of the process of molding and preparing youth to enter the adult world. In the context, then, of Greco-Roman literature of the same period, the term *pais* suggests a closer relationship between the military official and the child than would meet the eye. It is not concern for the military official's biological family that is at stake, but his strong emotional connection with a boy child whom he loves deeply. It is possible to identify the love as strong without knowing precisely how it was expressed.

Now we turn to the narrative itself. The narrative posits a trip to Capernaum, in all probability a town with a Roman military installation, after Jesus finishes giving oracles in some other unspecified city or town. In the context both of a universal mission to both Jews and Gentiles, this narrative frame makes perfect sense. Jesus travels from place to place, giving oracles, performing powerful deeds, and responding to the questions and needs of those he encounters.

The interaction between Jesus and the centurion remains peculiar. The centurion simply tells Jesus that his boy child suffers some ailment. He does not ask for anything; the centurion simply describes the situation. Jesus introduces the subject of healing when he asks the question, "Since I am coming (that way), shall I heal him?" Jesus reaches out directly to the implicit request of the centurion and offers healing. But Jesus engages with the centurion through a question, and questions force readers/hearers then and now to stop and to take stock of the situation. Readers must answer Jesus' question, or at least consider the options. How would a person then (or now, for that matter) have responded to the question? Would they (or we) have encouraged a healing in such an ambiguous social, religious, political (not to say potentially sexual) environment? The form of the question raises the subject and leaves it hanging until the centurion replies.

There are two parts to the military official's response, both of which Jesus affirms in his final climactic affirmation of the official's trust. First, the military official acknowledges his inferior status to Jesus ("Sir, I am not [sufficiently] acceptable for you to come under my roof"); then he acknowledges Jesus' ability to perform powerful deeds from a distance ("but [simply] say a word, and my child will be healed"). These two acknowledgments set the stage for Jesus' potential healing of the child. The military official does not demand a healing or insist that he deserves a special act of kindness from the healer. He presents a humble request in a military and social setting that does not require him to kowtow to any local person. At the same time, he understands the power of Jesus' words. Now here's the connection with the completion of the oracles of Jesus. The sayings collected here have already covered hearing oracles (Saying 17) and calling upon Jesus while not acting upon what he says (Saying 16). The centurion represents someone who has not heard a word yet knows that Jesus' words are powerful and effective, someone who has not heard the oracles or words of Jesus and yet implicitly trusts them enough to present a situation that he expects Jesus will rectify. So the centurion tells him simply to say a word and the healing, the powerful deed, will be accomplished. The narrative justifies the centurion's trust.

The military official, then, becomes the mouth of the oracle in presenting the rationale for Jesus' words and deeds. He, not Jesus, provides the lesson to be learned: "For I myself am a person under authority, and I say to one person, 'Go!' and he goes, and to another person 'Come!' and he comes, and to my servant, 'Do this!' and he does it." The follower here provides the important lesson. The military official argues that a person in authority who commands power can simply give an order and it is done. His words are powerful and dramatic. He recognizes the nature of true power and authority and ascribes such power and authority to Jesus. It is a remarkable moment when the person requesting help teaches others (including Jesus) about the true nature of power and authority. And the centurion performs this function well.

Jesus responds with both astonishment and affirmation. Nothing about the encounter suggests that Jesus finds the situation problematic or unclear. The narrative does not tell readers whether the healing ever takes place; instead, readers are left to consider the question on their own. How do readers/hearers react to the power and authority of Jesus after they learn of his civilized engagement with the leader of an occupying force? Can one learn from one's occupier? Will Jesus heal a beloved child in such a social, political, religious, and possibly sexual environment? Jesus leaves us with the thought that trust is important, central, and worthy of affirmation wherever it is found.

Saying 19
Q 7:18–19, 22–23
Matthew 11:2–6 and Luke 7:18–19, 22–23

When he heard about all these things, John, sending [a message] through his disciples, said to him, "Are you the one who is coming, or should we look for another?"

And answering, he said to them, "Go announce to John that which you hear and see: the blind see again and the lame walk about, those with scaly skin are cleansed and the deaf hear, the dead are raised, and the poor receive good news, and blessed is the person who is not offended by me."

This saying is redolent with prophetic references. Isaiah 61:1 in the LXX reads: "The spirit of the Lord is upon me, for which reason he anointed me; he sent me to announce good news to the poor, to heal those who are crushed in heart, to preach release to those in prison and to the blind sight." The saying invokes not only the style of the announcement of the day of the Lord (Isaiah 61:2) in this list of liberative proclamations and actions, but also some of the specific elements (the blind seeing, the poor receiving good news, and implicitly the healing of the sick). The saying provides intertextual conversation between Jesus and the prophet Isaiah's announcement of the day of the Lord, establishing a link between Jesus' description of his own mission and the prophet's vision. In a more suggestive than literal manner, the passage also invokes the prophet's reference to the "coming one" of Malachi 3:1 for whom people search. And of course, the narratives of the gospels identify John the baptizer as a prophet preparing the way for the coming one who is greater than he is (Saying 2). The reference to the raising of the dead invokes Elijah's revivification of the son of the widow at Zarephath (1 Kings 17:17–24) and Elisha's revivification of the Shunammite woman's son (2 Kings 4:17–37).

These intertextual references to prophetic literature and John the baptizer as prophet indicate that the saying intends knowledgeable readers to understand Jesus' statement as a comment upon them. The references create a filter through which we read Jesus' description of what occurs around him: the blind see, the sick are healed, the poor receive the good news. These significant deeds cloak Jesus with the prophetic mantle and suggest that Jesus is indeed the expected one, the one who will proclaim the day of the Lord. The saying demands that readers/hearers create in their minds a narrative that explains the suggested correlation by using these elements: (a) Jesus is the one who was expected by the prophets; (b) Jesus does the work that the prophets established as signs of the day of the Lord; (c) Jesus inaugurates the expected new day of the Lord; (d) Jesus has greater stature than even his contemporary prophet, John the baptizer; and by implication (e) the powerful deeds of those who follow Jesus (healing the sick and debilitated, raising the dead, proclaiming liberty to captives, for example) connect them through Jesus with the prophetic revelations of previous generations and further extend the day of the Lord into the future. This constructed narrative draws a direct line from the communities of followers of Jesus, through Jesus and John the baptizer, back to the prophetic expectations of previous generations.

The narrative of the saying, however, moves in another direction, complementary to the readers' constructed narrative based on the intertextual references. John sends his disciples to ask Jesus the question: "Are you the one, or do we look for another?" The question itself holds some interest. Would it not have been obvious that Jesus was doing the prophetically expected miraculous deeds? Could John and his disciples not have readily seen the deeds that announced that Jesus was the expected one? Obviously not. The deeds themselves seem not to have given definitive proof of Jesus' prophetic identity and function. John's question, however, arises in prophetic expectation of one who would announce the day of the Lord, so by invoking the prophetic expectation through a scriptural suggestion, we find a parallel situation to the quoting of scriptural material found in the temptation story (Saying 3). The question arises out of the scriptures for John, and John's followers communicate it to Jesus. We have a mild form of the contest between John and Jesus, John's followers and Jesus', set up around prophetic exegesis and application.

Jesus' response, also referencing scripture, provides definition to the issue. He does not answer the question directly but by listing the powerful deeds he has performed. All of the deeds align themselves with the prophetic text from Isaiah. In Jesus' response, his deeds speak for themselves. In other words, the response gathers up the deeds into an articulated narrative that constitutes a prophetic message. This means that Jesus' deeds make sense only as they become part of a discourse, in this case a discourse about prophetic expectation. The powerful deeds are not self-evidently revelatory but become revelatory in discourse about the scriptures relating both to the day of the Lord from the prophets and the empire of God from Jesus' own mission. The discourse, grounded in scriptural knowledge, gives meaning to the powerful deeds. Without the discourse, the meaning of the deeds would remain opaque; the transparency comes only through conversation. The question that John poses and sends through his disciples inaugurates the scriptural discourse that enables discernment about the day of the Lord in their own times.

This discursive emphasis explains the final statement: "blessed is the person who is not offended by me." The discourse removes the offense. This conversation, based in scripture, seeks to understand the prophetic expectations in the context of John and Jesus' own times. The fact that both John and Jesus relate through a prophetic textual reference grounds their conversation and gives it a context that reflects not their own status or understanding of themselves, but the meaning and significance of scriptural texts and expectations. They both refuse to speak about themselves personally, but speak only about the way that they approach the interpretation of their own experience in light of the prophetic writings. The offense would have been for Jesus to say directly, "Yes, I am the expected one." But having engaged in a scriptural contest as a means of interpreting contemporary experience, Jesus has removed the scandal. The person who understands this is truly blessed.

This saying is the first in a series of three sayings about John the baptizer. John's presence and mission seem to have been important to Jesus' mission and words. John and Jesus may have represented two different movements of the day, sometimes collaborative, sometimes competitive, but they were always closely associated with each other, at least in the eyes of the followers of Jesus. We have no independent information from John's circle.

Saying 20
Q 7:24–28
Matthew 11:7–11 and Luke 7:24–28

(1) After they left, he began to speak to the mobs concerning John: "What did you go out into the desert to view [as spectators]? A wind-tossed reed?

(2) So what did you go out to see? A finely dressed person? Don't you get it that those who wear refined clothing live in kingly palaces!

(3) What, then, did you go out to see? A prophet? Yes, I tell you! Even more extravagant than a prophet.

(4) This one is he about whom it is written: 'Behold I myself send my angel into your presence; he will prepare your road ahead of you.'

(5) I say to you, there has not been raised up among those born of women one greater than John, but the one who is the smaller in the empire of God is greater than he is."

The saying presents Jesus as very defensive about John to the mobs or the multitudes, whom Jesus seems to be upbraiding. The narrative connects this saying with the previous one concerning the message from John to Jesus carried by John's students. Now Jesus turns to the mobs and begins to ask a series of questions that seem hostile in tone and presentation. The fact that Jesus provides his own answers indicates that these questions have a different function from the more open-ended questions we have become accustomed to hearing in these sayings. Jesus asks the questions with an edge and answers them pointedly and mockingly. He is making a point about John. After the narrative introduction, the saying consists of three series of questions (1–3) followed by two pronouncements (4–5).

The saying portrays the mobs as mere spectators who go out into the desert for a theatrical or sporting event. In the first set of questions, Jesus confronts them for their voyeuristic tendencies and mocks them with the silly suggestion that they went out to see grass blowing in the wind. The saying portrays their voyeurism as obviously insignificant and petty.

The second set of questions (2) shifts the subject, but maintains a mocking attitude. Jesus confronts the mobs for going out to an inappropriate place, the desert, to engage in social voyeurism. He upbraids them for looking in the wrong places for finely dressed people who more properly may be observed in their finely appointed houses.

These two sets of questions set the stage for the third question, which has both content and significance. The third question raises the proper subject: if the mobs went out to see a simple prophet, they actually observed a far more spectacular prophet than their small imaginations could possibly fathom. The answer to this question indicates that even the mobs' voyeurism remains misplaced, because even when they see, they cannot understand the true significance of what they are watching. This question also taunts the mobs, mocking their inability to understand or to observe closely.

The previous saying was redolent with biblical intertextuality, but here we find no such thing. These mobs have clearly not honed their eyes to see and their minds to understand scripture or the scriptural implications of the things they observe. The mobs remain outside the discourse established by John and Jesus and their respective followers, the scriptural and prophetic discourse so necessary for understanding. That the mobs find themselves onlookers to the discourse makes their expectations and motivations suspect and laughable. They simply do not understand, even when they see.

Jesus changes the course of the conversation to make it truly revelatory by reciting a passage of scripture that invokes three possible biblical moments: the first, Malachi 3:1, in which the prophet tells the people that a messenger will be sent to prepare the way; the second, Exodus 23:20, in which God tells Moses that he will send an angel to protect the Israelites on the way; and the third, Isaiah 40:3 (LXX), where the Lord tells the people to prepare a road in the wilderness. These biblical references become the proper subject of the discourse, providing the lens for the mobs' understanding of what they seek. Without such discourse, the mobs will never understand their own yearning, their experiences, or the events of the day of the Lord and the empire of God. The mobs, like all the followers of Jesus and John, must engage with the scriptures to understand. The mobs must understand John as the messenger, the angel that God sent to prepare the way for something or someone else. Scriptural discourse helps them understand that they went out into the wilderness to witness the necessary preparation for the empire of God.

This empire of God is the subject of the final statement in this saying. Jesus argues that John and his movement remain preparatory to something that has a far greater value and importance, the empire of God. So the least person entering God's empire has greater value and stature than John, even though John stands as the greatest of those who pointed toward the empire, but like Moses in Exodus, never actually entered it himself. The suggestion that John and his followers had not entered the empire of God seems somewhat polemical in the context. John has been validated but simultaneously placed in a secondary or subservient role to the empire of God and to the work and words of Jesus.

This saying suggests to readers of the sayings and hearers of the voice of Jesus that important and significant discourses exist that stand at the heart of the Jesus movements. The sayings and Jesus' voice encourage readers and hearers to enter the discourse, to avoid appearing like the mindless mob, and to focus their attention on the revelation that occurs around them. Jesus' mocking and scolding tone provides a clarion call to discursive engagement not only with the scriptures but also with daily life. The discourse that Jesus describes here as well as in the previous saying does not simply read scripture at its literal level, but rather promotes the engaged reading of scripture interactively with the continuing revelation of God in later times. This is no biblicism, but rather an engaged, meditative, reflective, critical, and evaluative discourse, bringing life to the scriptures and the scriptures to life.

Saying 21
Q 7:[29–30]
Matthew 21:32 and Luke 7:29–30

For John came into your presence, and the [sinners and] tax collectors received him, but [the mobs did not].

This very fragmentary saying portrays John, at least the way I reconstruct it, as being received by sinful and cheating people (symbolized by the designation that they were tax collectors), but rejected by the mobs. The editors of the critical edition have assumed that it was the religious authorities who rejected John, but I think this saying, following directly on the previous saying, continues a conversation with the mobs. Sinners flocked to John and understood that they had something to benefit by listening and responding to John's message and actions. They received his word and presumably transformed their lives. The mobs, as we have just seen, seem not to understand. Their ignorance and lack of engagement with scriptural discourse make them unable to respond to John's words and message, while despised people—tax collectors—seem to "get it."

Readers of the sayings and hearers of Jesus' voice must consider where they stand in relation to the ongoing revelation of God in history. John's mission, inspired by God, formed one element in a chain of revelation that links Jesus to the past and links Jesus' followers to the future. The revelation of the divine empire continues, connecting events that readers and hearers may only properly understand as they engage in the discourse of the empire and in the manifestation of the empire in their own personal and corporate lives. Because revelation continues and never stops, discerning people must learn to read the signs, to understand the scriptures in new ways, to look for evidence of what God may be doing to connect scripture and life in new and often disturbing ways. Otherwise, readers and hearers will resemble the mobs who are locked out, not the sinners and tax collectors who had eyes to see and ears to hear.

Saying 22
Q 7:31–35
Matthew 11:16–19 and Luke 7:31–35

(1) To what shall I compare this age and to what is it similar?

(2) It is comparable to children sitting in the market streets calling out to the others saying, "We played the flute for you, and you did not dance; we sang a dirge, and you did not cry."

(3) For John came neither eating nor drinking, and you were saying, "He's demonic!"

(4) The human one came, eating and drinking, and you were saying, "Here is an eating and wine-drinking person, an associate of tax collectors and sinners."

(5) Wisdom is determined by her children.

This last saying in the series about John returns to an open-ended question format. Jesus asks how he should characterize the present generation. The odd response seems to indicate that the children of this age are either petulant or noncooperative: petulant in that they call out to others expecting them to respond; noncooperative in that they do not respond appropriately to callers. The saying compares this age to children playing with each other in the market streets. That children play in the marketplaces should not surprise anyone, either in antiquity or now. So this age resembles children playing in the shopping malls, calling out to their friends.

The callers want to set the stage for the response of their playmates and so they play the flute to make them dance or they sing a dirge to make them wail. The callers want to control the mode of playing. But the other children do not dance, nor do they wail. Petulance meets obstinacy. This peculiar image suggests that those who live in this age, who find themselves busy in the marketplaces buying and selling, attempt to control other people's performance and their response with a kind of petulant demand for control, but they fail because the responders are as obstinate as the callers are demanding. The situation creates a stalemate. There can be no advancement because there is no pleasing anyone, and because the participants play, they do not even buy and sell in the marketplace. The entire scene is one of frustration, of children trying to control other children who refuse to be controlled, while all are playing in a work environment.

This description of the age leads to two explanations of this petulance and obstinacy. The first explanation relates to why John was rejected: "John came neither eating nor drinking, and you were saying, 'He's demonic!'" Instead of treating John as an authentic ascetic who denied himself food and drink for the sake of his religious mission, people rejected him for his ascetic discipline and condemned him as one possessed. The outsiders maintained their petulance and obstinacy, refusing to acknowledge what was in front of them.

The same thing happened to the human one: "The human one came, eating and drinking, and you were saying, 'Here is an eating and wine-drinking person, an associate of tax collectors and sinners.'" The phrase "the human one" translates the Greek that means literally "the son of the human one." In the sayings tradition, this title seems to have multiple references: it refers to a figure mentioned in Daniel as coming at the end of time (Daniel 8:17); it could also simply be a euphemism for all human beings, for anyone who is born human; and it is frequently a self-referential way that Jesus speaks about himself. In this instance, I think that "the human one" represents a self-referential euphemism that Jesus uses to describe himself. I say this because this saying continues the comparison of John and Jesus, and the saying makes sense as a further instance of that comparison. But the tables have been turned: the saying portrays John as an ascetic, while it portrays Jesus as a glutton and a drunkard who keeps bad company.

The references here to impure and improper eating reflect the importance of meals to some of the early Jesus movements. Jesus worked at meals, which included the drinking of wine and which gathered unsavory, unacceptable, and unclean people. So the people accepted neither the ascetic nor the self-indulgent reprobate, neither John nor Jesus. They remained obstinate, petulant, and incapable of discerning the truth about people. They refused to understand John and Jesus: they played in the marketplace rather than shrewdly conducting their business.

The final statement summarizes: "Wisdom is determined by her children." Their deeds, their followers, their words, their impact on others, the offspring (children) of their lives demonstrate the wisdom of both John and Jesus. Folly and ignorance, it is implied, also will be known by their children, like those playing in a workplace or those giving orders to friends who do not receive them nor act on them. The message takes the reader back to Saying 15 about the connection of the fruit to the tree. The fruits of wisdom's labor will show the wisdom of John and Jesus.

This concludes this small section of sayings on John and Jesus. From the perspective of the Jesus movements, a strong connection exists between the two religious sects, and yet the Jesus movements consistently see themselves as superior to John and his disciples. The Jesus people are stronger and worthier than John's people, who always must take second place to Jesus. It would be interesting to know how John's followers understood Jesus and his followers.

In this saying about the ascetic and the glutton, John and Jesus, readers and hearers of the voice of Jesus can examine their own attitudes toward work and play as well as their own petulance and obstinacy. Rigid attempts to control others as well as rigid categories of thinking lead to distressing results in these sayings. Rigidity does not enhance understanding, but seems instead to prevent it. Both the sayings and the voice call readers and hearers to consider the ill effects of their rigidities. John and his disciples provide a good opportunity for considering the ill effects of rigid categories of revelation as well as rigid expectations about the leaders in God's continuing revelation.

Saying 23
Q 9:57–60
Matthew 8:19–22 and Luke 9:57–60

(1) And a certain person said to him, "I will follow you wherever you might go!"

And Jesus said to him, "Foxes have dens and the birds of the heavens have protective covering, but the human one does not have anyplace to lay his head."

(2) Another person said to him, "Allow me first to return and to bury my father."

And he said to him, "Follow me and let the dead bury their own dead."

These two connected sayings portray the realities of entering one of the Jesus movements, especially as one of the itinerant missionaries who must leave everything and everyone (including family; see Saying 69) in order to proclaim the divine empire. The sayings talk about people in generic terms: "a certain person" and "another." In this way, the wisdom saying does not refer to specific groups of people such as religious leaders, the mobs who have been following Jesus, or John and his followers, but to everyone who has an interest in joining the movement.

The first section raises the question of itinerancy, beginning with the enthusiastic, direct, unambiguous comment of a potential member of Jesus' community: "Wherever you go, I will go!" Jesus' response sets some serious parameters on the process, saying that other animals have logical and proper resting places (foxes in their dens and birds in the trees), but those joining the movement have no such places for protection. Those who join this movement leave behind their protective environments and simply follow. This theme will be developed to a significant degree later in these sayings, where Jesus tells his listeners not to worry about food or clothing (Saying 55), not to fear persecution and punishment (Sayings 5, 6, and 49), and not to worry about what they should say in court (Saying 53). Those who join the movement cut themselves off from others and become vulnerable, without support and without protection. And in this first part of this saying, they become homeless. They literally have no place to lay their heads.

Itinerancy seems to define the earliest promoters of the empire of God that Jesus and his followers proclaimed. They followed Jesus without regard to their own security and provision, and they had certain rules to follow about how to be received and what to do when they were rejected (Sayings 27 and 28). Put positively, these itinerant missionaries moved about unhindered, unimpeded, and unrestrained by concern for themselves or for life's necessities. But joining the movement involved much more.

The second part of the saying develops the social implications of itinerancy. Social and familial obligations bind a person to place and relationship. In this part of the saying, Jesus demands that his followers sever those relationships and social obligations. Jesus gives the example of burying one's father, an important familial responsibility demanded by others in the society as well. This obligation hits at the heart of the demand for social independence. One does not simply leave and reject family (as in Saying 69) in order to join the movement, but a true follower consciously and deliberately rejects other social and religious obligations. The dead cannot bury themselves, and so the participant in the Jesus movements leaves the dead unburied, untended, and discarded, for the sake of following Jesus. This would have struck an ancient person as just as barbaric and inappropriate then as it does now. But it dramatically presents the demands of following Jesus.

This radical withdrawal from Roman social, political, and religious life marks the early Jesus movements. Those of us who have known Christianity as an established and legitimate religion find this difficult to understand. In the early days of the movement, the separation of one empire from another, or Roman society from the society of those following Jesus, stood as a dramatic statement about how extensive and comprehensive the true empire of God really was. Jesus' early followers did not simply select a different religion, they embarked on an entirely different way of life—a different understanding of themselves, their social and political relationships, and the nature of the physical and spiritual universe as a whole. A true follower, a strong follower, could not live in both worlds at the same time (see Saying 73); he or she needed to make the painful choice between the Jesus movement and family, between the Roman government and the government of God, between the economic system among the close community and the practices of the marketplace (see Saying 9), and ultimately between God and every other sort of power and authority. This saying underscores the radical nature of that withdrawal and separation. The next few sayings explore additional implications of this radical withdrawal in favor of itinerancy.

Saying 24
Q 10:2
Matthew 9:37–38 and Luke 10:2

He said to his students: "While the harvest is great, the laborers are few! So beg the master of the harvest to send out laborers into his harvest!"

The short narrative introduction to this saying sets the stage as a teacher (implied) speaks to his students (identified as such in the text), establishing the context as educational. Ancient authors frequently refer to education in farming metaphors to describe the various aspects of teaching and learning. This saying participates in that tradition.

The first part of the saying is simple: the harvest is great; the harvesters are few. This would not be the case in an agricultural setting where a great harvest provides sufficient resources for the farmer to hire harvesters to bring in the crop. In an educational setting, however, this metaphor presents the notion that despite the great riches of learning, few actually engage with it enough to bring home the benefits. It says that while education remains very valuable, few students do the necessary work to benefit from its abundant riches. I am sure teachers of every generation say basically the same thing: much needs to be learned; few put themselves to the task. This first part of the saying, then, presents a commonplace issue in education, ancient and modern.

The second part of the saying seems to apply this educational metaphor to another context. This part of the saying refers to a process of recruiting and commissioning. If we stay within the educational context, it sounds as if this part of the saying instructs the students to beg the master of the harvest to recruit more students. That does not make sense. More teachers, yes. More students, not likely.

The clue that the context of meaning shifts rests in the word "master," Greek *kyrios*, meaning lord, master, or a person in authority. It is a title most frequently applied in Jewish and Christian literature to God, and in Christian literature, it is a common title for Jesus. Now we can assume that the saying means: ask God to send laborers into the harvest. The harvest seems not to refer to education but to some other process. It denotes the end of the growing season, when farmers gather the fruits of their labor into barns. In this religious context, it refers to the end of the age, or the end of a person's life, or the end of a movement, when one gathers into reserve the fruits of one's personal or corporate labor. The harvest signifies an eschatological ingathering of the fruit of moral, intellectual, and social endeavors. So now the saying shifts from education to an eschatological ingathering, both oriented to reaping the benefits of labor, both educational and religious.

Not only has the signification of the harvest changed, so has the referent to the laborers. These laborers who bring in the harvest are those who have been in the fields, working to produce the rich harvest. They represent missionaries, working the metaphoric fields of those being groomed for the empire of God. These laborers gather people into the barn of God's empire. The saying means, then, that the missionaries should ask God to provide more missionaries to bring in all the people ready to be gathered into the empire of God.

This shift from student to evangelist and from educational to missionary metaphor displays the development of the movement. We can well imagine that at first the students closely studied the philosophy of the empire of God under Jesus' tutelage. They needed to understand its thought patterns, mores, ways of living, principles, values, theology, political orientation, religious practices, and many other things. Having learned, however, they then became teachers themselves. Their learning represents a recruitment to the movement and at the same time a commissioning for further educational work among those not yet in the movement. The processes flow easily and fluidly from learner to teacher, from student to missionary, and from passive participant to active leadership. The saying tells us how the various Jesus movements spread from person to person, group to group, and society to society. This saying begins a series of sayings that give particular and specific instruction to missionaries. Scholars collectively call these sayings (24–30) Jesus' "Mission Speech."

Education and evangelism seldom conjoin in the postmodern context. Evangelists often regard education with suspicion, as educators do evangelism. But in these sayings, the two functions seem to combine easily and fluidly so that education becomes a means of evangelizing and evangelizing becomes an opening to education and learning. Perhaps this saying is encouraging the hearers of Jesus' voice and the readers of his sayings to join education and evangelism into one fluid discourse, honoring both the work of extending the divine empire and extending the understanding of those both within and without the empire.

Saying 25
Q 10:3
Matthew 10:16 and Luke 10:3

Go! Look, I send you as sheep among wolves!

Dangerous politics defined the imperial period during the life of Jesus and the period covering the time of the collection and elaboration of his sayings. The Romans did not consider the kind of missionary activity discussed in the explanation of the previous saying as benign. Talk of empire remained risky even for Romans, let alone for people in the occupied provinces. People talking about empire (whether Roman or otherwise) in Judea or involved in internecine fighting and opposition to Roman authority would have found themselves suspect or even prosecuted for treason. Rome did not entertain pretenders either to the imperial throne or to the Roman Empire. It remained a dangerous world.

Jesus inaugurated his movement in this volatile religious and political context. His proclamation of an empire of God made him and his followers suspect and liable to arrest and persecution. After all, this is what happened to Jesus: he was arrested, tried, and killed as the emperor (the word is *basileus*, which also means king) of the Jews. The Romans condemned Jesus as a pretender to the Roman or Judean throne. And Judea was a war zone and had been for a number of years by the time Jesus began his mission.

I take this to be the background of this saying. The wolves signified the Romans and their empire. They devoured any weak prey. Their force overwhelmed anything smaller and they squelched anything that might threaten. The sheep, on the other hand, signified Jesus and his movement. They proclaimed a new empire of God and God as a new emperor. That defined vulnerability in the Roman context.

In this saying, Jesus sends out his hearers/followers with an imperative: "Go!" Jesus commands them to leave and to begin their commission with the understanding that he sends them as vulnerable agents in a powerful hegemonic Roman environment. The missionaries' engagement with hostile and powerful foes is an important part of the mission. They expect hostility toward themselves and their mission; they value their vulnerability as central to their mission. Jesus sends them out as sheep among wolves, with their eyes open and their marching orders secure. Vulnerability and danger characterize the context into which Jesus sends them.

As part of the Mission Speech, this saying commands the mission itself, sending out the laborers mentioned in Saying 24 to the harvest that stands ready for gathering.

Saying 26
Q 10:4
Matthew 10:9–10a and Luke 10:4

Don't carry a pouch, nor lunch bag, nor shoes, not even a walking stick; and salute no one on the road.

The vulnerability of the missionaries extended further than simply the Roman context. This might be called "extreme" vulnerability and dependence. Jesus here sets the parameters for the itinerant missionaries' travel. The itinerants should make no provision for clothing, food, or comfort on the road. They literally travel with the clothes on their bodies and with no provision for the journey. As part of the Mission Speech, this saying provides details of the personal state of those itinerant missionaries.

The prohibition of baggage seems a strange one. The saying seems to intend to keep the movement of the itinerants easy and simple, unencumbered by any sort of baggage, which would make sense both literally (take no suitcase) and figuratively (travel light in order to be able to move quickly and efficiently from place to place). The itinerants ought to be just that, not simply people who move about, but people who have no place to lay their heads (Saying 23). Having no abode, they have no place to store their things, and so should not carry them.

The prohibition of food speaks to another issue: dependence upon God (Saying 55) and upon the hospitality of those to whom the missionaries go (Sayings 27 and 28). The degree of trust in God's provision either directly or through others must be sufficiently high that the missionary does not take food along on the trip. The saying articulates a radical dependence and simultaneous vulnerability: dependence upon God for provision and vulnerability to the exigencies of the reception of the message by those receiving the good news brought by the missionaries.

The prohibition of an extra pair of shoes also seems strange, especially given that these are itinerant missionaries. But again, this Mission Speech espouses a radical poverty as well as radical dependence. This stipulation indicates that the early people in the movement did indeed have suitcases, food, and extra shoes, but that they were forbidden to use them for the mission. The saying prevents those who have these resources from using them; it indicates that the movement included those who did have resources. If all the missionaries were already poor, or living in dire poverty, this issue would never have been raised. The fact that it is raised points to other ways of understanding the social and economic organization of the early movement. The missionaries voluntarily embrace a level of poverty that does not necessarily represent their normal social or economic status. They become poor, dependent upon God, and dependent upon the hospitality of those to whom they go for their all their resources and provisions.

The prohibition of the walking stick speaks to the issue of comfort: the missionary travel should not be comfortable or easy, but strenuous and unaided. The difficult walking, unassisted by a stick, insures that the missionary experiences the danger and discomfort of the road without a buffer and without aid. The missionary is not a casual traveler, or even a business or imperial authority using the Roman roads, but rather a vulnerable agent on a divine mission.

It is precisely the divine mission that makes salutations on the road problematic. The missionary has been commissioned for serious work. The prohibition against chatting on the way and against engaging with others outside the mission itself depicts the travel as intentional, determined, and comprehensive. It is so all encompassing that nothing can intrude. So the missionaries must not greet anyone on the way.

This saying portrays the seriousness of the missionary efforts of the early Jesus movements. These missionaries sacrificed everything for their commission to extend the empire of God and to gather the people into the safety and blessedness of that divine empire. The manner of the missionaries' travel underlines the difference between the Roman Empire and the divine empire. In the divine empire, new social and religious systems come into being: adherents embrace poverty freely; they gladly submit themselves to dependence on God for support and provision; they gladly receive their traveling provisions from others without complaint; they risk their safety and health for the mission; and they trust that other individuals and communities will supply their needs and fulfill their desires. This saying implicitly criticizes the Roman Empire and its means of operation and promulgates another system for those working for the empire of God.

The Christians, however, were not the only social critics of the Roman world. Other itinerants also embraced a similar poverty and renounced social interaction and politics. These were the Cynics, a philosophical movement that criticized Rome by their performances in the public arena. They, too, embraced poverty. Many Romans might have looked at these missionaries and assumed not that they were Christians, but that they were philosophical critics of the Roman political regime and Roman social mores. Their appearances would have been remarkably similar. Perhaps it was Jesus and the Christians who imitated the Cynics in their mode of dress and behavior as a means of criticizing the Romans while announcing the presence and advocating the expansion of the empire of God.

Saying 27
Q 10:5–9
Matthew 10:7–8, 10b–13 and Luke 10:5–9

(1) If you should enter into a house, say first, "[May] peace be upon this house." Then, if a child of peace is there, let your peace be upon him; but if not, let your peace be turned back upon yourself.

(2) In that house remain eating and drinking their [food], for the laborer is worthy of his salary.

(3) Do not travel from house to house.

(4) And if you should enter a city and they receive you, eat the things placed before you, and heal those who are sick in the city, and say to them, "The empire of God is close to you."

The Mission Speech moves from the personal circumstances of the itinerant missionaries to some principles governing their reception by both individual houses and cities. The saying founds these principles solidly on the preference for poverty, vulnerability, and dependence, as noted in earlier sayings, and it fleshes out the implications of those values in relationship to the missionaries' reception while traveling.

The first circumstance relates to entering a house. Syntactically, the conditional clause presents a general condition. The form does not indicate whether the condition is real or probable. It simply presents a general statement that indicates that if a missionary should enter a house, the missionary should send peace to it. The missionary bestows peace upon the house without knowing whether or not the missionary will be received positively or negatively. The entrance into a house demands the bestowing of peace regardless of reception.

Syntactically, the following conditional phrases also present general conditions; that is, they merely state what will happen under certain circumstances. The first condition stipulates that if a peaceful person resides in the house, the missionary should let the peace remain upon the house, but if a peaceful person does not reside there, the peace should be turned back onto the missionary. Peace here functions almost like a positive curse or spell. When cursing someone, a person sends out a verbal spell that binds and wounds the person being cursed. A verbal pattern or spell has a deleterious effect upon the person being cursed. Peace here functions in the same way, but positively. The missionaries must send out their peaceful spell and put it on the house before knowing how they will be received. If the house has peaceful residents, the blessing may stay upon it, but if the house has violent or evil residents, the missionary must withdraw the blessing. Peace is treated as a physical commodity that can be sent out and turned back by the will of the person bestowing it.

The second part of this saying provides instruction on eating and a rationale for that instruction. The saying advocates simply eating whatever the host offers. This injunction could function in a number of different ways. At one level, it releases the missionary from any purity or dietary restrictions. This means that the missionary, if presented food offered to idols, may eat it without any pain of conscience, as Paul argued in 1 Corinthians 8. Or it may mean that any Jewish dietary restrictions that may have been in existence at this time would not apply to the missionaries. Or it could also refer to Roman vegetarians, who on philosophical principles would not eat meat; they should eat whatever their hosts provided. Or it could simply mean that the itinerant missionaries should not be discriminating about their food and that they should eat whatever everyone else in the household eats. In any event, the saying instructs them to eat what is put before them.

The second part of this saying also provides a rationale: "for the worker deserves a salary." This rationale does not exactly match the principle that it justifies. The principle states that the missionary should eat whatever; the rationale states that the missionary deserves to be fed. They correlate but actually state different aspects: the principle is addressed to the missionary, and the rationale is addressed to the host. The same issue was raised by Paul as well. In 1 Corinthians 9:14, Paul argues that the apostles deserve to be supported by their local hosts. It seems that this principle of supporting the itinerant apostles and missionaries was important in the various early Jesus movements. In a sense, the principle and its rationale made it possible for the movements to spread farther and farther across the ancient Mediterranean to the west, along Northern Africa to the south, and as far as China to the east.

Two aspects of these Mission Speech sayings so far deserve mention. The correlation of instructions in Jesus' sayings to letters of Paul indicates that these principles found wide circulation in the early movements among a very diverse group of apostles and missionaries. Paul does not refer this principle or its rationale to a saying of Jesus, but clearly he understands them and expects others both to understand and to act on them. The second point is that Paul clearly understands the instruction about the laborer deserving support to refer to apostolic itinerants like himself and like his apostolic opponents who seem to be following him around and trying to subvert his mission. That implies that the Mission Speech may refer not only to generic missionaries, just people called out to traverse the world spreading the good news of God's empire, but to those designated by the community as apostles and to those whose own experience of Jesus after his death sent them out to begin to proclaim God's empire known through the death and resurrection of Jesus. The apostolic overtones, perceived only by reading the Pauline parallels, add weight to these instructions.

The third section of this saying tells the missionaries not to move from house to house. Like the seriousness of purpose expressed in not greeting anyone on the road (Saying 26), this part of the saying reinforces the seriousness of the mission by discouraging the missionaries from shopping around for better, more hospitable, or more receptive homes. The missionaries ought not to consider themselves shoppers looking for the best place to live. They have a serious purpose that requires a level of stability in their itinerancy. The stability provided by staying in one house, not moving about from place to place, again invokes the Pauline scheme, which demanded that Paul support himself by his trade and stay put in one community until the churches were fully established. This part of these instructions argues for just such a stability in the midst of an itinerant way of living.

The fourth section of this saying describes the itinerant missionaries' work: they travel and find hospitality on the way, eating whatever is provided; they heal the sick and proclaim the immediacy of the empire of God. We have just encountered the first three elements (travel, reception, and eating whatever the host offers) in the earlier sections of this saying. So this must be a kind of summary of the mission project that encapsulates the entire program. The saying includes two important new elements: powerful deeds and the announcement of the empire of God. The references to the healing of the sick and other powerful deeds have already been explored

(Sayings 18 and 19) in some detail, and they will continue to be central themes in these sayings. So also with the announcement of the empire of God. These elements have been central to the way these sayings of Jesus describe the mission and the various functions of leaders within the multiple movements that have formed. The final statement, then, encapsulates the entire missionary agenda and succinctly describes the mode of being a missionary and the primary works to be performed among the various people to whom the missionaries go.

I would like to raise one final point here. This saying and others seem to indicate that there were both itinerants and hosts involved in the early Jesus movements from the beginning. Not everyone traveled; some stayed in one place and offered hospitality to those who did travel. This points to two different kinds of community organization in the early movements: stable households of sufficient means to support visitors, and itinerants dependent upon them. For readers and for those who hear the voice of Jesus in these sayings, this Mission Speech provides two ways to support missions—to become a missionary and travel with the message or to become a household supporter of the mission. But the speech itself goes further and suggests that no matter how one lives, the extension of the divine empire remains a central task. In antiquity, that extension took place through itinerancy or hospitality; in later times, that extension occurs through service to the poor, intellectual work, the establishment of social services for the relief of the indigent, and many other notable works that require an equally strong commitment to embracing personal vulnerability and radical dependence upon God.

Saying 28
Q 10:10–12
Matthew 10:14–15 and Luke 10:10–12

But if you were to enter a city and they do not receive you, on leaving that city, shake the stirred-up dust from your feet. I say to you that it will be more tolerable for those living in Sodom than for that city.

The question of inhospitality would plague the itinerant missionaries and threaten their success. One cannot gather people into the empire of God if they are unwelcoming to its emissaries and to their deeds and message. This saying provides the pattern for responding to such inhospitality, and it constitutes a continuation of the previous saying (sections 1 and 4).

On entering a house, Jesus instructed the missionaries to send their peace upon the residents. This peace functioned as a blessing that placed a kind of verbal spell on the people of the house. The peace ritual effected a change in the people living in the house provided their lives were congruent with the ritual intent, to bring peace. Most societies practice such ritual actions, both verbal and sacramental.

Here we have a sacramental ritual action. When the missionaries encounter inhospitable cities in their work, the saying instructs them to shake the dust off their feet as they are leaving. The saying does not interpret the meaning of the ritual. Readers must create the interpretation. If the ritual action relates to the verbal action of the previous saying, where the peace was sent and returned if the people were not receptive to peace, then shaking off the dust enacts a way of symbolically returning to them all of the inhospitable city's substance. In other words, the missionaries take nothing from the city that would connect those left behind with the missionaries' powerful deeds and their proclamation of the empire of God. The ritual act displays the utter rejection and condemnation of those inhospitable to the emissaries of God.

The story of Sodom (Genesis 19:1–28) and its inhospitality toward the two angels (messengers) of God metonymically rehearses this situation. Lot received and hosted the two messengers of God, but the people of Sodom were inhospitable. God saved Lot but destroyed the people of Sodom and Gomorrah, telling Lot and his family not to turn back, not to look at what they had left. All obeyed, except Lot's wife, who was turned into a pillar of salt. The missionaries of the empire of God identify with the angels (messengers) of God sent to a foreign city. Lot embodies the hospitable reception of God's messengers, while the people of Sodom embody those who act inhospitably toward God's messengers. Lot's wife represents those who still hold on to their communities, despite their inhospitality and rejection of the messengers of God.

Shaking the dust from their feet prevents the itinerant Jesus missionaries from suffering the fate of Lot's wife's. The missionaries, for fear of holding on to the anger or the joy of the city, must separate completely from a place that has been inhospitable, leaving its fate, like that of Sodom, to the judgment of God. The act of shaking off the street dirt ritually separates the missionaries from the fate of the inhospitable city and ritually curses the people, subjecting them to God's wrath.

But the saying shows an increment of anger. Those who reject Jesus' missionaries will receive worse punishment than Sodom received. God punished Sodom with destruction by "sulfur and fire from the Lord out of heaven" (Genesis 19:24 NRSV), thoroughly destroying the city. God will intensify the destruction for those who reject the emissaries of the empire of God. There is real anger expressed here. This signifies that the missionary efforts were not always pleasant or successful and that the missionaries needed to entrust their anger at rejection to God's wrath. God would vindicate their anger and disappointment at rejection with a worse fate than Sodom. We will encounter more of that anger in the next saying.

Beyond the content of this saying, readers and hearers of Jesus' voice enact a process of reading scripture by entering into the story and living there. The reference to Sodom does not function as a proof text here, but as a parallel experience described in scripture through which later seekers may understand their own contemporary experience. Seekers comprehend their own experience by entering into the scriptural experience and making connections. Such reading constitutes a means of experiencing one's own life as refracted through the scriptures without necessarily requiring the scriptures themselves to address every possible life situation until the end of time.

Saying 29
Q 10:13–15
Matthew 11:21–24 and Luke 10:13–15

(1) Curses on you, Chorazin! Curses on you, Bethsaida!

(2) If the powerful deeds that were done in you were produced in Tyre and Sidon, they would have changed course in sackcloth and ashes. To be sure, it will be more tolerable for Tyre and Sidon at the end of the trial than for you.

(3) As for you, Capernaum, will you be exalted up to heaven? [No] you will fall into Hades!

In this saying, we find anger expressed in graphic language against cities that rejected the missionaries. The Mission Speech uses the blessings and curses tradition to bestow blessings on the hospitable and receptive while heaping curses on the inhospitable and unreceptive. This saying dramatically articulates the missionaries' anger and frustration with rejection.

Chorazin and Bethsaida (1) are on the shores of the Sea of Galilee in the region of Galilee, where the early Jesus movements probably originated. The missionaries probably experienced rejection there and so this saying curses the cities for their inhospitality and rejection, consistent with the condemnations outlined in Saying 28. The Greek word that I have translated "curses" is usually translated "woe," but this misses the dramatic sense that the Greek *ouai* suggests. The Greek connotes strong emotion, wailing, and intense disappointment. Chorazin and Bethsaida have incurred the wrath, anger, and condemnation of the missionaries thwarted in their effort to work powerful deeds and announce the coming of the empire of God.

The issue for Chorazin and Bethsaida (2) concerns their refusal to enter the empire of God when powerful deeds were performed within their walls. These cities did not understand. They did not comprehend the message. They did not find the powerful deeds compelling. They did not engage through them with God's empire. The saying offers another comparison, this time with the ancient foreign cities of Tyre and Sidon, who, had they seen what Chorazin and Bethsaida had experienced, would have changed course and followed the ways of God. These ancient cities, about which we know very little except that they were often reproached in the Israelite scriptures (see Joel 3:4–5 and Ezekiel 32:30, for example), did not have the benefit of powerful works of divine emissaries to make them change course. Chorazin and Bethsaida have been the recipients of these deeds but did not join the movement.

This part of section 2 envisions a trial at the end of time when every city will be judged according to its reception or rejection of the emissaries of God. On that day, the saying envisions that the despised Tyre and Sidon will fare better than the cities visited by the emissaries of God's empire in Jesus' time. The judgment will be harsher on those who had the opportunity to enter the empire of God but did not than on those who did not have the opportunity to enter because they did not have the emissaries, their powerful deeds, or the proclamation of the reign of God.

Capernaum (3) is also a city in the Galilee, near Chorazin and Bethsaida. The saying confronts Capernaum in a question, which we know to be a way of asking the readers/hearers to enter into the discourse and to survey their own lives and reactions. Will we, the readers, imitate Chorazin and Bethsaida and reject the message? Will God exalt Capernaum? Capernaum has the opportunity to enter the empire of God and has presumably seen the powerful deeds. So what will happen? The saying answers for the readers: no, if Capernaum rejects the emissaries of God, then it too will be plunged into Hades at the final judgment. Only those places that see and understand the powerful deeds as well as hear and respond positively to the announcement of God's empire will be exalted and justified.

It is not often that modern people have the opportunity to look into the experience and anger of ancient people. These sayings provide a window into that frustration and anger, the rejection and the cursing, the blessing and the joy of these early missionaries. It is a precious window indeed. For later hearers and readers, such anger demands attention because it demonstrates the strong emotions felt by those who were involved in the divine empire. As hearers of Jesus' voice, we cannot ignore emotions now considered destructive, such as anger and hatred, but must engage with them in the context of the divine empire. This saying guides the way.

Saying 30
Q 10:16
Matthew 10:40 and Luke 10:16

The one who receives you receives me, and the one who receives me receives the one who sent me.

This saying articulates the principle of inherent presences. The principle maintains that one person becomes so identified with another that the distinction between them disappears and no means of differentiating them exists. One person's presence so inheres in another that they become one undifferentiated being. It is not simply representational, that one person represents the personality of another, but inherence in that one person becomes so identified with the other that they present themselves as one being coexisting in one another. It also does not function as a metonym, where one stands in for another whose characteristics transfer from one to another, but rather a very intense identification of one being with another so that they become virtually indistinguishable.

This saying presents a threefold series of inherent presences: the itinerant missionary, Jesus, and the one who sent Jesus. These three persons so inhere that to receive one is to receive all three. When a host receives the itinerant missionary, the host receives not only the missionary, but the one who sent the missionary (Jesus) and the one who sent Jesus (God). The saying presents an implied question to the reader: "How do I find God?" The answer works backward from the question. To find God, find Jesus as Jesus manifests himself in the work of the ones he has sent. To receive God into one's household, one receives Jesus inhering in the missionaries doing the work of the empire of God. The inherence of one in the other two makes this possible: to receive the missionary means ultimately to receive God.

This principle of inherent presences plays an important function in these sayings of Jesus, and it continually emerges in a variety of contexts in this collection of sayings. The sense of intimate communion one with another among the participants in the Jesus movements, as well as the intimate relationship established between the readers and hearers of the sayings and the Jesus who speaks them, makes this sort of inherent presence a touchstone of the inhering relationships among the various participants in the empire of God. Such relationships tend to collapse the hierarchy of relationship prevalent in the Greek and Roman worlds and to establish more familial or closely knit communities as the norm. Those familial connections bind community members to one another and the individuals and communities to Jesus and through Jesus to God. The interconnection does not mean simply that members of the community may represent God to others, but that each member, because the divine inheres within him or her, carries the divine presence to other members of the community and to those outside the community as well. The missionaries do not simply represent Jesus to those to whom they preach and among whom they perform powerful deeds, but they also make Jesus present in their persons, so that in effect it is not they who heal and preach, but Jesus himself. The principle of inherent presences makes this possible.

Saying 31
Q 10:21
Matthew 11:25–26 and Luke 10:21

In [that hour] he said, "I give thanks to you, Father, Lord of the heaven and of the earth, because you concealed these things from the wise and intelligent, and revealed them to infants. Yes [I praise you], O Father, because in this way it became well-pleasing before you."

The sayings of Jesus have not preserved many of his prayers. This prayer, together with the prayer in Saying 34 (the Lord's Prayer), are the only ones among the sayings sources. In both these prayers, Jesus addresses God as Father. This prayer, however, does not seem to present a model for praying. It presents a kind of proclamation to God in prayer form; its message relates to those to whom "these things" have been revealed. The prayer functions not as an exemplar because the readers and hearers overhear the message in a private conversation between Jesus and the Lord of heaven and earth.

This oblique overhearing of a prayer surprises the hearer and reader. Although Jesus has accustomed the readers and hearers of his voice to puzzle over things, to think through the implications of a proposition or question, and to apply them to their own circumstances, Jesus usually speaks directly to the people around him (then and now). The shift in mode of communication makes this saying even more puzzling. The point seems to be that the listeners hear Jesus' private thoughts and conversations about his mission to let them know that they are insiders, important participants in the movement, close colleagues of Jesus and his Father, and intimates of the divine plan that is being revealed. That intimate communication and close proximity emboldens the hearers to think of themselves as part of the inner circle of the empire of God.

The brief narrative sets a stage. We are told that Jesus prayed in these words "in that hour." The sayings collector, or whoever this narrative voice represents, locates the prayer in time, not in geography (as the healing in Saying 18) or in chronological sequence (as in the narrative frames concerning John in Sayings 19 and 20). The narrator implies that this "hour" is an important one, with significance, albeit opaque. Jesus prays this prayer to be overheard at a turning point, a time of transition or conflict when the insiders of the movement need to understand something about the divine plan.

Jesus addresses the prayer to the Father, the Lord of heaven and earth. In early Christianity, the appellation "Lord" was applied to Jesus, as Paul readily attests in numerous places in his letters. Here Jesus applies that title to the Father, whose rule extends over both heaven and earth. This Father, ruler of all creation, is Jesus' intimate conversation partner. Jesus ascribes the dominion not to himself, but to the Father. It can be assumed that this Father is the same as the "one who sent" Jesus (Saying 30). So the hearers overhear a prayer addressed to the Father, the one who sent Jesus.

The content of the overheard prayer revolves about the Father's hiding information from some and revealing it to others. That God reveals God's self does not surprise. That replicates part of the great epic story of Israel, that God chose the Israelites, guided them through the wilderness, revealed the law, made a covenant, and brought them into the promised land. That revelatory relationship articulates the modality of the relationship of chosen community to God. It is the hiding, or concealing, that stumps the reader. Why would God conceal God's self, plan, or purpose from anyone?

The concealing of God's purposes from some speaks to the question of overhearing the prayer. The readers understand that some people do not understand or appreciate the empire of God as announced by Jesus and the itinerant missionaries of the movement. Some, as we have heard in the previous sayings, do not receive the emissaries, reject the message, do not understand the purpose of the powerful deeds, and refuse to enter the empire of God. It appears as if God hid the meaning or concealed the significance of the movement and the revelation from them. Those who reject the movement simply do not see what God has done in front of them, and this must be part of God's plan. The concealing of revelation from some and the giving of revelation to others testifies to the reality of a movement in process, a movement growing while still encountering opposition.

In overhearing this prayer on the lips of Jesus, readers gain an insight into two things: first, why some people do not understand; and second, that God has ordained their lack of understanding. This puts the reader/hearer in a position of being among those who both have received the revelation and have understood it. The participants in the movement stand at the center of God's plan revealed to them.

The characterization of the two groups is interesting. The insiders who understand are infants, while those who reject God's plan are wise and intelligent. Those who think they already understand the ways of God and God's revelation reject the empire of God, as opposed to those who see themselves as infants, growing and learning the ways of God. The infants have a lifetime of growth and revelation ahead of them, and God showers them with glimpses to keep them developing and maturing in the revelation. Those who think they already know have rigid minds and cannot see the revelation presented to them. They are hardened in their minds and understanding and, therefore, cannot enter into the empire of God. The infants, however, receive, understand, appreciate, and live in the empire, moving constantly toward maturity and more developed understanding. This growth and development mark God's plans for the infants.

The last phrase of the saying is "Yes [I praise you], O Father, because in this way it became well-pleasing before you." The grammatical structure in the original Greek often implies words or phrases that must be repeated in English for the sentence to be a clear and accurate translation of the Greek; the bracketed phrase "I praise you" is one such instance. This prayer continues with the affirmation that this intentional concealing and hiding has a very beneficial result. The Greek noun *eudokia* has a range of meaning, from well-pleasing, good will, contentment, and the object of desire. It expresses the good effect of God's concealing and revealing, God's contentment, or God's desire for the predicated outcome of God's actions. God's plan takes shape in the process of concealing from those who think they understand and revealing to those who are willing to mature in their understanding.

The rhetorical strategy of communicating this information obliquely through an overheard prayer again puts the reader in the situation of puzzling over its meaning. Not being the addressee of the discourse, readers/listeners learn that Jesus addresses God as Father and Lord of the heavens and earth. The rhetoric creates a direct connection between the infants in the prayer and the readers who are privy to listening to the prayer. The oblique message emboldens its readers while at the same time causing them to think about those from whom the revelation has been concealed and about the others to whom it has been revealed. How are these other infants related to the hearers? Why do the wise and intelligent not get it? The rhetoric solves none of these issues, but raises them in such a way that readers may approach them with confidence about their own status and importance.

Saying 32
Q 10:22
Matthew 11:27 and Luke 10:22

All things have been transmitted to me by my Father, and no one knows the son except the Father, nor [does anyone know] the Father except the son, and the one to whom the son wishes to reveal (him).

This saying articulates directly what Saying 31 spoke obliquely. The sayings have an obvious connection, yet their rhetorical strategies differ. This one builds on the principle of inherent presence to establish a pattern of revelation from Father to son and then from son to those to whom he passes on the revelation. The word that I have translated "transmit" also functions as the word for tradition, referring to things handed down from one generation to another. The saying strongly contends that what the Father knows has been transmitted, handed over, made a part of the son's tradition.

The identification of the Father's knowledge or plan with Jesus raises Jesus' stature and importance. Jesus does not normally project himself into these sayings, nor does he overtly ascribe to himself divine status or being. Such a saying would be more comfortable in the thought world of the Gospel of John, where Jesus' divinity finds constant expression and reinforcement. So this saying presents an unusual portrait of Jesus as the one to whom the Father has transmitted all things. The saying presents Jesus as God's vicegerent.

The basis for this vicegerency emerges from the special knowledge that the Father and the son have of each other. The saying advocates a kind of knowledge peculiar to the Father known only to the son, and knowledge peculiar to the son known only to the Father. The Father and the son know each other by a peculiar knowledge inherent in their relationship, and that understanding can only be communicated to others by revelation from the son. While the Father and son have an innate knowledge, others must receive that knowledge not by nature of the relationship, but by revelation.

The saying conjoins knowledge and revelation, providing the origin of knowledge in the mutual relationship of Father to son and connecting that knowledge to revelation to those selected by the son to receive it. The question of election by the son displays the intentionality of the process.

Revelation happens by choice, to selected people, for specific purposes known to God and passed on to Jesus, and through Jesus to those elect.

But Jesus' vicegerency has an omnipotent aspect. The saying emphasizes that "all things" have been transmitted. This leaves no room for partial authority or limited power. The totality of knowledge and power has been given over to Jesus by the Father. No one may know either Jesus or the Father except through election by Jesus to receive knowledge that only he has of the Father. The progression, the pattern of revelation, moves from the elect hearer to Jesus and to the Father and involves a comprehensive knowledge founded upon an omnipotent and universal authority.

While other sayings underscore the intimacy of the hearers of Jesus' voice and the readers of the sayings with Jesus, and through Jesus with the Father, this saying seems harsher and more distant. Jesus paints a different picture of the relationship, one that at once confounds an earlier intimate relationship and simultaneously demands that hearers and readers consider the fragility of that intimacy. Conflicting information in these sayings deliberately guides those who read them and who seek to hear the voice of Jesus in them to reflect on themselves, their commitments, and their relationships from different perspectives to achieve their goal, a deeper understanding of revelation.

Saying 33
Q 10:23b–24
Matthew 13:16–17 and Luke 10:23b–24

Happy are the eyes that see what you see, for I say to you, that there were many prophets and emperors [who desired] to see what you see, but they did not see [it], and to hear what you hear, and they did not hear [it].

Every educational context has an elitist orientation. Students consider their teachers the very best, and they consider themselves extremely fortunate to be able to study with their teachers. An increment of privileged educational opportunity and status creates a sense of a privileged and elite group of students studying under a gifted teacher. Few students have ever described their good fortune to study with mediocre or poor teachers—they would not expend the energy. Good and exceptional teachers create a learning community among their students and give them the intellectual and social tools necessary for them to learn to the fullest of their abilities. This seems only proper. The elitism is not about the personal status of the students, but about their expressed good fortune to be able to work with gifted teachers.

This saying articulates that good fortune for the followers of Jesus: "Happy are the eyes that see what you see." Those who gather around Jesus the teacher find their blessedness together in seeing what they see. Here seeing is learning. The learning takes place not simply in intellectual activity, although, as we have seen in these sayings, that is an important element, but also in the observation of a way of life, of certain activities and ways of relating to one another, of certain specific practices, and of ways of thinking about the self, society, and the world. These students are blessed to see what they see and to learn from observation and imitation. Such an orientation toward learning makes sense when the educational environment includes the working of powerful deeds that prepare the way for the energetic proclamation of the empire of God. Seeing is learning.

To underscore the importance of this select group of students of the empire of God, Jesus compares them to prophets and emperors who have longed to see what they see and hear what they hear, but have not been able to do so. But why prophets and emperors? The prophets represent the ones who know and reveal the mind or will of God in critical circumstances and times. They are the friends of God, often persecuted for that friendship and intimacy with the divine intent, who show the people a new way. The prophets make present the religious knowledge of the past. They desired to see and to hear, but had not been able to do so until Jesus inaugurated the empire of God at the time of Caesar Augustus. The happiness of Jesus' students relates to their good fortune to be alive and engaged at the right time when they could see and hear the best of all divine teachers.

There were many imperial figures in the ancient Near East–Macedonia, Persia, Babylon, Israel, and now Rome had kings and emperors (the Greek word *basileus* may be translated either way) whose courts sponsored scribal schools. These emperors and kings all had religious functions and statuses ascribed to them: the ancient world did not make the distinctions modern people make between the religious and the political realms, because they were understood and experienced as one and the same in antiquity. So these kings and emperors desired to see the establishment of a universal, omnipotent, extensive, and comprehensive empire over which they would rule and upon which their divinity or divinities would bestow wealth and power. Here Jesus proclaims such an empire, not human, but divine. Jesus announced and inaugurated the kind of empire they all sought to create and to sustain in order to solidify their wealth and power, but under the imperial authority of God and among people who were elite only because they could see and hear the oracles of God. The elites of this imperial court do not gain power because of their wealth or their genealogy or their social standing, but by their ability to hear and to learn about the empire by studying with their magnificent teacher, by imitating his way of life, and then by inviting others of every race, gender, nationality, and social status to enter into the empire with them. This empire is a decidedly different empire; this emperor, a decidedly different emperor. Those who see and hear the difference receive the blessing and find their happiness.

But the blessing extends from Jesus' immediate context to readers of these sayings and hearers of Jesus' voice in other times. The written sayings and their recitation put people born later in touch with the same reality. Through their reading, their hearing, and their imaginations, they receive the blessing that Jesus announces. Later readers and hearers find themselves more fortunate and happy than the many prophets and emperors of years past precisely in this entrance into the eternal moment of the divine speech enthroned in these sayings.

Saying 34
Q 11:2b–4
Matthew 6:9–13a and Luke 11:2b–4

Whenever you pray, say, "Father, may your name be holy; may your imperium come. Give us today our daily bread, and forgive us our debts just as even we have forgiven those indebted to us. And do not lead us into [mere] experimentation."

This prayer, so familiar to Christians, carries a message far more radical and compelling than most have heard. The familiarity and frequent liturgical use of the prayer have dulled modern ears to hearing that radical and compelling message. The economic, political, and social dynamics articulated in this exemplary prayer ought to be as confounding now as they were in antiquity. If you look closely at the way that both Matthew and Luke have transmitted this prayer, you can easily see the way that communities have struggled to appropriate, and often to dilute, the meaning of the prayer. Here I will only deal with this reconstruction, leaving the comparison to the reader's own intellectual and spiritual pleasure.

Jesus' instruction presents the prayer as a model: "Whenever you pray, say. . . ." These five petitions cover a wide expanse of theological, political, social, and economic topics. Jesus presents them as the normative topics of prayer. The narrative introduction intends this to be the basis of prayer "whenever" a participant in the movement prays. The topics also reveal the values that formed the community, so that the prayer tells its members what ought to be central to their concerns. Together these topics constitute the central values of the movement when it is at prayer. It is interesting to note what is not here as well as what is included.

The first topic is the holiness of God's name. The Greek word *hagiazō* means to make sacred or holy with special reference to doing so by offering a sacrifice to the divinity. It is a term that arises in the context both of Jewish and Roman sacrificial temple practice, as well as in personal and social pious sacrifices in other contexts. The statement implies a personal and social sacrifice of some sort that makes God's name holy. The participants in the movements Jesus inaugurated make sacrifices that make God's name holy and sacred. The passage is in the passive voice: "May your name be hallowed." The focus shifts from those who are sacrificing to the holiness of the divine name. Although the hallowing of the name belongs to those who worship God, the emphasis rests not on those hallowing the name, but upon God's own self. The passive voice suggests that the sacrifice that sanctifies God's name is only instrumental, pointing not to the benefit of the sacrificer, but to the glory of the divine name.

The second topic presents a dramatic image of God's empire: "May your imperium come." The statement suggests treason because it advocates an alternative empire, an alternative governmental structure, to that of local rulers, kings, or emperors. This governmental rule belongs to God and to God alone. The participant prays for God's empire to become the ruling force in society, an empire that thwarts and subverts all other empires. The first topic relates to sacrifice that hallows, while the second topic proclaims a radical political message. There can be no other emperor than God, no other empire than God's empire.

The third topic introduces radical dependence upon God, a dependence that we have encountered frequently in these sayings: "Give us today our daily bread." The Greek word describing the bread, *epiousion*, is very rare, so it is difficult to know precisely how to translate it. It could mean either bread sufficient for today, for the coming day, or for every day ("daily bread"); or it may mean, as certain of the early church fathers described it, the super-essential bread of the divine empire. So whether it is some special bread, as manna from heaven was in the Israelite scriptures (Exodus 16), or the bread sufficient for today (or the coming day, tomorrow), this petition asks God not for permanent provisions and support, but for just enough to get through the day. It restates the radical dependence upon God that the itinerant missionaries were instructed to maintain (Sayings 26 and 27) and that Jesus enjoined upon all the participants in the movement (Saying 55). Whenever one participant or the entire community prays, they must ask simply for what is sufficient food for the day, nothing more, nothing less. They must be absolutely dependent upon God in their living and working, without any other means of support and without any provision for setting aside anything for a difficult time. This petition defines radical dependency.

The fourth petition states a very radical economic policy: "forgive us our debts just as even we have forgiven those indebted to us." Just about every Christian era, beginning with Matthew and Luke, tried to change the meaning of this petition either to spiritualize it or to make it refer to something other than monetary debts. But not so here. This petition states boldly that participants in God's empire forgive the debts owed them, just as their debts are forgiven. No more indebtedness. No more interest on money loaned. No more engagement in the economic system of lending, interest, and repayment.

This petition asks God, the divine emperor of the realm, to forgive debts in the same way that participants in the movement forgive others' debts. But notice the chronology. First, participants forgive debts. This is the first step and it happens prior to the request that God do likewise. The community norm demands that there be no indebtedness, no holding of others in debt. This is a given. Then the community asks God to treat them in the same way they treat each other within the community and in the same way that they treat those outside it. The prayer does not stipulate that the forgiving of debts is for insiders only; the saying states that all debt is forgiven to those who owe without any restriction or boundary placed on that forgiving. God is to do unto others as others do unto others (see Sayings 8 and 10).

The prayer concludes with a dramatic last petition: "And do not lead us into [mere] experimentation." The Greek word *peirasmon* suggests a wide variety of meanings: a trial, a temptation, a worry or concern. In this context, it has eschatological implications, the trial or temptation standing at the end of time—at least this is how it is usually understood. But I take the word back to its root, *peira*, which means a trial, an attempt, an experience, a testing out of an experience, so translate the word as "experiment." I think this petition does not refer to the end-time or to final judgment at the end of time, but to a way of living in the current time. The petitioner asks God to establish the way of living encapsulated in this prayer—this forgiving of debt, this dependence upon God for food and support, this divine imperium under the holy emperor God, and these sacrifices both corporate and individual that hallow God's name—something real, something tangible, something substantive and actual. The petition asks that all these things not simply function in the realm of some divine experiment like the one inflicted on Job, but that all these petitions encapsulating a distinct and radical way of life become real like the empire of God, like the holiness of the divine name. This petition prays that God not make this whole program a mere experiment.

Such a petition captures the readers (and the reciters of the prayer in every age) off guard. The introduction of the possibility of a divine experiment, one that might on the face of it have a chance of failing, puts pressure on those participants to risk all, to take a chance even given the possibility of failure, and ultimately to step into this new empire of God no matter what the consequences. This petition closes not with a final *deus ex machina* before the final throne at the end of time, but with a call to decision, to risk, to know that there is no guarantee of success, no guarantee of food for today, no guarantee of money paid back to provide for tomorrow, no guarantee that the emperor God will ultimately be victorious. It is that risk, a divine risk, which ends this rather dramatic prayer, leaving the final choice to the reader or reciter to make. "And do not lead us into [mere] experimentation."

This exemplary prayer does indeed speak radically. It posits personal and corporate sacrifice that makes God's name holy. It places a divine empire over all other empires of the world. It places the participants in this divine empire in a relationship of radical dependence upon God for food and provision. It opts out of the economic system of lending and interest in order to show that radical dependence, and then begs God to treat the petitioners in the same way. And it suggests that this just might be a divine experiment, a testing of the mettle of the participants by a God who merely wants to know if they can give up everything (like Job) and remain faithfully dependent upon God. The prayer in its radicality gives little comfort, but it most certainly presents the values and internal systems that make these Jesus movements vital and alive.

Saying 35
Q 11:9–13
Matthew 7:7–11 and Luke 11:9–13

(1) I say to you: "Demand and it will be given to you, examine closely and you will discover, knock and it will be opened to you. For the one who demands, receives; the one who investigates, finds; for the person knocking, it will be opened.

(2) What person among you, of whom his son demands bread, would rather give him a stone? Or even if he were to ask for a fish, would give him a snake?

(3) If you, then, being worthless, know how to give good gifts to your children, by how much more will the Father in heaven give to those who demand of him?"

I have deliberately avoided familiar language in this translation in order to resist a facile assumption of meaning. The saying promulgates such a strong statement of affirmation, which familiarity with the traditional language destroys, that the reader needs to find different ways to engage the saying. The simple and direct narrative frame, "I say to you," directly confronts the readers and hearers. Jesus speaks directly to them then and now, jumping off the page to speak directly to every participant in the Jesus movements. The "you" is plural, so he speaks to the readers as a community, as a group. This saying speaks to the readers' corporate needs and communal desires.

The saying consists of three parts. First, an injunction to demand, to investigate, and to knock at doors. Each of these acts achieves success. The second part, again in the traditional modality of these sayings, confronts the communities with a series of questions. The third part provides the theological rationale for the question of giving raised in the second part and the issue of demanding raised in the first part. It is an eloquent saying intended to confront the reader and to make a theological point.

Jesus tells his followers to demand, to investigate thoroughly, and to knock. For itinerant missionaries and for people eager to extend the boundaries of the empire of God, knocking at doors makes sense. All the participants in the movements probably knocked on closed doors not knowing whether the response would be hospitable or condemning. Jesus assures them in this saying that if they knock, the door will be open to them. They will receive a positive response, at least to the extent that someone will acknowledge their initial attempt at beginning a conversation. Obviously, this part of the saying also has a metonymic quality: the door may stand in the place of anything that shuts out a participant in the movement. The closed door could be social mores, religious practices, political realities, social taboos, or anything that clearly separates one group from another and shuts out some people while enclosing and including others.

The injunction to investigate thoroughly, to seek, has an intellectual component not often associated with Jesus or the early Jesus movements. Jesus instructs his followers to seek, to investigate, to look into matters thoroughly. No blind faith here. Seekers must use their intellectual faculties to delve deeply into the realities of the empire, the meanings of the sayings, the mystery of the divine presence, as well as into other aspects of their lives and their participation in the Jesus community. They must think, search, look for answers and connections, and Jesus assures them that their investigations will be successful. They will discover what they're searching for. They will find the meaning that they desire. But only if they engage their minds in the enterprise.

The first statement also confronts the readers and hearers. "Demand and it will be given to you." The key to this saying is the need for the community, for the seekers, to know what they truly need and want. Before seekers can ask, they need to know and clearly articulate their needs, and when they do demand what they wish, Jesus guarantees that they will receive it. For that reason, I use the stronger translation "demand" rather than "ask," which seems less intentional, less focused, and weaker than the more forceful "demand." The seeking community and those around them, including God, have such a relationship that they may mutually make demands upon each other and upon God with full assurance that their demands will be met.

Just in case the community missed the point, the saying reiterates the message of this first section: "For the one who demands, receives; the one who investigates, finds; for the person knocking, it will be opened." Jesus categorically insists that these efforts will be successful. The saying does not raise the issue as a set of conditions, "if you ask, you will receive," but as a series of declarative statements, all intended to validate the success of the endeavors, the success of demanding, investigating thoroughly, and knocking at closed doors. Both with respect to the community of the followers and with God, these actions will be successful.

The second part of the saying confronts the readers and hearers with provocative questions intended to model proper responses to requests. The first question posits a situation in which a son requests bread and the person (presumably a parent) gives a stone. The request for something edible elicits something neither edible nor related to eating, a complete disjunction between request and response. Similarly, the request for fish results in the proffering of a snake. This again reinforces the disjunction. Posed as questions, they dramatize the inability of the community, or for that matter, God, to respond negatively or inappropriately to the requests of others. As questions, they encourage readers and hearers to examine their own responses to requests. How does a participant in these movements really respond—by giving a stone when bread is requested or by giving a snake when the request is for fish? Does the response create a disjunction between the values of the community and the response of its members? Does the response show a conjunction between request and response by community members and even by God? The question forces readers to consider their own lives and responses in relationship to the injunctions of the first part of the saying—to demand, to investigate thoroughly, to knock at closed doors.

The third part of the saying offers a theological position. The saying characterizes those who respond inappropriately to requests, that is, those who would give a stone instead of bread or a snake instead of fish, as worthless, debased, or evil. The saying argues that even those who respond inappropriately give good things to their children. Their inappropriate response does not include those close to them, in their own families or in their own close communities. In these circumstances, they respond appropriately, while in others they create a disjunction between request and response. The saying creates a correlation between the father who is useless, but still gives good things to his children, and the Father in heaven, who is not useless and gives even better things to his children. The community of followers have become God's family, and the paterfamilias of the family, God, will provide appropriate and good responses to God's children's requests.

The final statement of the saying again confronts its readers and hearers: "If you, then, being worthless ..." Are the readers part of the corrupt family that gives good things only to its own members, or are they part of the larger heavenly family where requests receive appropriate and immediate response? The challenge demands a choice, a decision, or at least an exploration of readers' values and connections. The saying underscores the theological point, however, that to the degree that there is goodness in every parent, the divine parent exceeds all expectations and provides abundantly for those who join the empire of God.

Saying 36
Q 11:14–15, 17–20
Matthew 9:32–34; 12:25–28 and Luke 11:14–15, 17–20

(1) And he exorcized a demon of muteness, and when the demon was cast out, the mute person spoke, and the crowds were astonished.

(2) And some said, "He exorcizes in [the name of] Beelzebul, the commander of the demons."

(3) Knowing their thinking, he said to them, "Every empire split into factions against itself is laid waste, and every household split into factions against itself will not survive.

(4) And if I myself exorcize demons in the name of Beelzebul, in whose [name] will your sons exorcize? For this reason they themselves will be judges over you.

(5) If then by the finger of God, I myself exorcize demons, then indeed upon you has come the empire of God."

This saying appears to have undergone some expansion and development. The subject matter, though on the whole cohesive, shifts from perspective to perspective. The heart of the saying seems to be section 3, which talks about the destruction and downfall of divided empires and houses. To this saying has been added a narrative context (1), which has been expanded by the addition of dialogue (2). Section 4 applies the central saying of section 3 to the narrative context and the central saying around which it has been constructed, while section 5 concludes the saying with a theological explanation and application.

This saying displays a complex developmental history that instructs readers on the complexity and uses of the sayings themselves. Even though these sayings are attributed to Jesus, they were remembered and passed on to others within particular contexts. The sayings functioned in various circumstances, and communities applied them to their own lives and issues freely. People connected this saying about a divided empire and house to the question of exorcism and authority for exorcizing. The central saying in section 3 does not actually refer to anything specific about exorcism: it simply makes a statement about the inevitably destructive effects of factionalism and division. This statement could be applied to any number of different circumstances, especially given the contentious impulse of formative Christianity evidenced in the letters of Paul (see the opponents of 2 Corinthians) and in the description of Paul's meeting with Peter and James in Jerusalem (Galatians 2:1–14). But here in this saying, the community applied the central saying to the question about exorcizing and other powerful deeds.

The exorcism contains traditional elements of a healing: the description of the ailment ("he exorcized a demon of muteness"), the healing ("when the demon was cast out"), the effect of the healing ("the mute person spoke"), and the response of witnesses ("the crowds were astonished"). This small narrative creates the interpretive context for the central saying, which has nothing to do with exorcism and everything to do with the destructive effects of division. The interpretative context has to do with the ability of a healer to perform a powerful deed, an exorcism. The crowds' amazement highlights the power of the deed, while the exorcism itself receives very little description. The narrative is simple: there was a man who had a demon that made him mute; it was cast out and the man spoke again. The narrative itself is not what is important: it simply provides the setting that introduces the dialogue.

The second part of the saying moves from setting to the besetting issue. Among those who were amazed, a few commented: "He exorcizes in [the name of] Beelzebul, the commander of the demons." Nothing in the narrative thus far prepares us for this statement. Either it is an assumption (because of the nature of the deed) or it is an attempt to disparage the powerful deed of exorcism. These "few" ascribe the authority for the exorcism to a highly placed and powerful demon: they identity the demonic figure by name, Beelzebul, and they describe him as the "commander of the demons." The discussion is not about the power of the deed or whether it was accomplished. Rather, the argument is about the authority of the healer and the origin of the power that expelled the demon of muteness. Like the debate in Saying 3 between Jesus and Satan, this saying squares off one ultimate authority against another, Beelzebul against the authority Jesus invoked.

The central saying, applied here to the question of the origin of the power to exorcize, has two parts. First, the narrative speaker ascribes a kind of omniscience to the healer: he knows what people are thinking and, knowing their thoughts, he can bring forward a wisdom saying to present to them. The point of the saying itself remains clear: division destroys an empire; division ruins a household. The language, however, is dramatic: "Every empire split into factions against itself is laid waste." Internal factions become an internal military enemy capable of destroying the empire. The language invokes a military campaign, as does the description earlier of Beelzebul as "the commander of the demons." The second example makes the same point with respect to a household: "every household split into factions against itself will not survive." Jesus characterizes Beelzebul as the leader of an empire or the head of a household. If the demon can be exorcized by a demon, then the exorcism indicates that the household of demons is divided, that the empire has split into destructive factions. If done by the "commander of the demons," the exorcism signifies that the empire and the household of the demons will be destroyed and cannot survive. Jesus simply takes the supposition that the exorcism occurred under the authority of Beelzebul to its logical conclusion.

The fourth section of this saying, seemingly a response to the central wisdom saying of section 3, remains opaque: "And if I myself exorcize demons in the name of Beelzebul, in whose [name] will your sons exorcize? For this reason they themselves will be judges over you." This does not follow the logic of the preceding section. It moves in another direction, seemingly speaking to the few who questioned, but actually also turning to the readers through the reference to "your sons." This section of the saying presumes that the onlookers will replicate Jesus' powerful deeds. They, too, will exorcize demons, just as Jesus has. The question Jesus presents, however, asks by whose name they will exorcize, if Jesus does it through Beelzebul. The assumption in the Jesus movements is that healing and exorcism would take place in the name of God. The sons of the onlookers would imitate Jesus' actions and exorcize in God's name. In such imitation, the sons of the onlookers would show that their authority and knowledge surpass that of their parents. They will become judges over them. The sons will rule over the parents. The spiritual authority of a divine household and a divine empire undivided will destroy and undermine the authority of the divided household, the empire of Beelzebul, and all who exorcize in his name. As the previous section of the saying indicated: if demons expel demons, it signifies a divided empire that cannot prevail, but if the divine emperor expels the commanders of an enemy's army, then that household remains strong and will prevail.

This last point is made explicit in the final section of the saying: "If then by the finger of God, I myself exorcize demons, then indeed upon you has come the empire of God." The victorious and prevailing household, the united empire, stands able to destroy its enemies, to exorcize the forces of the opposing empire. And this opposition signifies something quite different from the divided household of Beelzebul. This exorcism indicates the immediate presence of the divine empire that has descended into the realm of everyday living. Even though the narrative setting points toward the existence of two empires in opposition to one another, that of God and that of Beelzebul, in the end, only one empire stands undivided and without factions, only one household remains solid and unified, and that is the household and empire of God, whose strength is so mighty that exorcisms may be accomplished through his finger alone. Jesus and his followers represent the inauguration of the divine empire on earth. Their exorcisms display their unity with the divine forces and their power over all their adversaries.

For the readers of these sayings and for those who listen to the voice of Jesus in them, this saying creates a whirlwind: the context shifts; the various parts move fluidly within the shifting contexts; controversies erupt between Jesus and his adversaries and between Jesus and Beelzebul; Jesus speaks directly to readers and hearers outside the immediate context; and the resolution of the problem seems almost anticlimactic in its positive assertion of the final authority of Jesus and the divine empire. This whirlwind models a kind of engagement that does not evade controversy and conflict but embraces them as a means of revelation and renewal. The saying meets conflict head-on in order to articulate precisely the theological perspective and realities of the empire of God. This articulation becomes a revelation developing from the real conflicts and pains of everyday living and struggling to understand the ways of God in the midst of a combative and confrontational world.

Saying 37
Q 11:[21–22]
Matthew 12:29 and Luke 11:21–22

No one is capable of entering a strong person's house to steal from it without first tying up the strong person. Only then can the house be robbed.

This saying operates at a number of different levels. The literal level makes clear sense: a thief may only rob a strong person's house by immobilizing the strong person, making him incapable of defending his house. Thievery requires inhibiting those capable of preventing the crime, because a strong person can resist the thief and thwart efforts to plunder his house. The literal level presents a brief statement of a truth regarding the problem a thief faces before a householder capable of defending his or her property.

At another level, the description of the householder as a strong person, a powerful person capable of defending what properly belongs to him, suggests one of the people who participates in the Jesus movements. Such a strong person—strengthened by a trust in divine providence and care (Saying 55), aware of a divine mission supported by the power of God (Sayings 24–30), assured of divine election and of true knowledge of God (Sayings 32, 33), enfolded in the empire of God (Saying 82), capable of working powerful deeds and announcing that divine empire to others (Saying 27), assured of the presence of the spirit to guide and direct (Saying 53), and not fearful of those who can kill the body (Saying 49)—knows the meaning of real strength. No one may prevail against that person. There is no power strong enough to bind such a person.

The little narrative, then, assures participants in the movement that by claiming and building upon the strength given to them, as those who put the foundation of their houses upon rock (Saying 17), they will prevail against every person who seeks to immobilize or hurt them. The narrative guarantees that they cannot be plundered if they remain strong, because a thief cannot rob a strong person's house unless he subdues the strong person.

However, the saying comes from the perspective of the thief. It is not a direct statement, but one that talks about the weakness of the thief who would like to subdue the strong householder. The saying bolsters participants in the Jesus movements not by making them strong, but by referring to the weakness and inability of the thief to plunder the strong person's house. It argues for the weakness of the opponents in the face of the participants' strength.

At yet another level, this saying makes a point about the empire of God, also referred to as the household of God, with God at its head (see Sayings 32, 35, for example). God, arguably the strongest person in human activity, cannot be plundered by anyone, because God cannot be subdued, immobilized, or vanquished. God's strength so far surpasses that of all God's enemies and foes that God's household, the empire of God, can never be robbed or plundered by anyone. The empire stands on the strength and power of the divine person who stands as its head of household.

The three levels of meaning in this short saying display the way in which each of these sayings may often hold divergent and rich alternative meanings, all of which may be supported by the text. That is to say, the text is multivalent—in a deliberate way, it presents different perspectives and provocative words and images that suggest a limitless variety of interpretations and applications.

Saying 38
Q 11:23
Matthew 12:30 and Luke 11:23

The one not with me opposes me, and the one who does not gather [people] together with me drives [them] away.

This saying plays with the concept that not acting functions as an action. It consists of two parts, the first relating to the work of Jesus, the second relating to the work of the participants in the movements that continue the work that Jesus started.

The first part of the saying presents a mysterious proposition: anyone who does not join Jesus does not remain indifferent or neutral to him, but becomes an active agent opposing him. Not participating in the empire that Jesus announces and inaugurates constitutes a rejection and opposition to Jesus and God's empire. The saying suggests an ultimacy to Jesus' work that demands attention, that cannot sustain neutrality or refusal to participate, and that cannot be ignored. It also suggests that those whom Jesus invites to join him must make a choice: either to join him or to oppose him. Like the person in Saying 23 who wanted to follow Jesus but first wanted to bury his father, the person in this saying has a choice—either to follow Jesus or to oppose Jesus. The saying admits of no middle ground, no time of equivocation, no evasion of the empire that Jesus activates through his speech and powerful deeds. Jesus states it boldly: "the one not with me opposes me."

The second part of the saying turns attention not to Jesus, but to those who follow Jesus. In a sense, the saying turns from outsiders to insiders in the movement. Outsiders who do not join Jesus announce themselves as opponents, but insiders who do not gather people together, who do not bring them to the banquet or the festival of the empire, actually drive people away. This second part indicates that those involved with the Jesus movements must continue to gather people together for eating as in a symposium (this concept of the meal is implicit in the Greek word *synagōn*) or in a study group (the same Greek word applies to meetings of Jewish people for the practice of their religion). Those involved in the movement become its opponents by not performing the central acts of the community of those inside the empire of God: to gather people into the empire and to nurture them in the practices and principles that define it. One either gathers people in or drives them away. Again, the saying admits of no middle ground, no equivocation, no prevarication. One either gathers or disperses people.

This saying provides an interesting insight into the social dimension of Jesus' mission. The collection of people into groups is central to the divine empire. It works in two ways: the first consists of the frontline social grouping of those who gathered themselves into the empire by responding directly to Jesus' words and deeds. The second way that the construction of community happens requires those who have already entered the divine empire to gather others into it. In both systems, the formation of communities of people who relate to each other and to God as participants in the divine empire is the central factor to living in the empire. The social dimension of living in the empire takes precedence over all other individual and personal issues: the community of those in the divine empire, those who join Jesus or those whom Jesus' followers invite into the movement is central to the instantiation and embodiment of the empire of God in the human realm. People either join the empire or oppose it; they either gather people into the empire or drive them out. No one remains neutral.

Saying 39
Q 11:24–26
Matthew 12:43–45 and Luke 11:24–26

Whenever the foul spirit has been exorcized from the person, it passes through arid places seeking rest, and it does not find it. It says: "I will return to my house from which I was exorcized." And returning, it finds [the house] swept clean and beautified. Then it goes out and it associates with itself seven other spirits more useless than itself and they come together to set up house there, and [so] it is that the last state of that person [is] worst than the first.

In a small narrative, this saying elaborates a process of reversal, the first and the last, with respect to the state of being after an exorcism. It compares the first state, characterized by the cleansing and beautification that follows an exorcism, with the last state, where the foul spirits return in strength to take control of the person again, only now more fiercely. It is the reversal that drives the narrative.

People in antiquity knew that they shared the physical universe with a wide variety of spirits, which could be bad or good, clean or unclean, positive or negative. The physical universe reverberated with beings in various states of embodiment, from the fully embodied state of the human person to the semi-embodied state of various spirits to the completely disembodied and spiritual state of the angels or divine beings who dwelled in the heavens. Belief in these beings formed an important part of the psyche and mentality of people in antiquity—they were part of everyday life.

Certain places provided particularly fitting environments for various spirits. At home, the spirits of the gods or of deceased family members properly functioned around the hearth, the place where the family assembled both for the extension of its own life and for ritual observances that honored the spirits. The desert and other arid places properly housed spirits that had a more pernicious or devious nature. In these sayings, the desert as a place of temptation or of educational debate plays an important role (Sayings 3 and 20). The desert provided an arena where people could discern spirits and understand spiritual forces, good or evil. Spirits could not simply be dissolved or expelled; they needed to have a place to go as partially embodied beings in the physical universe. Place formed an important part of the lore of spirits in antiquity.

Now this saying begins to make more sense. A foul or unclean spirit is expelled from a person. But no place has been designated for the exorcized spirit to go. So it travels in search of a resting place. It goes to the place where spirits are properly housed and discerned, but does not find a proper place there. This foul spirit disrupts precisely because it has no place; the person who expelled the foul spirit did not deal with it properly by sending it to some other place. This produced the situation in which the foul spirit remained a potential threat.

The narrative switches from the person to the house. The space where spirits live takes center stage and becomes the primary concern of the saying. In other words, the saying does not relate primarily to the fact of exorcizing an unclean spirit from a person, but the question of where those unclean spirits dwell once they have been expelled. The issue is location, not personal health or cleansing. The foul spirit reasons with itself that, since it could find no place to live, it would return to its own house, the house from which it was expelled. In the meantime, the house has been cleaned and

ordered, restored to its earlier beauty and sanctity. The place has been transformed. The cleaning and beautification of the house makes sense. The person cleanses the house to restore its original beauty, the beauty that the foul
spirit compromised by its presence. The cleaning makes the house all the
more attractive to the unclean spirit, who upon seeing it, gathers up its foul
cronies to live in the house with it. The one foul spirit gathers to itself seven
more foul spirits and all eight of them take over the newly cleaned and beautified house. The eight foul spirits undo the positive work of cleaning and
beautifying the house and make it even more foul than it was before. This is
the reversal, the last state of the person is worse than the first.

So what happened? Why did this reversal take place? No explanation is
given, nor any rationale, nor even any principle that should be applied to the
situation. So the readers must apply the principle of the saying just prior to
this one. The last saying argued that those who do not gather, dissipate.
Refusal to gather becomes an active means of dissipating energy and force.
In this circumstance, only the foul spirit gathers others. The exorcized person cleans, prepares a space, but does not gather people of the divine empire
into it, nor does the person invite good and clean spirits into the house. By
not gathering, the house becomes foul, unclean, useless, while the foul spirit,
by gathering seven other useless and foul spirits, performs the duty of gathering and joining together. This saying again asserts that gathering other
people into the divine empire is mandated; if the participants in the movement will not gather, then the foul demons will, and the movement will not
have benefited those whom it has cleansed and renewed.

So this saying reinforces the previous saying. If a person is not with Jesus,
that person opposes him; if the person does not gather, the person dissipates.

There are probably other principles that readers could apply to make
sense of this short narrative of the exorcized foul spirit and its overtaking of
a purified house. Without any suggestion from the narrative itself, readers
must import principles from other sayings to construct meaning. The only
direction in the narrative that suggests something specific is the turn from
person to space. The saying suggests that the cleansing of the space that took
precedence over the gathering of clean and positive spirits into the house
made the difference between permanent and mere temporary cleansing. The
saying moves the reader toward understanding community as taking precedence over space and corporate identity as more important than individual

identity. But these are just suggestions to help make sense of a narrative that does not disclose its own point.

Saying 40
Q 11:?27–28?
Gospel of Thomas 79:1–2 and Luke 11:27–28

And a woman cried out: "Blessed is the womb that bore you and the breasts that fed you."

He said to her: "Blessed are the ones who heard the oracle of the Father and cherished it."

Although later participants in the Jesus movements and in the early church focused their attention on the person of Jesus, those christological concerns did not interest Jesus himself or many of his early followers (at least those who preserved these sayings). The later ecclesiastical concern revolved around Jesus, Jesus' relationship to the Father, his self-understanding as the Christ (Jewish Messiah), his divine personality (whether from birth or by adoption later at his baptism by John), the nature of his humanity (fully like other humans or simply using a human body to house a divine nature), and, of course, the relationship of Jesus to the spirit. But these concerns arose later, in the third and fourth centuries CE. Jesus himself seems to have consistently pointed toward the divine empire and the rule of God, focusing not on himself (even to the point of referring to himself with the circumlocution "son of humanity"), but on the Father and the Father's household, the empire of God.

Having said that, the woman who cries out in this saying sends a blessing to the mother that bore Jesus. It is precisely that, a blessing. It reflects her joy at hearing what Jesus says and at seeing what Jesus does. In a manner quite traditional in Near Eastern and Mediterranean cultures, she blesses the mother that bore and nurtured the gifted and godly child. The woman pronounces a commonplace blessing upon Jesus' mother to reflect her enthusiasm and support.

Jesus' response, however, shifts directions. Even such a blessing upon his mother, and indirectly upon himself for whom the woman has given thanks, detracts from the announcement of the Father's empire and from the divine words that the Father speaks through Jesus. Jesus is the Father's oracle, the one who speaks the Father's words among the people, announcing the divine empire that the Father has called into existence through his emissary and son, Jesus. But the attention remains on the Father, not on Jesus. Jesus pronounces a blessing upon others who relate primarily to his mission, not to his person.

Again, the Greek word I translate "oracle" may mean word, discourse, conversation, and communion (among many other meanings). The one who is truly blessed is the one who hears the divine oracle of the Father and cherishes it. The Greek word translated here as "cherish" may also mean keep or preserve. So the one who hears and guards the meaning, or hears and cherishes, or hears and preserves, or hears and acts upon the oracle of the Father, is the one who is truly blessed. Blessings come to those who listen to divine revelation and enclose themselves within it. Blessings come from hearing the divine word and cherishing it. Blessings come from hearing the divine conversation encapsulated in these sayings and preserving the discourse within oneself and among one's friends. Blessings come to those communities of gathered people who preserve the words of God in their midst and feed upon them.

Jesus deflects attention from himself to his mission and insists upon changing the significance of even commonplace blessings. From within the revelations and oracles of God, every cultural, social, and individual pattern must be reconstructed to reflect its true meaning derived from its relationship to the empire of God. Not even seemingly harmless and traditional actions can retain their significance and meaning outside the divine empire. Everything must be re-thought, re-contextualized, and re-signified to reflect its true meaning within the empire of God. Such a perspective gives the divine empire a totalizing function. The sayings of Jesus leave little room for social convention or social propriety, or even for people to consider their options before joining one of the movements. Nothing can stand outside God's empire, and God's empire bestows meaning and significance upon every aspect of living.

Saying 41
Q 11:16, 29–30
Matthew 12:38–40 and Luke 11:16, 29–30

Some desired a sign from him. He answered, "This generation is a worthless generation. It seeks for a sign, and a sign will not be provided it except the sign of Jonah. For just as Jonah became a sign to the Ninevites, thus even the son of the human one will be to this generation."

The desire for a sign makes perfect sense in this saying since so many of the sayings discuss powerful deeds and wonders (for example, Saying 19 in the report to John's disciples; Saying 27, which tells the missionaries to heal the sick; Saying 29, which talks of the powerful deeds performed by Jesus and his followers). In a theological context, the Greek word *sēmeion* means such things as a sign from God, a means of prognostication (such as a portent), an omen, or a powerful deed. Jesus and his followers set up the desire for signs by their own performing of powerful deeds that announced and inaugurated the empire of God. The wonderful deeds functioned as a kind of advertising for the movement when they entered a town or village. Jesus and his followers would perform them to signify that a new empire has come into existence under the rule and authority of God. The signs point to the positive presence of God. This saying does not disparage the signs but the desire for signs. It is the desire, the searching, not for the empire, not for God, but for the splashy performances that dazzle the eye and the mind, that causes the difficulty. It might even be said that these onlookers demand the performance of powerful deeds for the sake of performance alone and not for entry into the reign of God.

The saying offers Jonah as a sign. This introduces a different meaning to the word "sign." Jonah is more a sign in the sense of a prognostication or portent of things to come. The ambiguity of the term makes for interesting reading because the reader expects signs to refer to powerful deeds. That expectation is thwarted by the introduction of Jonah as the sign, the indicator of future things that will come to be.

In what sense, then, is Jonah a portent? The historical Jonah does not portend the future; the saying uses the historical Jonah proleptically as a sign of events to come in the lifetime of the hearers/readers of this saying of Jesus.

Although later Christians employed Jonah's stint in the belly of the whale (Jonah 1:17–2:10) as a sign of the resurrection of Jesus, this saying refers to other parts of the Jonah story, specifically to his effective and successful preaching of repentance to the Ninevites (Jonah 3:1–10). Two parts of the Jonah story do not correlate to Jesus, "the son of the human one," in this saying: Jesus does not attempt to avoid his mission as Jonah does (Jonah 1:1–7), nor does Jesus resent the effectiveness of his preaching and the repentance of the people around him as Jonah did (Jonah 4:1–11). This means that the correlation between Jonah and Jesus relates to the transformation of the people around them as a result of a preaching of repentance and renewal. The sign of Jonah that this saying presents is the sign that Jesus, like Jonah, will be effective in his mission and succeed in calling people to change their lives. For Jonah, this was faithfulness to God; for Jesus, this means entering the reign of God.

Now the saying begins to make more sense. This "worthless" generation, a generation that demands signs for signs' sake, seeks demonstrations not to repent but to entertain themselves. That is why the saying characterizes them as worthless or evil. They simply do not get the point of the powerful deeds. Jesus, however, takes up their demand for a sign, but gives them Jonah, the successful preacher to the Ninevites, rather than a powerful and entertaining performance. Jesus switches from one sign to another and treats the sign of Jonah as a portent of their own repentance despite themselves. Jesus, referring to himself through the circumlocution "son of the human one," offers himself as the same sort of sign to the current "worthless" generation. But even here, the words are hopeful and not condemning, because the worthless generation, like the sinful Ninevites, will repent and find renewal. The same will happen with the onlookers to Jesus' mission.

Signs only have meaning when someone or some group reads them. This saying reinforces the central importance of reading and interpreting. Those who engage these sayings, either as readers or hearers, must search not on the surface for entertainment, but below the surface for deep meaning and significance. Signs should lead to revelation and understanding, not simply to entertainment. The use of signs such as Jonah here, a proleptic sign taken from the scriptures to articulate an experience and its future meaning for a later group of people, demands just such a search for the deep meaning of the saying. Jonah's presence here subverts literal interpretation and forces readers and hearers then and now to search out meaning below the surface by engaging with the historical situation in the context of their immediate circumstances. This is hard but necessary work for those who take seriously the divine empire, as the next saying clearly shows.

Saying 42
Q 11:31–32
Matthew 12:41–42 and Luke 11:31–32

(1) The Queen of the South will arise at the judgment with this generation and give sentence for it, because she came from the boundary of the earth to hear Solomon's wisdom, and behold, here is something more than Solomon.

(2) The Ninevite men will arise at the judgment with this generation and give sentence for it, because at the preaching of Jonah they repented, and behold, here is something more than Jonah.

This saying (as does the previous one) exemplifies a process of thinking through the scriptures, which the saying then applies to a particular situation in the life of the community. The thinking through scripture occurs through the exploration of the Queen of Sheba story (1 Kings 10:1–10) and the preaching of Jonah to the Ninevites. The Queen of Sheba, a province south of Israel and Palestine, came as a foreigner and outsider to the Israelite King Solomon to learn his wisdom. Although she had heard of his wisdom, she did not believe it until she herself traveled to his court to learn from him. What she had heard was true: Solomon was both a wise teacher and a graceful ruler. After experiencing his wisdom, she praises the God of Israel and offers Solomon rich gifts. The process of thinking through the scriptural story seems to relate to the common experience of being outsiders to great wisdom. Just as the Queen of Sheba was a foreigner who marveled at the wisdom of Solomon, so the followers of Jesus should marvel at Jesus' wisdom. The experience of wonder and awe at wisdom holds the two stories together. By thinking through the scriptures at the level of experience, readers can get a sense of the emotional and intellectual dynamic of the saying.

The same process applies to Jonah. Jonah preaches to outsiders and they repent. Jesus preaches to Gentiles, and they should repent as did the Ninevites. The Ninevites repented at hearing the word of God, responding to the divine message delivered by the divine messenger. Just as the Ninevites repented, so must those hearing Jesus' preaching repent and enter the reign of God. The same experience holds these two references together.

The application refers to the eschatological day of reckoning when the dead will rise (see 1 Thessalonians 4:13–18) and pronounce judgment on the living before the great throne of God (see Saying 29). This final day will separate the just from the unjust, the good from the evil, the faithful from the unfaithful, granting life and salvation to those judged worthy and damnation and death to those judged unworthy. This eschatological narrative provides the background to the process of thinking through the scriptures. On that eschatological day of judgment, both the Queen of the South, representing the experience of outsiders who recognize true wisdom, and the Ninevites, representing outsiders who heard the word of God proclaimed to them by the messenger of God and repented, will arise to pass judgment on "this generation," on those people living at the time of the Jesus movements. The eschatological narrative provides a context for thinking through two scriptural references.

The saying affirms, however, that the present experience far surpasses that of the Queen of the South and the Ninevite men. "Something more than Solomon . . . , something more than Jonah" stands in their midst. Jesus, the speaker of these sayings, far surpasses the wisdom of Solomon and the words of Jonah. Jesus and his followers constitute a superlative wisdom and a sterling preaching of the word of God. In fact, for the readers of these sayings then and now, Jesus is divine wisdom and Jesus embodies the discourse or word of God, and thus he far surpasses the gifts and effectiveness of both Solomon and Jonah. But this means that the judgment will be greater. Those who did not have the benefit of hearing these sayings of Jesus will judge the people who do have that benefit, because even without Jesus they had an inkling, which the current generation has missed.

Readers need to know both the process of thinking through the scriptures and the meaning of the application in order to understand the saying. The scriptural references operate at a more complex level than simple typology or example; the characters exemplify a pattern of living, a way of responding, and thus model a kind of behavior and experience for the hearers. The saying then places that experience into the context of the final judgment, when they will arise to pass judgment and to give sentence upon those who did not recognize the wisdom before them and who refused to repent and enter the empire of God. At the same time, those who have recognized the superior wisdom that Jesus articulates and who repent to enter the empire of God receive affirmation that, on the same eschatological day, they will be justified. On that day, those who understand as the Queen of the South and repent as the Ninevite men will find themselves positively evaluated not only by the two biblical figures raised from the dead to pass judgment, but also by Jesus and God. The fact of judgment affirms those who joined the movements, while threatening those who still refuse to hear and to repent. The readers, as insiders, identify with the group that receives positive judgment, and they join their ancient colleagues in enjoying the experience of their own election and participation in the divine empire.

Saying 43
Q 11:33
Matthew 5:15 and Luke 11:33

No one lights a lamp and places it in a hidden place but instead places it on a lamp stand, and it provides light to all those in the house.

The truth of this statement is so self-evident that it should give readers pause. Of course, if one lights a lamp, one intends it to give light to those who gather around it. One does not light the lamp in order to hide the light. This perfectly straightforward statement rings true at the literal level. Given that simplicity and directness, why was the saying preserved as part of the sayings of Jesus? There must be alternative ways to read and understand this saying.

It might be best to begin by reading from the end. A person places a light on a lamp stand in order to provide light for those in the house. The word "light" itself suggests spiritual illumination or intellectual enlightenment. The house, as has been noted before in these sayings, often represents the divine empire filled with those who have chosen or have been elected to enter it. The illumination, then, can be of the household of God. But light does not shine only on elect people. It simply shines without differentiating that upon which it shines. The goal of lighting a lamp may also be to help other people who may have gathered around in need of seeing. The light may also shine on those outside the household who are invited guests, clients, or servants. The saying does not suggest a definite direction for interpretation, so both directions of interpretation remain possible. The light shines upon anyone, both insider and outsider.

It is easy to imagine that some participants in the Jesus movements might have been skittish about displaying their knowledge, their spiritual gifts, or their elect status in a divine empire that subverted the Roman imperium. It would be easy for such wary practitioners to try to hide their light, their gifts and knowledge, from those around them. They might have wanted to hoard what they knew and not disclose their status in the divine empire. This is a hidden place indeed.

It might also be easy to understand that some people would want to hide their knowledge or status from others because outsiders either would not understand or simply are not considered worthy of the knowledge. In other words, the hiding of the light bespeaks real entitlement and superior status. So this entitled person lights the lamp but puts it in a hidden place lest others see it and make the elect knowledge common.

The saying argues against both of these kinds of hiding and all others. Jesus proposes that illumination, spiritual and intellectual enlightenment, must be dispersed within the house so that all can see. It must not be kept private, or secret, or in one's individual domain, but rather it must be made public, transparent, widely known, and socially beneficial. All those in the house must be able to benefit from it, and in this way, the lighting of the lamp becomes a sign of communal sharing in intellectual and spiritual enlightenment.

So this very simple statement speaks about much more than the simple lighting of a lamp. It talks about making manifest, to those both within the movements and without, the gifts and knowledge given to those who participate in them. The saying articulates the value of spreading the light as far as possible and never hiding or hindering it.

Saying 44
Q 11:34–35
Matthew 6:22–23 and Luke 11:34–35

(1) The eye is the lamp of the body.

(2) If your eye is clear, all of your body is luminous, but if your eye is useless, your whole body is dark.

(3) So, if the light that is within you is dark, how great is the darkness!

This saying uses the physiology of the eye as it was understood in antiquity (1 and 2) to make a point about the presence of metaphorical light in those who participate in the Jesus movements (3). The analogy encourages readers and hearers to think about physiology as revelatory of a theological process. Engaged readers and hearers can then make other connections between the eye and light and between physiological processes and theological realities.

The statement that the eye is the lamp of the body compares an eye to a lamp and the body to a house, as we saw in the previous saying. Having introduced the topic of light, this saying develops it in another direction, talking now not about the social function of lighting a lamp as in Saying 43, but rather about the way that illumination or light enters a participant in the Jesus movements.

"The eye is the lamp of the body." The eye enables the transmission of light from outside to inside the body. Ancient people thought that the eye put out a beam of light to the object seen and attached to it so that it could be perceived from within the body. As a transmitter of light, the eye functions as a lamp to the body, the organ that enlightens the body and makes it capable of perceiving and interpreting external physical realities. Since light also functions as a metaphor for spiritual and intellectual realities, as we have seen in Saying 43, it could also be said that the eye enables intellectual and spiritual light to enter the body as well. This first statement in the saying establishes the basis for the analysis that follows in the second part.

The physiological analysis continues in the next statement: "If your eye is clear, all of your body is luminous." The eye "works" only if it is healthy, clear. The body becomes full of light precisely because the eye functions well. The healthy eye becomes a conduit of light from outside to inside, from the body to the outside perceptible world and from the perceptible world to the body. Metaphorically and analogically, the same applies to spiritual and intellectual phenomena: if the eye is healthy, the person becomes enlightened, capable of spiritual and intellectual knowledge and also reflecting on it.

The contrary also stands: "but if your eye is useless, your whole body is dark." If the eye does not function properly, if it ceases to transmit light outward and guide light inward, it is useless to the process of seeing. As a result, the body becomes dark; no light enters. Metaphorically and analogically, the spiritual and intellectual eye, if no longer functioning properly, makes it impossible for the person to be enlightened, thereby condemning the person to the darkness of ignorance and spiritual depravity.

The last part of the saying departs from the analogy and makes a comparison: "So, if the light that is within you is dark, how great is the darkness!" This last saying posits a situation in which an eye functions properly and makes the body luminous, but then malfunctions so that the light in the body becomes darkness. The saying does not address those who never saw in the first place, whose eyes could never function properly, but rather those who could see, but whose eye became impaired, resulting in the darkness of the body. The expression "how great is the darkness!" laments the loss of precious light in the body and its replacement with the darkness that comes from a change in the physiology of the eye. Here the metaphoric dimension of the saying comes to the fore. Clearly, the saying does not simply argue a physiological point: physiology points to some other level of interpretation. This saying begins to make sense with the last part: it discusses those who could at one time see well, whose enlightenment made their bodies luminous with their spiritual and intellectual transformation, but who now cannot see and whose spiritual and intellectual gifts have been destroyed. The saying talks about backsliders—those who saw but see no more; those who rejoiced in the luminosity of the Jesus movements but who have withdrawn into a darkness of ignorance and nonparticipation. These are people who, in the reversal of the Johannine statement, were seeing but now are blind (John 9:25).

Now all of this discussion raises an important question that I have left to the end. What does the eye signify? To what does the eye refer? The answer emerges from the analysis of the third part of the saying, where its theological dimension emerges. The eye signifies illumination, the transmission of light from the divine realm to the personal and communal realm. The eye is the organ of illumination and therefore probably stands for such things as the repentance and renewal preached by both Jesus and John (Sayings 1 and 29), entrance into the empire of God (Sayings 20 and 34), the successful mission that extends the divine empire (Saying 24), or even sacramental rites such as baptism or the sacred meal eaten by the participants in the divine empire and in the Jesus movements. The eye seems to represent whatever instrument brought people into the empire of God, into relationship with these sayings of Jesus, or into the community of the followers of Jesus. The eye is the portal to engagement with God, and when it functions properly, the entire person becomes full of God. But when it becomes clouded and useless, the person experiences God's absence. The saying could have been expressed in just that simple declarative way, but instead engages the mind, science, theology, and physiology, keeping the followers of Jesus then and now fully engaged.

By using physiology as a revelatory instrument, the saying trains readers and hearers in reading the signs (see Saying 41). Every human function potentially reveals divine processes: earlier sayings used experiences described in scripture as revelatory, while this saying draws on physiology and other sayings employ observations of nature (Saying 59). The physical universe reveals the divine mind (as Paul writes in Romans 2); therefore, seekers can read its signs to understand God. For hearers and readers of these sayings, the universe is full of divine revelations.

Saying 45
Q 11:?39a?, 42, 39b, 41, 43–44
Matthew 23:1–2a, 6–7, 23, 25, 26b–27 and Luke 11:30, 41–44

(1) Damn you, Pharisees, because you tithe mint and dill and cumin and you chuck justice and mercy and trust. It was necessary to do these, not to chuck them.

(2) Damn you, Pharisees, because you cleaned the outward parts of the cup and the plate, but the inward parts are full of greediness and incontinent living. Clean the inside of the cup and the outside will also become clean.

(3) Damn you, Pharisees, because you love the prime seats at dinner parties, and the front seats in the synagogues, and greetings in the marketplaces.

(4) Damn you, Pharisees, for you are like invisible tombs, and people who are walking upon them do not know it.

Precisely who the Pharisees were in the time of Jesus as well as in the time of the early Jesus movements has challenged scholars for many years. The scholarly consensus of the past few years argues that the portrayal of the Pharisees in the Synoptic Gospels reflects more a sibling rivalry of similar movements (Jesus' and the Pharisees') than opposition based on radically different ways of living a religious life. For the purpose of these sayings, however, "the Pharisees" symbolize pompous people who affect superiority under the guise of pious religious observance and the proper social etiquette appropriate to persons of the upper classes. Probably the Pharisees got this reputation later in the Jesus movements, when the rivalry between Pharisees and Jesus people was strongest; it reflects a Christian polemical perspective rather than a historical one. Unfortunately, such characterizations of Jewish religious leaders, especially of the Pharisees, later led to the persecution of Jews.

The first saying condemns pompous and affected religious people for their misplaced scrupulosity regarding religious law while they ignore religious injunctions to establish justice for the poor and the needy. This religious hypocrisy takes tithing seriously but ignores issues of mercy and trustworthiness. In other words, these people freely give a tenth of their herbs, but do not freely give of themselves in merciful actions that display their trust in God. But having fulfilled their religious obligation to tithe, they appear pious while doing nothing to fulfill their social and economic obligations to the community. In order to be truly pious, these people need to perform acts of mercy, not dismiss them. God demands ("it was necessary") mercy and trust, not the appearance of religious propriety. Their own hypocrisy, however, condemns them; they are damned for their refusal to perform the works of mercy that mark true participants in the divine empire.

The second saying extends the condemnation to those who attend to the externals of purity concerns but ignore the internals. The case in point is the cleansing and purification of eating implements: they clean the outside but not the inside of the cup. The saying characterizes the inside of the cup as polluted with moral flaws: "the inward parts are full of greediness and incontinent living." The saying argues for external physical cleanliness as well as internal moral cleanliness. These dissemblers prefer, as in the previous saying, to take the easy way out of the purity issue—cleansing vessels without morally purifying themselves. The saying argues that purity begins with the interior, with moral cleansing, and that the interior cleansing extends to the exterior. The saying defines purity as a moral, not a physical state. The Pharisees' inability to understand this condemns them.

The first two parts of this saying refer to what might properly be called religious observance. The third moves into social practice. The characterization of the affected and pompous socialite recalls the roles and functions of a patron in the Roman system. Patrons, whose clients were dependent upon them for economic, social, and political benefits, demanded attention. Their clients lined up to greet them in the morning and accompanied them in the marketplace and throughout the day. The clients were sycophants who insinuated themselves in the good graces of the patron. The patron, on the other hand, expected the very best. Society entitled patrons to seats of honor, to social prominence at dinner parties, and to (somewhat enforced) greetings from clients and others in the marketplace.

In their pomposity and hubris, the people referred to in this saying expect front-row seats, the best place (and therefore the best food) at dinner parties, and greetings, manifesting their entitlement before others. The saying condemns them for this display of social status. In light of the first two parts of the saying, it could be argued that these socialites condemn themselves because they look to the externals and not inside themselves, to appearances and not to the moral rectitude that confers true nobility (2), and because they live a life of ease and do not perform works of mercy (1).

The saying ends with yet one more curse on pompous social elites. It does not follow the pattern of the first two sections in appending a rationale, but rather begins with a further damnation of them and a description of them as invisible tombs trampled upon by people who do not know of their existence: "Damn you, Pharisees, for you are like invisible tombs, and people who are walking upon them do not know it." For people who like to "see and be seen," this is the worse sort of anonymity and invisibility—first to be dead and buried; then to be buried in an unmarked tomb along a road; and, finally, to have people walking on the road and desecrating it. Certainly rich and entitled patrons would find this a horrible antidote in death to their social privilege while living. The saying reverses their privilege and transforms it into extreme humiliation, tying their fate with that of the destitute poor buried along the Roman road.

The anger expressed in this saying cannot be ignored. It is dramatic and graphic, especially in the final statement. Given the missionaries' absolute dependence on the hospitality of others (see Sayings 24–30), the missionaries and their hosts certainly would have encountered opposition and social ostracism at the hands of those who rejected the message, the powerful deeds, and the existence of a divine empire. The missionary situation invites opposition, mockery, and persecution by its very countercultural nature. New things, then and now, remain difficult for the vast majority of a society. Eventually, the missionaries began to feel resentment and anger at the rejection they experienced, and this saying certainly expresses that anger vigorously. In this particular case, it seems to be anger at the continued opposition in later years of the movement from other Jews, the Pharisees, who in all likelihood did not accept the direction that the Jesus movements were taking. We do not know the precise details, but we get an inkling of such opposition from Paul's opponents in the Corinthian correspondence. The rivalry and contention between one Jesus movement and another, between one form of Judaism and another, and between Jews and Jewish followers of Jesus as well as between Romans and the varieties of Judaism (including the Jesus movements) defined the religious environment, eventually leading to the anger expressed in this saying.

Saying 46
Q 11:46b, 52, 47–48
Matthew 23:4, 13, 29–32 and Luke 11:46b–48, 52

(1) And damn you, legal scholars! You bind up loads and place them upon human shoulders, but you yourselves do not want to move them with your finger.

(2) Damn you, legal scholars! You lock up the empire of God in front of people. You did not enter nor did you permit those who were coming to enter.

(3) Damn you! You constructed tombs for the prophets, but [it was] your

fathers [who] killed them. You yourselves acknowledge that you are sons of your fathers.

The early Jesus movements as well as other contemporary Jewish movements argued about the Jewish law. Just as many perspectives on the law emerge in the early Christian period, from the law-abiding and temple-oriented James and Peter to the Pauline dismissal of the law so that Gentiles inherit Jewish privileges (see Galatians 2:1–14), so too does contemporary Judaism display a similar assortment of understandings, from the highly allegorized interpretations of Philo of Alexandria to the more traditional interpretation of the early rabbis, the forebears of rabbinic Judaism. Every variety of sectarian Judaism, from Jesus to the early rabbis, had to consider the law and formulate a strategy for honoring it. This particular saying, with its inherent critique of observance and study of the law, seems to align Jesus more with the Pauline perspective as articulated in Galatians than with the perspective of Peter and James, which argues for the observance of purity and other codes of the law. Obviously, the saying, however, does not address the question of the law directly, but obliquely, through scholars of the law whom it angrily condemns.

The first statement condemns legal scholars for a kind of overinterpretation of the law that burdens people. The argument in many respects is similar to those in the previous section, except that here it seems to concern a scrupulosity imposed upon other people that exempts the scholars themselves. The saying condemns the lack of mutuality between legal scholars and their students in their lifestyles, research, and teaching. The dramatic comparison of heavy loads on human shoulders with the unwillingness to move a finger makes the egregious disparity graphic. This statement could apply equally to scholars in the Jesus movements and to scholars in formative Judaism.

The second part of the saying, however, imports the criticism of the legal scholars into the arena of the empire of God. This now becomes an issue fundamental to Jesus and the movements that followed him. Again, the argument could apply as well to James and Peter as to the early rabbis. The issue is that the legal scholars keep people out of the empire of God. Their rulings and understandings lock up the empire for only certain people, keeping others out of the divine empire. James and Peter, according to Paul, tried to do this with the Gentiles before an agreement could be reached, an agreement not appreciated by more observant "false brothers" in the Jesus movements (Galatians 2:4–5). This saying condemns the scholars for their attempt to close the door to the empire right in front of people, in their very presence, and to lock them out. But in restricting others' access, the scholars shut themselves out of the divine empire. Their strategy backfired. In fact, their restriction of access to the divine empire means that they had not entered it in the first place. The nature of the divine empire requires access for all, preaching to all, powerful deeds for all, and certainly entrance for all seekers.

The last section (3) posits one of the reasons for the controversy over the law within both the early Jesus movements and early rabbinic Judaism: tradition, those things that one generation hands over to subsequent generations to guide and direct their lives. These scholars relied on the traditions of their forebears and claimed authority based on their inheritance of the tradition. Section 1 has already condemned such reliance upon tradition or election. This saying further impugns the validity and sanctity of tradition. Following tradition, the scholars honor the prophets; they build tombs to commemorate them and to give them physical space in the community. But the younger generation's building of tombs does not disclose the fact that the ancestors actually killed the prophets. The legal scholars "acknowledge that [they] are sons of [their] fathers," but do not acknowledge the damage and evil performed by their fathers. They claim inheritance without responsibility. This saying of Jesus criticizes the use of tradition on the basis that the tradition itself is at best of ambiguous status and at worst a cover for evil deeds.

Again, the issue of the law, its interpretation, application, and status, remained a hot question for Jesus, the Jesus movements, and the early church, as it did for formative Judaism. The level of anger at the legal scholars shows the depth of the debate, its critical importance to the lives of religious practitioners, and the intensity of the relationships of people on both sides of the issue who lived in close proximity to one another. This argument was central to those living out their religious identities in ancient Roman Palestine.

In fact, throughout the history of Christianity, and perhaps of Judaism as well, religious practitioners have tended to move precisely toward the type of rigidity and pomposity this saying deplores. Rigidity and self-righteousness are endemic to the human condition. Humans seem to move toward religious rigidity with ease and speed. This saying directly confronts that seemingly natural tendency, condemning it as destructive of the very heart of the divine empire. Readers of these sayings and hearers of the voice of Jesus in them must actively resist such tendencies, overcoming the natural propensity with a supernatural one.

Saying 47
Q 11:49–51
Matthew 23:34–36 and Luke 11:49–51

For this reason also Wisdom said, "I will send prophets and sages to them, and they will [choose to] kill and to banish from among them, so that an account of the blood of all the prophets that was spilled from the creation of the world may be demanded from this generation, from the blood of Abel to the blood of Zechariah who was killed between the altar and the house. Yes, I say to you, an account will be demanded from this generation!"

The killing of the prophets mentioned in the last saying segues to this statement. But this saying addresses not only the legal scholars, but the people of "this generation." The audience has been expanded and universalized. So although the sayings are connected, they still remain separate sayings addressed to different groups of people.

Wisdom appears as a character in these sayings of Jesus only here and in Saying 22, where she is "determined by her children." In the Israelite scriptures, Wisdom serves a twofold function: theologically, Wisdom becomes a hypostasis of God who aided in the creation and directs humans to virtuous and godly living by embodying divine goodness in human action; historically, Wisdom guides and directs every generation of human beings in the right way, manifesting the mind of God to those entrusted with directing God's people. In this saying, the historical function of Wisdom dominates. Just as in Wisdom of Solomon 10–19, Wisdom directs the leaders of Israel from Adam through Moses and the Exodus by presenting the mind of God to them, so in this saying Wisdom continues to send prophets and sages to the people of God to guide and direct them.

Although the sayings of Jesus refer to prophets in a number of different places, this is the only mention of Abel (Genesis 4:8–10) and Zechariah (2 Chronicles 24:20–22), neither of whom rank as prophets in the Hebrew scriptures. (The prophet Zechariah, whose prophetic book bears his name, does not fit the description of one whose blood demands a reckoning, so the reference to Zechariah must be to that of 2 Chronicles.) Again we interpret contemporary experience through biblical figures, as explained in the analysis of Saying 42.

According to the biblical narrative, God preferred Abel's meat offering to his brother Cain's cereal offering. In a jealous plan, Cain killed Abel, and God said to Cain: "What have you done? Listen; your brother's blood is crying out to me from the ground . . . which has opened its mouth to receive your brother's blood from your hand" (Genesis 4:10–11 NRSV). So Cain "went away from the presence of the Lord" (Genesis 4:16). Abel's narrative is about the murder of one whom God cherished, one whose blood cried out to God from the earth upon which it was spilled. Election and cries of blood mark this story. The Abel story proleptically anticipates the experience of the followers of Jesus and their persecution—even murder, in the case of Jesus himself and some of his followers—with their blood as well demanding an accounting from God.

Similarly, in Zechariah's case, "the spirit of God took possession" of him and he proclaimed the word of God to the people, who took him out and killed him. Joash, who killed Zechariah, experienced similar retribution: "his servants conspired against him because of the blood [of Zechariah,] the son of the priest Jehoiada" (2 Chronicles 24:25). Again, God demands retribution for the persecution and killing of a person ordered and ordained to speak the word of God to the people, even a word they do not want to hear. Jesus and his followers spoke the word of God to many communities and were persecuted for their proclamation. Their suffering, and sometimes their deaths, demanded retribution from God and punishment of those who persecuted them. The followers of Jesus connected this saying with the danger of proclaiming God's word and the retribution God had in store for those who rejected and persecuted them.

With this clarification of the significance of the biblical characters mentioned, the meaning of the saying becomes clearer. The narrative identifies the speaker of the saying as Wisdom and connects the saying to the previous saying about the killing of the prophets. Wisdom, the hypostasized emanation of the divine mind, speaks in the voice of God to the people of this generation, including the legal scholars mentioned in Saying 46. The intense identification of Jesus with Wisdom (see John 1:1–18), both in the early period of the Jesus movements and later, enables this saying by Wisdom to be included among the sayings of Jesus. Both Jesus and Wisdom relate to God in the same way, as embodiment and revealer of the divine mind.

Wisdom, speaking for God, tells the readers and hearers that she will send prophets and sages to the people ("this generation"), even knowing that the people will elect "to kill and to banish" them. The identification of the people as "this generation" holds negative connotations: "this generation" tends to describe those who have not entered into the divine empire; nor have they responded properly to Jesus' announcement of God's empire or conformed their lives to the presence of the empire among them. The designation identifies them as outsiders. To these outsiders, Wisdom will send prophets and sages to reveal the mind of God to them. But these outsiders will respond, typical of their standing as opponents to the divine empire, not by hearing and responding positively to the message, but by killing the prophets and banishing the sages.

The rejection of prophets and sages by this generation has a definite purpose: "so that an account of the blood of all the prophets that was spilled from the creation of the world may be demanded from this generation." Thus, the current generation bears the responsibility for the actions of previous generations. They do not simply act on their own; they represent the entire history of people from the beginning of time who have thwarted the divine way and rejected the divine word. Such a statement adds an eschatological dimension to their rejection. The end-time being sufficiently near, those who repeat previous generations' recalcitrance become responsible for it—for persecuting those like Abel, who were the select of God, and for killing those like Zechariah, who spoke an unpopular yet fully divinely ordained word to the people who rejected it. The accounting demanded of this generation is severe because it persecutes the elect who have joined the empire of God in the various Jesus movements and rejects those who have been sent to them in Jesus' name to proclaim God's word and empire.

Just in case readers have missed the point, the saying ends with a strong affirmation that this accounting will indeed happen.

The fact that this saying attributes this harsh and judgmental perspective to Wisdom and not to Jesus himself shows that at some level the followers of Jesus wanted to distance him from the saying. Yes, Jesus and Wisdom are closely related in the thought world of formative Christianity and Judaism, but they remain separate characters. To ascribe this saying to Wisdom rather than to Jesus himself puts the responsibility on the traditional character who acts in God's stead in the scriptures. It takes Jesus off the hook for the harshness of the saying. But by placing this saying of Wisdom within the sayings of Jesus, the saying transfers the harsh message into the Jesus movements' thought world and suggests the close connection between Wisdom and Jesus without collapsing them into the same person.

People and societies that value individuality often miss the importance of group responsibility. Simply by virtue of one's participation in a social or religious group, one comes to bear responsibility for the group's past and present actions. God holds each responsible for the actions of the whole and judges the whole by the actions of each participant, past and present. Readers and hearers of these sayings, therefore, bear responsibility for both those who embraced the divine empire and those who opposed it. The judgment pronounced in this saying and the insistence upon accountability extend to all the people in subsequent generations.

Saying 48
Q 12:2–3
Matthew 10:26–27 and Luke 12:2–3

(1) Nothing is veiled that will not be unveiled and hidden that will not be made known.

(2) That which I say to you in the dark, tell in the light and that which you hear in your ear, preach upon the housetops.

Two categories describe the kind of knowledge found in the first part of the saying (Greek *gnōsis*): esoteric knowledge is knowledge restricted to the initiated elect that is not to be disclosed to anyone, and exoteric knowledge is unrestricted knowledge that is available to anyone. This saying advocates exoteric knowledge and instructs the participants in the Jesus movements to reveal everything they know. Nothing must remain undisclosed to those outside the movements and, conversely, everything, no matter how secretive it seems, must be disclosed.

The saying is rather elegantly arranged: its two parts each consist of two grammatical units joined by a conjunction. Rhetorically, the topic flows easily from veiled to unveiled, hidden to seen, dark to light, and whispered to preached loudly. And each part underscores the importance of the other and adds to the seriousness of the injunction to disclose everything.

"Veiled" and "unveiled" suggest a kind of eschatological scenario in which God or the participant in the movement pulls away the veil of illusion to reveal everything hidden behind it. The revelation discloses everyone's and everything's true nature. The metaphor of veiling and unveiling provides a dramatic setting for the disclosure of all things. The second part of section 1 continues with less flair, making explicit the significance of what was just said metaphorically: everything hidden will be revealed.

The saying switches perspective in the second part, leaving metaphors behind. The two units of this part are direct: what a participant hears in the dark must be spoken in the light, and what a participant hears in secret tones must be publicly proclaimed. Again there is an esoteric element: things heard in the secrecy of darkness, things whispered in the hushed tones of private communication. And again, the saying enjoins participants to speak out in broad daylight and to preach what they know from the rooftops.

Each of these four units creates a connection between those inside the movement and those outside it. The insiders cannot hold onto what they know, or even to the community of which they are a part, for themselves alone; the community of those with access to knowledge must extend it to enfold those outside, who must be given access. Jesus instructs the community of participants in the Jesus movements always to move outside their inner circle to embrace those beyond the boundary of knowledge and community. The direction of knowledge moves outward.

This understanding of the exoteric nature of knowledge conforms to the image of a movement growing and expanding its horizons by gathering more people and new perspectives into its community. Some in the early Jesus movements, like those in the Corinthian community, attempted to keep their knowledge and spiritual lineage intact and preserve themselves as identifiable communities of participants with a restricted identity (see 1

Corinthians 1:10–17). This saying thwarts the impulse to exclusivity and both Jesus in this saying and Paul in 1 Corinthians support exoteric over esoteric knowledge, even though the original revelation may have come to the participants in esoteric contexts.

Saying 49
Q 12:4–5
Matthew 10:28 and Luke 12:4–5

And do not be fearful of those who kill the body, but are not able to kill the soul. Rather fear the one capable of destroying the soul and body in Gehenna.

This saying may be connected with the previous saying to the extent that it argues to not fear making public what originates in an esoteric context. The saying encourages boldness and courage. It differentiates between a number of different kinds of death—the body, the soul, and the soul and body together. The saying creates a progression of deaths from body to soul, then to soul and body together, in an incrementally increasing sequence that culminates in the worse of all deaths: that of the soul and body together being thrown into hell. The saying posits degrees of death. The lesser fear is of the death of the body, which ought not to be a consideration at all for participants in the Jesus movements. Self-preservation for them does not simply relate to the preservation of their bodies, to which (as Saying 55 instructs) the participants give little attention regarding food and clothing. The body alone does not sustain interest or care. The real fear is of the death of the soul, the part of the person connected to Jesus and his sayings as well as to the divine empire that Jesus announced. The inner person must be preserved, and the death of the inner person commands greater fear than the death of the outer person, the body.

The saying also distinguishes between two killers: the one capable of killing the body only but not the soul and the greater killer who can destroy both soul and body. One must presume that the greater killer refers to God, albeit in a rather unusual mode of speaking of God. God is the killer who has the capacity to destroy both soul and body by casting them into the pit, the hellfire, or hell (all of these are signified by the word "Gehenna"). The hearers of this saying must fear God above all other killers, who have only limited power. This is not a very pleasant image of God, but it is the one the saying projects.

This saying advocates fearlessness before lesser killers, whose dominion and power rule only the body. Participants in the Jesus movements ought not to fear the imperial authorities or even the emperors, who only control their bodies. Rather, they must fear the true emperor, God, whose dominion extends to the entire cosmos, including Gehenna, the place of damnation and the abode of the unjust. The fearlessness also relates to what is truly valuable. The body does not hold value in itself, at least according to this saying, but gains value by its relationship to the soul. Participants in the Jesus movements should protect their souls while acting fearlessly with respect to their bodies.

The saying ultimately advocates courage and boldness because it asserts the supreme authority of God over all other powers and authorities both in the human realm and in the cosmos at large. As long as God reigns, God's empire will finally succeed, and those associated with the divine empire will ultimately achieve victory over every opponent and authority. This saying guarantees them that victory and urges them to be fearless, bold, and courageous.

Saying 50
Q 12:6–7
Matthew 10:29–31 and Luke 12:6–7

(1) Are not five sparrows sold for two coins? And one from among them will not fall down to the ground without your father.

(2) And even all the hairs of your head are numbered.

(3) Do not fear: you yourselves excel over many sparrows.

This saying continues the theme of fearlessness and courage. It shows the high value that God places on God's creation and especially on those who participate in the Jesus movements. The saying progresses from sparrows to humans and then to those people participating in the Jesus movements.

The first saying begins with a question about the relative inexpensiveness of buying five sparrows for a small amount of money (two Greek *assaria*). Although they have little value in human commercial terms, God does not allow even one of them to fall to the ground without attending to it. God values God's creation and looks after it assiduously.

The saying argues in the second part that God does this for humans as well. Just as God attends to the lives of the relatively inexpensive sparrows, so does God attend to the lives of humans, who rank higher in the hierarchy of being than birds. The minutest aspect of human bodily existence, including the number of hairs on someone's head, warrants God's attention.

The final part of the saying summarizes the argument: do not fear, because humans have far more value than sparrows. God's attention to all creation extends not only from the insignificant parts of the creation and to the insignificant parts of the human person, but also to the most excellent parts of creation, the human person involved in the divine empire to which God has called them. In the hierarchy of being, the participants in the divine empire rank higher than those people who have not entered the empire of God. God attends to these elect more, so that they need not fear any harm from anyone. Their election guarantees their preservation and protection by God.

Readers of these sayings and hearers of Jesus' voice experience the extravagance of God's exultation of those who have heard and understood the message. God's faithfulness and trust can make them bold, fearless, and courageous. When Jesus speaks directly to the readers/hearers in the third part of this saying, he transcends his immediate audience to address this affirmation to subsequent generations of hearers and readers, who similarly should rejoice in the divine affirmation.

Saying 51
Q 12:8–9
Matthew 10:32–33 and Luke 12:8–9

(1) Whoever would agree with me before people, the son of humanity will agree with that person before the angels.

(2) Whoever would deny me before people will be denied before the angels.

The concept of reciprocity, articulated so clearly in Saying 8, emerges here in another form. Again, Jesus refers to himself obliquely as "the son of humanity" who will stand before the judgment seat of God at the end of time, giving evidence about people's lives. The sayings acknowledge others who will also be present and doing the same thing: the Queen of the South and the Ninevite men of Saying 42, who will arise to judge the outsiders. Jesus, however, will commend or condemn insiders based upon their defense or denial of Jesus in public. The scene envisioned in the saying involves the throne of God (unmentioned), with the angels surrounding the throne, before which stands Jesus giving testimony. The saying, in typical fashion, presents the same concept in two forms, positive and negative.

The first part of the saying presents the concept positively. The reciprocal relationship extends to those who agree with Jesus before other people. If they articulate their agreement, if they stand up for what they know to be true, then Jesus will stand up for them at the last day, giving positive testimony in the eschatological divine court in the presence of the angels who surround God's judgment seat. The Greek word *homologeō* conveys a wide assortment of meanings, all related to the concept of thinking or saying the same thing. It can mean confess, acknowledge, concur with someone or something, as well as simply to agree with someone. Jesus demands not simply passive acknowledgment and concurrence from his followers, but also an active, energetic agreement with him. Those who do this will be justified in the last days.

The second part of the saying presents the same concept negatively. The Greek word *arneomai* conveys the sense of refusing, denying, rejecting, and renouncing something. Those within the movement who reject Jesus will find themselves rejected by Jesus on the day of judgment, in the presence of the angels who surround the throne of God. This is as strongly negative as the previous part was positive: the denial of Jesus, the refusal to acknowledge him and the empire that he inaugurated, the rejection of community with others who have entered the divine empire, will result in similar denial, refusal, and rejection by Jesus at the end of time.

The concept of reciprocity, that Jesus will do to others as others have done to him, demands this sort of judgment in the end. What astounds the readers of these sayings is that this reciprocity relates not only to humans, as in Saying 8, but relates as well to the relationship of participants in the movements to their founder and ultimately to God (see Saying 32). The strong connection between Jesus and his followers establishes such a high level of parity that it connects the heavenly court to earthly action. The barriers between earth and heaven, human and divine, crumble before the parity articulated in this saying. Human action in the human realm has consequences in the divine realm.

Saying 52
Q 12:10
Matthew 12:32a–b and Luke 12:10

And whoever would speak a word against the son of humanity, it will be forgiven that person, but whoever would speak against the holy spirit, that person will not be forgiven.

This saying contrasts responses to speech critical of divine figures. The phrase "son of humanity" may be a circumlocution for Jesus referring to himself obliquely and as an eschatological divine figure. The holy spirit appears in other sayings: in the contrast between John's and Jesus' baptisms (holy wind) (Saying 2); as the spirit who drives Jesus into the desert to be tested (Saying 3); and as the one who gives members of the Jesus movements proper last-minute instructions on what to say when brought before judges (Saying 53). The holy spirit is not mentioned often this collection of the sayings of Jesus but emerges at critical and important points in Jesus' and his followers' lives.

From Saying 3, the reader understands the holy spirit as the agent who guides and directs Jesus: "Jesus was led up into the desert by the spirit to be put to the test by the devil." This holy spirit appears to be a higher divine power than Jesus is, and yet not God's own self. The holy spirit may direct Jesus to engage in an educational testing bout with the devil, and it will (as will be seen later) advise the persecuted members of the Jesus movements (Saying 53). The holy spirit takes on the appearance of a director, a guide, a teacher to Jesus and to Jesus' followers, and as such has more authority, power, or status than those whom it guides. Saying 2 confirms the spirit's higher status by stating that Jesus will use it to baptize with a baptism more powerful than John's. The spirit as director is not only more powerful than Jesus or John or their followers, but also more holy and wonderful.

Jesus places himself among those mediators of the spirit like John and Jesus' own disciples, who must depend upon the holy spirit for their words, deeds, and authority. By including himself in this category of those subservient and dependent upon the spirit, Jesus acknowledges the superiority of the spirit over his own life. This saying states that those who speak against the spirit's mediators and agents will be forgiven, but not those who speak against the source of their power, the holy spirit itself. Any speech against the holy spirit enters the arena of actions so despicable as to be beyond forgiveness.

This saying is one of the most peculiar of the sayings of Jesus. Readers do not normally contrast Jesus with the holy spirit or put Jesus in a lower position to the spirit. Generations of Trinitarian theology have made that seem strange and uncomfortable to us, perhaps even heretical. But since this saying was promulgated long before the doctrine of the Holy Spirit (now capitalized) was formulated, readers must accept the positioning and perspective of the sayings without trying to fit them into later, more theologically acceptable terms. In this saying, Jesus understands himself as someone in a subservient role to the holy spirit, whose relationship to God is undefined.

The saying also conveys to later hearers and readers something of the mystery of God's direction. The way the holy spirit functions in these sayings suggests its role as a kind of mysterious and all-knowing guide to seekers, among whom even Jesus is counted. The holy spirit leads people to encounter situations in which they test their spiritual mettle, find God revealed, learn new skills, and advance in understanding in a way that confounds normal patterns of learning and growth. It is mysterious. This saying firmly rejects those who would in any way thwart that mystery.

Saying 53
Q 12:11–12
Matthew 10:19 and Luke 12:11–12

When they bring you into synagogues, do not have an anxious mind about how or what you might say, for the holy spirit will teach you at that time what you should say.

This is an interesting saying because of the situation that it presumes: undisclosed people would bring the missionaries of the Jesus movements to trial in a synagogue where they would be expected to give an account of their work and receive judgment. This implies that synagogues had legal or judicial standing either in religious or in imperial realms, neither of which has been substantiated by historians. The Greek word *synagogē* could simply refer to an assembly such as a city council, a religious council, or even the council of elders (*gerousia*) in Jewish cities in the Diaspora. The saying presumes that the missionaries would find themselves providing an account of themselves, their actions, and their beliefs before a hostile group of leaders.

This saying suggests that missionaries in such a hostile environment remain cool and wait for inspiration about what they should say to the leaders before whom they have been brought. They must not be anxious, nor should they cast about in their minds wondering what they should say, because the holy spirit will provide them with their defensive speech.

This radical dependence on the holy spirit for guidance in speech is added to the missionaries' dependence on the hospitality of their hosts (Sayings 26 and 27) and as their dependence on God for food and clothing (Saying 55). The missionaries mark themselves as those completely dependent upon God through others for their food, clothing, shelter, and speech, and in so marking themselves, they make themselves holy, set apart for God.

This kind of dependence on God and the inspiration of the holy spirit in the midst of troubles also characterized Paul's ministry (see 2 Corinthians 6:1–10 and 11:21–29). Although Paul prided himself in not being a burden to those among whom he announced the gospel of Jesus Christ, the apostles who followed him presumed upon the hospitality and support of the local community as a right and a privilege (2 Corinthians 11:12–15). Yet even Paul acknowledged the generous support of the church in Philippi (see Philippians 4:15–18), a support that made his mission to the Greek provinces possible. This dependence on God acting through the hospitality of others characterized the early Jesus movements and in that very vulnerability gave their members theological direction and impetus.

This saying indicates that the early missionaries did not learn one consistent message that they all proclaimed; they did not master a set of theological principles that they presented to others or have set of core beliefs that they rehearsed with each other and with those to whom they spoke. If they had learned such set pieces, they would not have needed to rely upon God so heavily before magistrates and leaders. This saying suggests that the content of the mission remained fluid and flexible so that the divine empire could change and adjust to local needs and circumstances. So the early missionaries were absolutely dependent on the holy spirit. The holy spirit guides and directs missionaries just as the spirit drove Jesus into the wilderness for his educational debate with the devil and just as it empowered Jesus' baptism to be more effective than John's.

The saying finally instructs the participants in the Jesus movements, then and now, to trust the mystery. Readers and hearers in later generations have resisted the impulse to trust the mysterious workings of God. Established religious organizations tend to distrust such mysteries. But the sayings tradition represented in this collection of Jesus' words promote the mystery as being trustworthy and faithful.

Saying 54
Q 12:33–34
Matthew 6:19–21 and Luke 12:33–34

Do not hoard for yourselves treasures on earth, where moth and corrosion destroy and where thieves dig through and steal, but hoard for yourselves treasures in heaven, where neither moth nor corrosion destroy and where thieves do not dig through nor do they steal.

The meaning of this saying hinges on the contrast between heavenly things and earthly things. The saying pits those things that can be destroyed or stolen against those things that last because they are unassailable and indestructible, while commanding hearers to treasure only the lasting things rather than the destructible ones.

So much of these sayings of Jesus relate to everyday living. The sayings for the most part do not advocate a withdrawal from the realities of daily life. Rather, these sayings engage life as a way to live in and enact the divine empire, whose reality connects the mundane world to the divine world and collapses them into one overarching reality. The radical dependence on God and on God's message for food, clothing, shelter, and speech affirms this direct connection between this world and the divine realm. They are inextricably bound together and form one constant stream of reality that embraces both seemingly discordant realms. So this saying probably uses the rhetorical contrast of earthly to heavenly treasures not to describe divided realms, but as symbols for contrasting two kinds of treasure, one appropriate to the divine empire and one not.

A person can hoard either destructible or indestructible treasures. The values articulated in these sayings forbid the accumulation of wealth, food, clothing, means of travel, and all other "consumables," things that can be destroyed or stolen by a thief who can dig through the walls of the house. They are destructible and therefore not worthy of human effort to amass.

Heavenly treasures, those beyond destructibility and thievery, are the enduring values of the divine empire. These sayings give a clue to those heavenly values: poverty and mourning (Saying 4), the endurance of reproach (Saying 5), loving enemies (Saying 6), generosity of response (Saying 7), reciprocal treatment of one another (Saying 8), the refusal of interest on or repayment of loans (Saying 9), enacting mercy (Saying 10), refusing to judge another (Saying 11), the itinerant and vulnerable proclamation of the divine empire (Sayings 24–30). These virtues govern living in the divine empire; they are the indestructible treasures acquired by a participant in one of the Jesus movements and they become a part of the participant's being. They cannot be commodified, nor can they be stored in a house. These treasures resist physical decay and cannot be taken away or stolen by anyone. These treasures surely demand the attention, the effort, and the energy required to develop them, because they last. These virtues, developed in the course of living on earth and in the divine empire simultaneously, become a heavenly treasure stored up for those who have amassed them. They will last forever, being virtues that adorn their owner even after death.

Saying 55
Q 12:22b–31
Matthew 6:25–33 and Luke 12:22b–31

(1) So I say to you, "Do not worry about your life, what you might eat, nor about your body, what you will wear. Is not life more than food and the body [more than] clothing?

(2) Consider the crows, they neither plant nor reap, nor gather into storage bins, and God feeds them. Are you not more excellent than birds?

(3) And who among you through worrying is able to add an arm's length to his height?

(4) And why are you worrying about clothing? Acquire knowledge from the lilies, how they grow: they don't work hard nor do they spin, but I say to you, even Solomon in all of his glory is not clothed as one of these.

(5) Then if God so dresses the grass in the field, present today and tomorrow thrown into a cooking pan, will [God not dress] you much more, O small-minded believers?

(6) So do not worry, saying, 'What shall we eat?' or 'What shall we drink?' or 'How will we be dressed?' Search first for his empire, and all these things will be delivered to you."

This saying is a well-crafted and rhetorically sophisticated argument for complete dependence on God, a recurrent theme in these sayings of Jesus. Sections 1 and 6 both tell readers/listeners not to worry over everyday life. The saying begins with a statement intended to confront readers and hearers about their anxiety. The statement then leads to a question that challenges not directly, through direct address, but obliquely, through a question intended to make the readers and hearers examine their own lives. (The sayings frequently employ such questions.) The final section asks the same questions but also provides a solution. The saying encloses other arguments within an envelope structure: three examples from nature (sections 2–4) and one theological rationale (section 5). Combined, they make this a tightly reasoned and cohesive argument for radical dependence upon God for food and clothing.

Only the financially rich have the luxury of not worrying about food and clothing. The vast majority of people consider food and clothing to be sufficiently important that they spend much of their energies providing them for themselves and for their loved ones. In this saying, Jesus makes an argument that even such basic and essential needs as food and clothing do not deserve the attention they receive by suggesting that life entails more than food and clothing. He contrasts mundane daily life with a life far surpassing it in value and depth: "Is not life more than food and the body [more than] clothing?" Jesus shifts attention, as in the previous saying, from one understanding of what humans must have to survive to another, from anxiety about surviving to interest in truly living. The question expects the response, "Yes, life is more than food or clothing." The question itself suggests that true living does not entail anxiety about food and clothing. The reader is drawn in and wants to learn more.

The interplay of questions and statements continues in the second part. Jesus instructs the hearers and readers of this saying to consider crows—loud, demanding, and intrusive. Although they are pests, God provides for them and does not demand that they plant crops, harvest them, and store them for use throughout the year. These vexatious birds receive God's provision, as do all creatures. They do not worry about their food. They are not anxious. If God provides for the crows, whom people find obnoxious, how much more will God provide for humans, upon whom God places a higher value? "Are you not more excellent than birds?" Jesus asks. Again, the question expects a positive answer: humans are more valuable than birds and so God will provide for them just as purposefully and richly as God does for beings lower on the ladder of being, indeed, for all creation. This part of the saying (2) addresses one of the questions introduced in the first part, namely, the need for food; section 3 talks about anxiety.

The question in part 3, which follows immediately upon the previous question, requires readers and hearers to answer for themselves. The question itself does not grammatically expect a particular answer, so it stands as a theoretical question of indeterminate response. But the answer surely would be impossible in the positive: it is not possible to extend one's height by worry. In fact, people can do very little to increase their height, because height comes naturally to the person, just as food comes naturally to the crows. Worrying has no effect on height. So the question most certainly must elicit a negative answer: no, it is not possible to increase one's height through worry.

The issue of anxiety is sandwiched between the need for food and the need for clothing. Section 4 takes up the question of clothing. Again, the saying intersperses questions with statements. This part begins with a question addressed directly to the hearers: "And why are you worrying about clothing?" In question form, it restates section 1: "do not worry about . . . what you will wear."

The saying suggests an answer using yet another situation from nature. Lilies do not create their own clothing, but God has clothed them gloriously. Lilies do not work for their clothing and yet they appear beautifully clothed, surpassing even the King Solomon's glory, whose riches and wisdom were legendary (1 Kings 2–11). From the lilies, people must learn the lesson that God has also clothed them gloriously already, without their effort, without their anxiety, without their planning, and without their skill.

The penultimate part of the saying upbraids hearers and readers for thinking small-mindedly. They lack the vision, the connection with the realities of God's provision evident in nature, and the capacity for imaging the way that God will provide for them. Continuing on the topic of God's provision of clothing but switching from lilies to grasses in the field, the saying makes the dramatic statement that if God so provides for things that live now and may ultimately be devoured by others, God will even more clothe humans, who have greater value and stature before God. This summarizes the theology of the saying and articulates the problem among those who have anxious minds about food and clothing. The anxiety they experience points toward the poverty of their understanding. They think that they need to provide food and clothing for themselves and do not rely on God's providential care.

The final part of the saying (6) is another injunction not to worry, but this time it includes a solution. The yearning for provision should lead hearers and readers to the divine empire, to the arena that guarantees God's providential care, to the place where God's protection and provision manifests itself. Upon entering the divine empire, and on joining with the others who have entered it, provision for real life is provided. But this is true life, not the superficial, outwardly appearing life of eating, drinking, and dressing, but the inward real life of vulnerable dependence upon God for everything. The saying rests on an ambiguity: just as the missionaries depend upon God through the provisions of hosts in every city, so here the community that manifests the physical empire of God on earth becomes the provider for those things necessary not only to bodily life, but to the spiritual life as well. The divine empire, encompassing things both earthly and heavenly, physical and spiritual, mundane and sacred, makes provision for all things necessary for living. By seeking the divine empire first, all the other needs will be satisfied by God in the community of those who have entered the divine empire. God will provide everything necessary for living, just as God has provided for crows, lilies, and the grasses of the field.

The way this saying weaves its message of reliance and trust in God instructs people in the art of meditation, an art of engaging with a divine subject from a variety of perspectives, all clearly focused on the centrality of the divine presence.

Saying 56
Q 12:39–40
Matthew 24:43–44 and Luke 12:39–40

(1) Understand this: If the master of the house knew in which night watch the thief was coming, he would not have permitted his house to be breeched.

(2) And you yourselves must be made ready, because the son of humanity comes at an hour you do not imagine.

This saying proposes a general state of preparedness for those involved in the Jesus movements. It develops the argument first with a short narrative about a thief breaking into a house to rob it, then with a general statement addressed to the readers and hearers of the saying. The general statement implies a narrative of the end of time, when the final judgment of all people will take place (see Saying 47). So two narratives, one explicit and one implicit, come together to make a strong case for preparedness.

The first narrative identifies the readers and hearers with a householder who, if he had known the hour of the thief's attempted robbery, would have protected his house from breaching and his goods from plunder. Thieves generally do not announce the hour of the night when they will do their work. The narrative suggests that specific knowledge would have saved the day, but in the absence of specific knowledge of the time of the robbery, the thief was successful. On the other hand, the householder probably could have prepared himself generally against a thief and thus been prepared for the robbery at any time that it might occur (even though this is not stated directly in the saying). That general preparedness seems to be the point of the second part of the saying.

The speaker addresses the audience of hearers and readers directly in the second part: "You yourselves must be made ready," moving from a theoretical perspective to reality. The saying tells the readers to be prepared generally, because they do not know the specific time when the "son of humanity" will come. In fact, they cannot even imagine the time when he will come, so they must always be prepared for the final judgment, to defend themselves before the throne of God, for the time when the heavenly "son of humanity" makes his case for and against those who have engaged with him.

The two parts of this saying do not correlate exactly. The comparison seems to be between the householder and the readers, on the one hand, and Jesus and the thief, on the other. The correlation between householder and a participant in the divine empire who has amassed the right kinds of treasures and who must protect them makes complete sense. They have stored up treasures that need to be secured against thieves.

The correlation of thief to Jesus, however, seems more complicated. Paul compares the day of the Lord to a thief: "For you yourselves know very well that the day of the Lord will come like a thief in the night" (1 Thessalonians 5:2). And he encourages his people to "keep awake and be sober" (1 Thessalonians 5:6). But here the comparison seems to be between Jesus and the thief in the night, not the occasion of the final appearance of the "son of humanity" for final judgment. Clearly, the saying describes the same scenario that Paul envisions for the end of time. And the robbery at night describes our inability to know the precise moment of the end-time. So the saying encourages the reader to associate the thief with Jesus, the son of humanity who will come at the end of time to judge the world.

By placing the two parts together, the saying helps readers and hearers to understand the analogy. The analysis of everyday experiences to discover the hidden meaning in mundane events propels readers and hearers into understanding the ways of God. Placing these two narratives together, even though they do not correlate exactly, enables readers to make the connection between daily life and the divine empire.

Saying 57
Q 12:42–46
Matthew 24:45–51 and Luke 12:42–46

(1) Who indeed is the trustworthy and sensible slave whom the master appointed over his household slaves so that he would serve them food at the right time?

(2) Happy is that slave whom, when the master comes, he finds [the chief slave] so doing. I am sure that he would appoint him over all his possessions.

(3) But if that slave should say in his heart, "My master takes a long time [to return]," and he will begin to hit his fellow slaves, [while he himself] eats and drinks with the drunkards, that slave's master will come on a day that he does not expect and in an hour that he does not know, and he will punish him severely and set his destiny with the untrustworthy.

This saying continues the discussion about preparedness raised in the previous saying. It examines the topic through an elaborate narrative about a slave entrusted with the running of the household in the absence of the master. The narrative examines the issue of preparedness from two perspectives: a positive one in which the master finds the slave doing his job and a negative one in which the slave neglects his duties and the master catches him in dissolute living. The saying also supplements the theme of preparedness with that of trustworthiness. The Greek adjective *pistos* can mean both trustworthy and faithful: it relates to the noun *pistis*, which is usually translated "faith," but also means trust. The preparedness advocated by the saying requires a level of basic faith and trust in the master, God, keeping the leader of the slaves in line.

The saying begins with a question that explores the responsibilities and authority of the faithful chief slave, whose duties include the feeding of other slaves among other administrative household tasks. The specific comment about food and eating, taken up again problematically in section 3, suggests a communal orientation among the slaves with one of them as their leader. The leading slave stands as the leader of the community of slaves with special attention to provision for their food. Readers and hearers of these sayings will find these themes familiar. The leading slave's obligations point to functions within the stable, non-itinerant communities of those involved in the Jesus movements. These local leaders are responsible for feeding the community at the right time and, it might be suggested, for feeding the itinerant missionaries when they arrive as well as maintaining the household for the itinerant missionaries while they are traveling. The question format enables readers to engage in reflection by situating themselves and their obligations within the frame of the story as it unfolds.

The first scenario (2) is positive. The master is truly happy when he returns and finds that the leading slave has done his duty. That slave will be rewarded with even greater responsibility and honor. This answer shows the result of faithful and trustworthy service. In the wider context of the early communities of followers of Jesus, this suggests that those who follow their master Jesus and provide well for those who have entered into the divine empire by feeding the community and wisely guiding the community, will be rewarded. It also demonstrates the central importance of meals and eating, not only to the community that stays in one place, but also to those who travel from place to place. Providing meals is important. Those who are faithful in this task will receive their recompense, including honor and more responsibility for their faithfulness.

The second scenario (3) is decidedly negative. Here readers encounter the unfaithful and stupid response of the chief slave who begins to question the length of the master's sojourn and, imagining that the master will not return, usurps the prerogative of the master to discipline the slaves. Additionally, he takes the place of the master at banquets. Again the meal, only here it is the debauchery of the banquet that the saying emphasizes: the slave "eats and drinks with the drunkards." Because the length of the master's sojourn is miscalculated, the social relationships among the slaves became abusive and the provision of food debased. That is, the illusion of delay led to social decay: slaves abused other slaves; meals became occasions not of refreshment but of excess and vulgarity.

The final statement in this negative scenario combines the master's delayed return with punishment for unfaithful service to bring the saying full circle to the subject of preparedness. At the literal level, the narrative explains that the master will return at an undisclosed and unknown time to punish the unfaithful slave severely and to place him among the faithless to whom no responsibility or reward is given. A switch has taken place in the narrative. Suddenly, readers understand that the delay refers to something more than the literal subject of the narrative. The delay must refer to the day of the Lord that will come as a thief in the night when people least expect it, as Paul describes it in 1 Thessalonians 5:2, 4: "For you yourselves know very well that the day of the Lord will come like a thief in the night . . . But you, beloved, are not in darkness, for that day to surprise you like a thief." Paul even predicts that those who are fooled by the delay will eat and drink with drunkards: "So then let us not fall asleep as others do, but let us keep awake and be sober; for those who sleep sleep at night, and those who are drunk get drunk at night. Be since we belong to the day, let us be sober" (1 Thessalonians 5:6–8a). Because the delay refers to the delay of the arrival of the Lord to inaugurate the end-time, the punishment the master metes out to the unfaithful slave invokes the judgment of all the unfaithful before the judgment throne of God, a situation mentioned elsewhere in these sayings (Sayings 47 and 51, for example).

Now this saying begins to take on depth. The little narrative about the chief slave in a household invokes the great themes of the early Jesus movements: meals, itinerancy, the divine empire, and judgment with punishment and rewards. Unlike Saying 45 and Saying 46, however, this saying does not frame these themes in anger. Instead, the saying is very matter-of-fact, not evoking anger or even fear, but simply stating that the faithful will receive rewards, the unfaithful, punishments. Readers see the consequences of choice.

The parts of the saying make a complete circle. Introducing the virtues of faithfulness and sensible thinking at the beginning, the saying explores the realities of both, ending with the fate of the unfaithful and foolish. The saying advocates faithfulness and good sense for those participating in the divine empire while dissuading them from the foolish behavior that comes from the self-deception that the master will not return. It reaffirms that moral choices determine rewards or punishments. In this saying, the moral choices involve community meals, the way members of the community treat each other, and the general transformation to a way of life that renders the members prepared at any time for the return of the master. Morals and community life fuse here, raising the question, "Who is the trustworthy and sensible slave?"

Readers and hearers of this saying may identify with the chief slave, with the abused slaves, with the master, or even with the drunken diners. Each of these provides a different point of entry into the narrative and a way to think about the meaning of the story. Likewise, readers and hearers may identify with the allegorical reading of the story, an allegory of the early church filled with itinerants and stable households. And finally, the narrative leads readers and hearers to consider the end-time, when the master Jesus will return to settle accounts.

Saying 58
Q 12:[49], 51, 53
Matthew 10:34–35 and Luke 12:49, 51, 53

(1) Fire! [That's what] I have come to cast upon the earth, and how I wish it had already burst into flame.

(2) Do you imagine that I came to cast peace upon the earth? I did not come to cast peace, but a dagger.

(3) I came to divide into two: son against father, and daughter against her mother, and [new] bride against her mother-in-law.

This saying raises the issue of choice to a more significant degree. Jesus speaks in the harshest of terms about his mission's effect on social and political life. The saying articulates in the most dramatic terms the distinction between the empires of the world, upon which God calls down judgment and predicts destruction, and the empire of God, which Jesus has both announced and inaugurated.

Section 1 dramatically calls down a conflagration upon the earth. Jesus merely kindles the fire and expresses his eagerness to have the fire destroy more quickly and more widely. The saying, however, positions Jesus above the earth, casting fire down upon it. This conceptualizes Jesus not as the itinerant teacher, but as a heavenly figure who operates from above. Yet at the same time, Jesus says, "I have come to cast fire upon the earth." Jesus' mission originates above, in the heavens from which he came, but operates on the earth, where the fire will consume and destroy. The conjunction of the positioning of Jesus above the earth and his mission on the earth invokes a mythical understanding of Jesus as a man from heaven come down to earth to guide and to judge the world. As Jesus functions as the heavenly figure with a divine mission to judge and to destroy, he eagerly anticipates the destruction that his mission brings to the earth.

The next part of the saying (2) articulates that eagerness in terms of the discord and division that the mission causes: "Do you imagine that I came to cast peace upon the earth? I did not come to cast peace, but a dagger." Jesus' mission, once envisioned as peace that is cast down upon the earth from above in the heavens, casts down not peace but an instrument of destruction and warfare. The people on the earth imagined that the heavenly savior would bring peace, like the emperor Augustus and his famous peace of Rome (*pax romana*). The divine imperium that Jesus inaugurated does not bring peace, but division, struggle, warfare, destruction. Peace is an illusion, not a reality. The dagger signals the divine empire and the divine purpose. These are strong words, but they indicate that the establishment of an empire, any ancient empire, depended upon the subjugation of the people by force. Augustus, for all his spin about being a prince of peace, actually spilled more blood than most of his predecessors in establishing his autocratic rule. Jesus' rule must be established in the same way—with the warfare that subjugates people and makes them choose to enter the divine empire while renouncing and fighting the empires on the earth of which they were a part. The saying affirms the destructive impulse that inaugurates any new empire.

The force of that division and destruction, the force of the dagger cutting through social ties, emerges from the third part of the saying. The family, the center of loyalty in antiquity as in postmodernity, comes to the fore of the struggle: family members will fight against one another, because some will chose to enter the divine empire and reject earthly empires, while others will choose to remain in the earthly empires. Such choices divide even the closest unit. But family, as the smallest expression of the empire, does not trump the divine empire. Family ties must be destroyed along with all else that does not find its center and being in the divine empire that Jesus brings. So father and son, mother and daughter, will contend with each other, as will new members of the family with older members. The saying affirms that the conflict, the destruction, the fire, the division stand at the center of the mission that God has inaugurated through Jesus.

This saying, as does the previous saying, insists that readers understand the divisive dynamic of encountering Jesus in his sayings or the divine empire in his deeds. People are forced to choose, to make a decision, to separate from all other bonds of empire or family in order to enter the divine empire.

Saying 59
Q 12:[54–56]
Matthew 16:2–3 and Luke 12:54–56

When it is evening, you say, "Fair weather, for the sky shines fiery red." And in the morning: "Today is winter, for the lowering sky shines fiery red." You know how to discern the appearance of the sky, but are you not able [to discern] the fullness of time?

This saying explores good discernment, the ability to see and to understand the underlying dynamics of a person or situation. Discernment often involves reading signs that indicate inner or hidden realities. This saying revisits the idea of reading signs for their hidden meaning (see also Saying 41).

Two different weather signs appear in the saying: a fiery red sky at sunset, and the fiery and low-appearing red sky of winter. Jesus commends his listeners on their ability to read the signs. They understand that at evening a red sky points toward fair weather, while a red sky appearing low on the horizon tells them it is winter. The interpretation of these weather signs probably exists in every culture and region of the world—people need to know what the weather will be. And their interpretation of the signs probably has a high level of accuracy.

Jesus puts this question to his listeners/readers: Given that they can interpret these signs in nature, why can't they understand the fullness of time that is before them? Why can't they read Jesus and the signs of the divine empire that Jesus inaugurates? Again, the question leaps from the page, from the ancient hearers to all other hearers; it urges readers and hearers to think about their lack of discernment regarding the fullness of time, the time of Jesus, his mission, and his divine empire. Time, as we have been reading in previous sayings, has come like a thief in the night, but there are signs of the presence of the divine empire that few have been able to read and interpret. Jesus questions his followers and our inability to discern, to look deeply at, and to understand the meaning hidden in the moment in which he is present and the divine empire is made manifest.

The same discerning skills necessary for reading weather signs make it possible to read the signs of the times. Discernment is discernment. Jesus does not upbraid his followers for their stupidity or their lack of ability to read signs. No, Jesus commends them for their skill. He does, however, upbraid them for refusing to apply the same skills to the work of interpreting the signs of the fullness of time. The problem is not lack of skill but lack of vision regarding what God makes apparent all around them. The people Jesus is addressing know how to read signs, they just don't know which signs deserve attention.

The process with which readers of these sayings and hearers of the voice of Jesus engage in interpreting these sayings replicates reading the signs of the times. The sayings, precisely as a complex set of communications, demand deciphering, decoding, and careful reading. Often their meanings do not lay on the surface, but must be discerned. The sayings weave a pattern of meaning while simultaneously training readers of these sayings and hearers of the voice of Jesus in discernment. Jesus affirms that the same interpretative skills necessary to read the signs of daily living, like reading the sky for weather, function to read the signs of the empire of God that he presents in his oracles and deeds. In the end, as I have already said, discernment is discernment. But discernment must of necessity pertain to the things of God as well as to the realia of daily living.

Saying 60
Q 12:58–59
Matthew 5:25–26 and Luke 12:58–59

When you meet your adversary in a lawsuit on the way, make it your business to free yourself from him, lest [the legal adversary] hand you over to the judge, and the judge [hand you over] to his underling, and the underling throw you into jail. I tell you: you will not escape from there, until you pay the last penny.

Sometimes participants in the various Jesus movements simply need to be shrewd about their affairs. Here Jesus takes up a frequent problem in

Roman society, being sued in a court of law. These legal procedures could be both financially costly and socially detrimental. They were serious business in the Roman world. Jesus talks about that reality to make a point about responsibility.

Jesus advises his hearers to settle a dispute out of court rather than take chances in legal processes. He argues that it is better to negotiate a settlement than risk a sequence of events that will eventually wind up with the defendant in jail. The plaintiff, the legal adversary with a presumed advantage of either a good case or a close relationship to the judge, can hand the defendant over to court officials who will take him off to jail. The narrative does not disclose the nature of the legal proceeding until the end: the defendant owes the plaintiff a sum of money, which he sues to regain. In the end, without negotiation, the defendant chances a stay in jail as well as the repayment of the debt.

Financial debt is often a focus in these sayings. At various points, they develop an economic policy for the empire of God. Saying 9 argues that participants in the Jesus movements ought not to expect to have the money they have loaned repaid, nor should they expect interest on it. Saying 26 instructs itinerant missionaries not to carry any cash, while Saying 27 tells these missionaries that their salary will be paid to them in kind as food, clothing, and shelter. And of course, the famous line of the prayer in Saying 34 asks: "forgive us our debts just as even we have forgiven those indebted to us." The economics of the reign of God operates on a decidedly different basis. The debt envisioned in this saying could not have been incurred within the community of participants, at least if they were faithful to the sayings themselves, so it must have been between a participant in the Jesus movements and an outsider. The outsider plaintiff will expect repayment and will demand justice in the courts, while the insider defendant anticipates the possibility of prison. In this case, Jesus argues for the participant to be shrewd. Negotiate. Find a way out. Get out of the debt.

Paul also gave instruction to the Corinthians regarding legal proceedings. In 1 Corinthians 6:1–11, Paul addresses the question of lawsuits between members of the believing community. He argues: "In fact, to have lawsuits at all with one another is already a defeat for you. Why not rather be wronged? Why not rather be defrauded? But you yourselves wrong and defraud—and believers at that" (1 Corinthians 6:7–8). Paul envisions a court within the divine empire consisting only of believers who will judge the whole world: "Do you not know that the saints will judge the world?" (1 Corinthians 6:2). He even envisions this court will have heavenly authority: "Do you not know that we are to judge angels—to say nothing of ordinary matters?" (1 Corinthians 6:3). In Paul's mind, the question of legal proceedings must be left for the divine court of justice where the saints judge things heavenly and earthly, deeds of angels and the ordinary disputes of every day. This court is no usual court. It has high standing.

When Jesus describes a courtroom scene in a narrative, readers become suspicious. He is probably speaking at more than one level. At the literal level of this saying, according to the analysis just presented, participants in the Jesus movements should negotiate their debts with their lenders, avoiding the courts and the possibility of jail. At the economic level, Jesus warns about those engaged in the economics of the earthly empire and not the economics of the empire of God, which places clear negative parameters on personal wealth and privilege. And at the theological level, Jesus argues for personal and corporate responsibility before the great judgment seat of God at the end of time. Accounting will be made and scores will be settled. So the participant in the divine empire should be shrewd, thinking through and negotiating the possibilities in order to avoid the judgment that prevents full participation in the divine empire. The multivalence of speech in a sayings collection make this interpretation, and probably many more, viable and possible.

Modern Western culture places a lower value on shrewdness than did ancient cultures in the Mediterranean and the Middle East. To be shrewd indicated a potential for survival in often hostile and difficult social, economic, political, and religious environments. Often the divine empire requires its participants, then and now, to embrace qualities and virtues at such odds with the dominant culture that they appear out of place, even rude, and perhaps disgraceful, in line with Jesus' own insistence that the empire of God does not coexist with other empires and other social systems, but rather stands as both supreme and separate from all others. Jesus clearly embraced shrewdness as a value of the divine empire, one that would enable its participants to survive.

Saying 61
Q 13:18–19
Matthew 13:31–32 and Luke 13:18–19

To what is the empire of God similar and to what shall I compare it? It is similar to a mustard seed, which a person, taking it in hand, threw into his garden. And it matured and became a tree, and the birds of the sky found covering in its branches.

Similitudes, or comparisons, engage the mind in a particular way. They bridge the known and the unknown. Like a metaphor, these comparisons take information about familiar and known things and create connections between what can be envisioned and articulated and what must yet be discovered. Readers discover meaning as they move from known to unknown and make the connections suggested in the comparison. The process can almost be endless in that the connections readers make may move in many different directions and incorporate many new experiences. This means that the interplay between known and unknown is not flat. Readers may connect with the comparison by identifying with any one of the elements or by analyzing the comparison from any one of the different perspectives made available. That's how it works in this saying: readers may identify with the person planting the seed, with the tree itself, or with the birds that find covering in the tree. Each identification, each perspective, each element provides a different point of entry into the known and produces a different understanding of the unknown.

The saying begins with a question inviting readers to connect something they know with the experience of being participants in the empire of God. Jesus' answer to his own question is strange for two reasons: the invasive mustard plant seems an unlikely candidate for intentional planting, and it matures not into a tree but into a bush. Perhaps the plant resembles the unlikely candidates for the empire who through membership in it grow beyond their natural capabilities—to be trees, not bushes. Participants in the empire of God recognize themselves as seemingly worthless, annoying, and invasive agents to society, yet they are planted by God to create the empire. Their election by God seems directly related to their invasive tendencies and mission. But they will not grow into bushes, which most people want to weed out of their gardens, but into trees that will provide shelter for many. Jesus seems to say this with a wink.

The narrative itself moves in a cohesive and simple direction. It describes a person taking a mustard seed (in the singular) and throwing it into his garden where it becomes a tree to shelter birds. Again, why would a farmer purposefully put the mustard seed into his garden? It makes no sense. Mustard plants are invasive weeds. So the farmer intentionally plants something that potentially will take over his garden in order to shelter birds, who potentially will eat the seeds that he plants, or the berries, or the fruit. Again, the narrative, though simple, does not make sense. And that is probably the point. God works in ways that surprise and confound the normal ways of the world in order to do new and even more confounding things. God has planted Jesus as an invasive weed in the Roman Empire's garden in order to take over the garden and to shelter many creatures in the divine empire that will replace the Roman one. Jesus plants the pesky missionaries as seeds within the surrounding world to do similar work—to invade the various political and social communities in order to build a subversive structure that will house many others in an alternative and invading empire. The narrative drives readers to make more and more connections. Perhaps the invasive seed represents the holy spirit that guides both Jesus and the participants in the movement, the spirit invading the garden so that new ways of thinking and relating emerge to shelter the lives of many. Perhaps the invasive seed represents the parts of a family (see Saying 58) that join the movement, then invade the family structure to create alternative and non-biologically based families. The mind races from possibility to possibility, based solely on the image of a man throwing a mustard seed into his garden.

A reader may connect with any one of the characters; for example, the seed—as a missionary or spiritual agent or the first in their family to join one of the Jesus movements. Or a reader might identify with the planter who casts the invasive message of the divine empire into social relationships or who builds a social and religious structure for other less-grounded people. Or indeed, the reader may identify with the birds of the air, flying about without a spiritual abode, wholly dependent upon God for food and shelter (Saying 55), for whom God provides an unlikely shelter in the branches of a bush that grows into a tree for their benefit.

Although modern people do not think of Jesus as someone who engaged in humorous conversation, the ancients valued humor and learning through humor. This saying accomplishes just that.

Saying 62
Q 13:20–21
Matthew 13:33 and Luke 13:20–21

To what shall I compare the empire of God? It is like yeast, which a woman, taking it, hid in three pounds of flour until it leavened it completely.

Again, the question captures our imaginations. Jesus again explores how daily events are revelatory of the divine empire. And he invites readers and hearers into this intellectual process.

Jesus leads the way by comparing the divine empire to a woman. For modern people, who have the narrative gospels as their introduction to Jesus and his early followers, the presence of women baffles. In the synoptic tradition, they remain peripheral. Although the narratives do not deny their presence, their place and importance remains secondary to the gospels' concerns. But from Paul we know that there were women involved in early Jesus movements and that they held important positions and performed critical missionary work (see Romans 16:1–16 for Phoebe, Mary, and Junia, among others). The examination, if not the erasure, of stereotypical gender roles was part of the earliest Jesus movements, as Paul attests in his famous statement: "There is no longer Jew or Greek, there is no longer slave or free, there is no longer male and female; for all of you are one in Christ Jesus" (Galatians 3:28). So the comparison of the divine empire to a woman probably would not have surprised anyone at the time of Jesus and in the formative Jesus movements. It only became surprising later. In any event, Jesus compares the empire of God to a woman doing a normal, daily task: making bread.

The saying has a simple narrative: a woman takes yeast and throws it into flour until the entire bulk of flour is leavened. She makes leavened bread. What is the analogy? The divine empire resembles leaven—a little of it goes a long way by invading the flour and making it rise. Paul writes: "Do you not know that a little yeast leavens the whole batch of dough?" (1 Corinthians 5:6). Paul takes the metaphor in another direction, however, when he argues:

"Clean out the old yeast so that you may be a new batch, as you really are unleavened" (1 Corinthians 5:7). Paul uses leavening to stand for the spiritual condition of a person who must clean out the old before engaging the new. So the divine empire or the holy spirit enters a person like leavening and remakes the person. Or the divine empire enters into society as a leavening that eventually will take over the entire society. In this reading, the empire of God represents an invasive agent like the mustard seed of Saying 61. Another interpretation sees the leavening as the presence of the holy spirit in the community of Jesus that sanctifies them and transforms them, making them into food for others.

There are other ways to look at this saying. We wonder why the woman hid the yeast in the flour. Is it not normal to put yeast in flour to make bread? Why hide it? Now readers begin to think about an agent hidden in a person, in society, or in the world who, without being seen, transforms the entire environment. The hiddenness of the leavening eventually will be seen in the expanding flour, but it starts out hidden and moves toward gradual revelation (see Saying 48).

This saying does not involve humor, as did the previous one. Instead, it inspires an intellectual engagement with the theological premise of divine agents present in and transforming environments.

Saying 63
Q 13:24–27
Matthew 7:13–14, 22–23; 25:10–12 and Luke 13:24–27

(1) Come in through the narrow door, because many will demand to enter and those who enter through it are few.

(2) Whenever the housemaster gets up and locks the door, and you begin to stand outside and to strike the door, saying, "Master, open for us!" and giving you an answer, he will say, "I do not know you!"

Then you will begin to say: "We ate and drank together, and you taught us on the main streets [of our town]!"

And he will speak to you saying, "I do not know you! Get away from me, you workers of iniquity!"

This saying presents a compelling image: a narrow door, much in demand, through which few pass. The Eastern Christian tradition interprets the command to enter by this narrow door as an invitation to the ascetical life, the disciplined life of self-reformation aiming toward a transformed and vibrant relationship with God. The early ascetics, both monastic and lay, gravitated to the interpretation of wisdom sayings as an ascetical discipline particularly suited to altering their understanding of themselves, of their social relationships, and of the symbolic universe in which they lived. In addition to meditating on the sayings of Jesus, these ascetics also meditated on the sayings of other ascetics, pagan and Christian, as well as philosophers, both ancient and contemporaneous with them. They engaged with these sayings and with the ascetic life in general as a struggle to enter a narrow door. They also understood themselves as the select few who could indeed enter through the narrow door by virtue of the effort they made and the understanding they acquired. Although later traditions of interpretation do not always indicate the meaning of a saying at an earlier period, in this case it seems that it does. The injunction to enter by the narrow door through which few others will enter directs the hearers and readers to strive to do something that few others can do. The basis of their ability to enter through the narrow gate is analyzed in the second part of this saying.

In the first part of the saying, Jesus commands that those capable few who can enter through the narrow door must do so. It's not a question but an injunction: "Enter through the narrow door." Readers, then, must figure out what the narrow door signifies. The saying provides no context, nor does it define the meaning.

The second part of the saying, however, helps us make sense of the first part. A narrative complete with dialogue, its narrator observes the action from a distance. Now the door is not only narrow; it is locked. The housemaster gets up and locks the door. The people who are knocking demand entry, as commanded in the first part of the saying. The housemaster denies entry because he does not know the people who are knocking. Those outside protest that they had eaten and drunk with the householder and he taught them in public places, but the householder still denies them entry. In fact, he not only denies them entry, he also expels them as sinful.

Entry into the locked room requires that we know one another. Those knocking presumed a level of knowledge and familiarity with the house-holder—they dined and drank together, and the householder taught them. They thought they knew the householder, but such a casual relationship was not enough for the householder, who does not say what kind of knowledge would suffice for entry. Here we learn what does not work, without any suggestion of what might work.

Readers must decide who the householder symbolizes. If Jesus, then entrance will not be gained by simply hearing him speak or eating with him or drinking with him. Such a casual relationship is not good enough. If God, then seekers do not gain entrance through eating or drinking, perhaps through ritual meals, nor through a study of scripture alone; God demands something more. If the householder represents the community of those who have entered into the divine empire, then simply attending liturgies, meals, and studying with them does not gain entry into the community. If the householder represents an individual seeker, then simply engaging with God, Jesus, or other participants in the divine empire casually does not transform him or her or help the person gain entrance into the divine empire. All of these and more are viable interpretations of this saying.

The two parts of the saying contrast two ways of trying to gain entrance: one is in the imperative, to "enter by the narrow door"; the other, right of entrance by casual knowledge. Action contrasts with knowledge. Action succeeds, while knowledge alone gains only rejection. The saying invokes Saying 16, in which Jesus questions why people listen to him without doing what he instructs. Hearing and interpreting is insufficient for those who wish to enter the divine empire through the narrow door, whatever that narrow door might represent.

Since the saying does not define the narrow door or the household that stands behind the locked door, readers must make their own sense of what those images signify. It may well be that each person and community face different narrow doors, that the locked-up households differ in their expectations of which actions make people worthy of entrance. The lack of specificity in the saying demands that readers begin to make sense of these elements in the context of their own lives. This perhaps explains why the ascetic tradition took this saying as the explanation of the ascetic life. Individuals must do different things to enact their new identity as participants in the divine empire. The narrow gate and the locked household signify malleable and mutable criteria for entry. But that malleability and mutability do not imply easy access—the narrow door suggests the need for real and intentional effort and striving, while the locked door suggests the householder requires shrewd and thorough knowledge of the knockers to unlock the door.

The saying ends by firmly rejecting those who do not enter, categorizing them as wicked people. Those who are outside, who have not struggled, who have not gone beyond hearing to action, find themselves expelled and distant from the source of true life and fulfillment. The saying suggests that the stakes are very high: the choice is either struggle or exile.

Saying 64
Q 13:29, 28
Matthew 8:11–12 and Luke 13:28–29

And many will come from the east and the west and will recline [to eat] with Abraham and Isaac and Jacob in the empire of God. But you will be cast into the outer darkness. [That is] where [there is] weeping and grinding of teeth.

The implied anger of the previous saying finds full expression in this saying. Again, the saying contrasts two kinds of people: those reclining (presumably to eat) with the Israelite patriarchs in the divine empire and those who have been cast out. No middle ground exists. A person either reclines to eat or is expelled into the outer darkness of wailing and teeth grinding.

The image of the divine banquet in which the faithful dead dine with God undergirds this saying. The saying describes those faithful dead as many from across the horizon from east to west or, as the Greek would allow, from sunrise to sunset. The entire inhabited world contains people worthy of this heavenly banquet. The banquet bridges the empire of God and the Israelite tradition. Abraham, Isaac, and Jacob, the heroes of Jesus' own religious tradition, merge with the image of the earthly banquet of those who eat and drink with Jesus, either in person or, as in Paul's case, through a ritual meal. Paul makes explicit the eschatological dimension of this feast when he writes: "For as often as you eat this bread and drink the cup, you proclaim the Lord's death until he comes" (1 Corinthians 11:26). Paul affirms the connection between earthly feasting and the coming of the day of the Lord, when all the faithful will presumably feast with Christ at the heavenly banquet.

The saying also affirms a universal invitation to the eschatological banquet. People come from east and west, a euphemism for the entire inhabited world upon which the sun rises and sets. This gathering includes, then, not only the patriarchs, but also faithful Jews as well as Gentiles and Romans and all those who have entered the empire of God. The boundaries remain fluid and open for all to enter the divine empire, at least those who make the effort.

The saying, however, threatens readers: "But you will be cast into the outer darkness." The rejection contrasts with the rather expansive view of those dining in the eschatological banquet. Why would the saying classify readers or hearers as those who will be rejected? Why does the saying describe the rejection that these readers and hearers will experience as a place of "weeping and grinding of teeth?" The saying provides no answer. Readers confront an expansive invitation or a stinging rejection and condemnation, hearing of the many who dine with the patriarchs contrasted with those cast into outer darkness. The saying contrasts heaven and hell, the presence of God with God's absence, and the divine banquet with a sad death and funeral. The saying describes two different ways of living and their results. Readers face a choice. And that is the point of the saying: to invite listeners and readers, perhaps even to frighten them, to consider their life choices as they ponder the final outcome of those choices—either a heavenly banquet or hell.

The saying expresses great anger at those who choose improperly, suggesting severe punishment for those who choose not to enter the empire of God. The divide seems rigid and permanent, with little room for neutrality or hesitation. The angry tone may reflect the frustration of those inside at those outside, the anger of the missionaries toward those who reject their message, or simply the reality of the divine judgment. In any case, the choice remains paramount.

Saying 65
Q 13:[30]
Matthew 20:16 and Luke 13:30

The lowest [person] will be [the] first [citizen of the city], and the first [citizen of the city will become the] lowest.

These sayings of Jesus consistently make a point about social dislocation in a variety of forms: the holy spirit drives Jesus into the desert for a contest (Saying 3); John lives in the desert and people visit him there (Saying 20); the missionaries of the movements function without provision, itinerant and vulnerable (Sayings 26–28). The sayings also make much of inversion: the poor, hungry, and grieving are blessed (Saying 4) and followers of Jesus should rejoice at persecution (Saying 5); scriptural scholars hold the keys to the divine empire but prevent people from entering (Saying 46); the hidden will be seen and private teachings will be publicly proclaimed (Saying 48). The two themes meet in this saying.

The Greek word used here for "first" suggests a social setting. It denotes a person who is socially prominent. The saying plays with the categories of the first and the least of the city, that is, with the most prominent as well as the most inferior persons who live in the ancient city. The saying implicitly contrasts a city of the Roman and Hellenistic world and a city of the divine empire. It indicates that the most socially inferior citizen of the Roman city will become the most prominent person of the city in the divine empire, because entrance into the divine empire confers status upon the members of that divine city. Correlatively, the most prominent person of the city in the Roman Empire will become the least in the city in the divine empire, because prominence in the divine city rests not on social status or wealth, but on poverty, hunger, grieving, and vulnerability. Once a prominent person experiences that social dislocation, he or she becomes a good candidate for election to the divine empire.

Place takes on importance only by virtue of its relationship to the divine empire: a city like Rome has no value except in its connection to the divine empire; social status has no value except in its connection to the divine empire. Likewise, low status in the Roman city does not indicate low status in the divine city, nor does poverty exclude a person from being a leader, even the primary leader, of the divine city. The saying inverts the category so that what seems despicable becomes honorable, and what seems depraved becomes holy. One's place in society and in the city does not predetermine one's status in the empire of God because God inverts all status to make the least the first. Even with all its wealth, the earthly city is still incomparably poorer than the divine city. Social dislocation and inversion define the empire of God.

Saying 66
Q 13:34–35
Matthew 23:37–39 and Luke 13:34–35

(1) Jerusalem! Jerusalem! She who murders the prophets and stones the ones sent to her!

(2) How often I desired to collect your children, in the way that a bird collects her chicks under her wings, and you did not want it.

(3) Your house is abandoned!

(4) I say to you: you will not see me until it comes [to the point] that you say, "Blessed is the one who comes in the Lord's Name!"

Jesus pronounces a lament over the central city of his region, the center of religious, political, and financial life in the ancient Roman province of Judea. Cities lamented their fate in time of war when destruction raged against the local dynastic authority and when the seat of power, the royal city, experienced burning and pillaging. A lament over the city, a genre of literature as well as a corporate expression of woe, grieved the loss, the pillaging, the rape, the capture of citizens to make them slaves of their conquerors, the killing of children, the looting of public buildings, the burning of public and private buildings, and the desecration of sacred temples. Those who witnessed the destruction poured out their emotions in laments. The Book of Lamentations provides an excellent example of the genre, although antiquity supplies many more examples of lament over a fallen city. In this saying, Jesus speaks a lament over the city of Jerusalem.

Jesus' lament over God's destruction of Jerusalem characterizes the city as "She who murders the prophets and stones the ones sent to her," the reason for her destruction. Jerusalem, a symbol for the political and religious leaders of the city, rejected the prophets and the missionaries sent to her, and therefore God vanquished her. The history of Jerusalem's rejection of the prophets, however, does not begin in the time of Jesus, but extends backward into Israel's sacred history and especially to its relationship with the prophets. Jeremiah, for example, speaks a prophetic word in the time of the Babylonian conquest of Judea: "I myself will fight against you with outstretched hand and mighty arm, in anger, in fury, and in great wrath. And I will strike down the inhabitants of this city, both human beings and animals; they shall die of a great pestilence" (Jeremiah 21:5). Jesus' judgment on the city gathers such ancient history into his own times as he joins the lament over a city still standing. His lament encapsulates the prophetic experience and becomes a prophetic word about the destruction of the city by God once again. Jerusalem rejects Jesus, just as she rejected earlier prophets' oracles.

The second part of the saying explains Jesus' own sense of failure. Jerusalem's children refused Jesus' attention even when he wanted to gather them and to protect them, like a mother hen with her chicks. It is a tender kind of image. Jesus, perhaps invoking Isaiah 31:5, which speaks of God's rescuing Jerusalem, proclaims his intent to collect the people of Jerusalem, including the leaders, and gather them into another imperium, another dynasty, the empire of God, where they would be safe, protected, nurtured, and fed by God. But Jerusalem spurned his efforts, so he pronounces this lament over the city that has rejected God's salvific action.

The statement that Jerusalem's house has been abandoned (3) suggests two possibilities. The house may refer to God's abandonment of the temple of Jerusalem, an act preparatory to God's giving Jerusalem over to destruction. In this case, the abandoned house could signify God's withdrawal from Jerusalem and his rejection of the people of Jerusalem. Unlike a hen gathering her chicks, this God is abandoning his children. The house may also refer to the leaders of the city of Jerusalem, who have abandoned the people they should protect, unlike a hen with her chicks, and have left the city in order to save themselves from impending destruction, leaving the people to fend for themselves. The abandoned and desolate house thus signifies the state of Jerusalem before her destruction—a place bereft of God, of leaders, and of hope.

Even given this hopeless situation, however, the saying does not leave readers abandoned. It ends by speaking of Jesus as the one who will return, who will indeed gather the people together and bring them into a new empire. Jesus is the one to whom the people will say, "Blessed is the one who comes in the Lord's Name," invoking Psalm 118:26. Despite their hopelessness and the destruction of their city, the people will not be abandoned. Jesus, like the mother hen, will gather the abandoned people, the destitute, and the vanquished into a new reign. But the people of Jerusalem must wait, because they will not see Jesus until they understand that the coming salvation that he brings comes only in the midst of the desolation, not to alleviate it or to prevent it, but to save those who accept the reign of God.

Saying 67
Q 14:[11]
Matthew 23:12 and Luke 14:11

Everyone who exalts himself will be humiliated, and everyone who is humiliated will exalt herself.

The theme of inversion introduced in Saying 65 reemerges in this simple statement. In a culture oriented toward honor and shame, as were both the Roman Empire and Judean society, issues of exaltation and humiliation loomed large, especially to the entitled and to rising social and political stars. The hope of glory challenged people to build magnificent theaters and other public works, to arrange for gladiatorial games, to show munificence to common people (the *plebs*), to display their many clients (people dependent upon them for social and economic good), and to manifest the virtues appropriate to a man (and I used that word advisedly) rising in the society. Fear of humiliation also drove them with equal energy, because in such a glory-and-exaltation-seeking society, the fear of being bested, of failing, of losing one's financial resources in a civil suit, of returning to Rome not as a military victor but as a loser, or even of incurring the wrath or indignation of a person socially and politically superior to them, was always possible. Exaltation or humiliation occurred daily in this complex world, making its members both vulnerable and suspicious.

Jesus, addressing the realities of the society in which he announced the divine empire, appropriately speaks about exaltation and humiliation. But here Jesus inverts expectation by subverting the desire for honor and glory. The inversion states a principle of the divine empire into which Jesus calls people: those who would seek glory as the Roman and Judean imperial structure would define it will find themselves humiliated. The divine empire and the empires of the world differ in their orientation—glory, honor, exaltation for those in the divine empire comes only to the humiliated, the humble, those at the bottom of the social ladder. The inversion redefines the meaning of exaltation, making it the result of humiliation or of being the lowest and humblest members of society. Saying 4 describes these as the poor, the hungry, and the grieving. They will not only enter the divine empire, but they will also be the leading citizens of the divine empire. Their fortunes will be reversed. Similarly, those whose worldly fortunes are great will be humiliated in the divine empire, where they will need to become the lowest, humblest, and most abased.

Jesus' wisdom does not reflect the traditional wisdom of either Roman or Jewish sages. This becomes evident by comparing Jesus' sayings to those of Musonius Rufus or Seneca (on the Roman side), or to Proverbs, Wisdom of Solomon, and Ben Sira (on the Jewish side). Their practical wisdom provides instruction for day-to-day living and recipes for success in the world. Jesus' instruction, however, moves in a decidedly different direction. Jesus' wisdom subverts the moral structures of society and encourages a counter-cultural engagement with it, a countercultural engagement that defines the new society and the new empire of God. That divine empire not only subverts the empires of the world—Roman, Jewish, and all others—it also redefines the meaning of imperial authority from a divine perspective. Jesus reverses normal social expectations to create a new divine empire based on a different code of conduct and honor and a different series of steps toward exaltation.

Whenever readers and hearers encounter this sort of inversion of expectation, they find themselves turning inward to understand the limits of their own capacity to embrace the lowest place. The saying forces seekers both corporately and individually to confront their defenses against humiliation. Not an easy task, especially in the postmodern context.

Saying 68
Q 14:16–18, ?19–20?, 21, 23
Matthew 22:2–10 and Luke 14:16–21, 23

A certain person made a great dinner, and invited many [to it]. At the dinner hour, he sent his slave to tell those who had been invited, "Come, because [the dinner is] now prepared." [One excused himself, citing the necessity of his] farm. [Another excused himself, citing the necessities of his business. And another excused himself because he was newly married.] [And the slave returned to his master and told him these things.]

Then the infuriated master of the house said to the slave, "Go out on the highways! As many as you find there, invite them to fill my house [with dinner guests]."

This little narrative exemplifies the invitation to the divine empire. A master of a household invites many people to dinner and proceeds to prepare the dinner. The guests, however, do not respond appropriately. They cannot attend because of farming, business, and marriage. So the master invites others to take their place. The story seems prosaic, but readers, having been trained by earlier engagements with the sayings, know to analyze them as revelatory of the new thing that God enacts through Jesus' announcement of God's alternative empire.

The previous saying suggests that readers look for inversions. This narrative does contain an inversion—those the householder invited in the beginning have been replaced by anyone who happens to be on the road. Strangers have replaced friends. The uninvited displace the invited. The table-friends enrage the master of the household, while strangers please him. The story is replete with inversions.

The banquet itself, however, is also suggestive. These sayings of Jesus talk a lot about food and eating: God's provision of food for the itinerant missionaries (Sayings 26 and 27), the request for daily food (Saying 34), the faithful father giving a child the food it asks for (Saying 35), the question of properly cleansed eating utensils (Saying 45), the injunction not to worry about food (Saying 55), the image of the banquet or eschatological meal as part of the mythology of the return of the Lord in the final days (Sayings 41 and 42), and the story about those who thought they knew Jesus well because, as they said, "we ate and drank together, and you taught us on the main streets of our town" (Saying 63). Eating and drinking together and providing food for others play a central role in the empire of God. Food and banquets become signifiers of the divine empire and especially of the last days of the empire of this world, before the Lord returns to establish the divine empire on earth. So the banquet has both liturgical and missionary importance as well as eschatological and apocalyptic significance. The liturgical and missionary significance relates to the meal practices of the participants in the Jesus movements; the eschatological and apocalyptic significance relates to the mythology of the eventual return of the Lord to reign on earth. So the invitation to a great dinner signifies at many levels: it replicates the banquet given for missionaries when they arrive in a city; the banquet of participants when they gather to celebrate the agape meal or Eucharist (1 Corinthians 11:20–34); the heavenly banquet of the divine empire; the final banquet that will gather all the faithful to the bosom of Abraham (Saying 64); and the banquet of daily bread sufficient to do God's work for the participants in the movements (Saying 34). Other possibilities certainly exist.

The invitation goes out first to those known to the master, then to strangers. The invitation in the end becomes universal. Even though the first people did not respond appropriately or positively to the banquet itself, the master had nonetheless invited them and, when they did not come, he invited others. The invitation takes on different meanings depending on who we think is the master of the household. If the master stands for God, then the invitation went out first to God's intimates, the Jews, and when they refused to come, God extended the invitation to strangers, the Gentiles (see Colossians 1:21–23 and Ephesians 2:11–13). If the master is Jesus, the passage could refer to Jews and Gentiles, but it also could refer to different degrees of separation from Jesus. In this latter circumstance, those who were closest to Jesus could not respond appropriately to his invitation, while some who were distant could respond appropriately and enter the divine empire (see Saying 23). If the master of the house represents the commissioned itinerant missionaries of the early Jesus movements, then the invitation went out first to their neighbors in their own hometowns and then to those people they visited. Many other interpretations would also work here.

Reasons for declining the invitation differ in Matthew, Luke, and the *Gospel of Thomas*, revealing the authors' biases. In the *Gospel of Thomas*'s Saying 64, Thomas's prejudice against business comes out in the reasons given for the rejection: business with merchants, purchasing a house, buying a village, and planning a marriage. Luke includes purchasing a field, buying oxen, and marrying, while Matthew simply has farming and business as excuses. Despite the differences in the reasons given in the narrative, the initial invitees refused because they were caught up in daily living. Their excuses do not justify their refusal to attend the banquet, which readers now understand as something much more important than a simple meal. Their engagement with farming, commerce, and marriage distracts them from accepting an invitation to enter the divine empire and from discovering that God provides all that is necessary for their lives. Their engagement in worldly endeavors prevents them from seeing the divine empire being put in place around them. Those who are free, those on the highways who are away from business, commerce, and family, readily respond to the invitation. They fill the master's house. Their lack of encumbrance makes them capable of hearing and responding to God's call. What matters to the master is that his house be filled and his banquet enjoyed, a delightful image for the work that God does for people: feeds them in abundance and provides diligently for their needs. The respondents, the invitees, simply need to say yes to God's invitation, and then all things belong to them.

Paul loved to call himself a slave of Christ (see, for example, Romans 1:1). For Paul, the word "slave" was his name for himself as an itinerant apostle. The slave who functions as an intermediary between the master and the invited guests (both intimate friends and strangers) seems to suggest the kind of apostolic mission that Paul articulates. Participants in the Jesus movements could place themselves in the narrative by identifying with the slave who extends God's own invitation, or Jesus' own invitation, to insiders first, then to outsiders (see Romans 2:9–11). These missionary slaves understand themselves as intermediaries who gather the people into God's banquet by extending the invitation to all whom they encounter.

An infinite set of possibilities exists for interpreting this saying. That is probably why Jesus spoke in parables—to make us think. The meaning depends on the reader/hearer and on his or her facility with the sayings traditions—the more experience one has with the sayings traditions, the more complex and intricate his or her interpretations become. Jesus expected us to engage in this kind of exploration or he would have spoken in simple statements, as he does, for example, in Saying 8: do unto others as you would have them do unto you.

Saying 69
Q 14:26
Matthew 10:37 and Luke 14:26

Whoever does not hate father and mother is not capable of being my student, and whoever does not hate son and daughter is not capable of being my student.

The imperative in the divine empire to construct alternative relationships finds no more radical expression than in this saying. The divine empire demands comprehensive and primary allegiance. Participants in the divine empire cannot engage partially, but must make serious choices to engage in it. As Saying 58 affirms, this will cause division and strife within families, society, and political structures. The empire of God, a subversive and alternative empire, must be accepted totally; it does not coexist with other empires, other social structures, or other ethics.

The divine empire also functions as a school that demands commitment to a process of intellectual, spiritual, social, and economic growth. Students learn to live in the divine empire by reflecting on complex questions and by living in new communities unencumbered by social and political mores; this lifestyle requires a radical dependence on God as well as freedom from traditional restraints. To be a participant in the empire of God is to be a student of living the divine way.

In this saying, Jesus articulates the most radical and, for postmodern people, the most difficult expectation of those who dare to enter the empire of God as students of God and disciples of Jesus: the rejection of family ties. Since the divine empire replaces biological family with filiation with God, normal family ties have no place. Father, mother, son, and daughter have no compelling relationship to a participant in the divine empire. Like the man who wanted to bury his father first before following Jesus (Saying 23), these ties just hold participants back. Because they enmesh followers in alternative relationships that are peripheral to God's empire, family ties must be despised and rejected.

The saying uses strong language: the disciple must hate father, mother, son, daughter, indicating the intensely affective nature of the divine empire. Although thinking, reflecting, and doing stand at the center of the process of entering the divine empire, the whole person, especially his or her emotions, enters. Fear (Saying 49), love (Saying 6), anger (Sayings 29 and 36), and now hatred describe the affective response of participants in the divine empire to the world around them. The divine empire calls forth such strong emotions because it demands the totality of a person's life—finances, security, political and religious allegiance, social relationships constructed only from within the divine empire, and family only as created in the divine empire.

Ascetic masters know that connections to an old self or identity prevent the emergence of the new, so they recommended withdrawing from family and social relationships to create a space in which to construct a new identity. If a participant relates primarily to his or her family, he or she will never be empowered or free to begin to live in a different way, to become a new person who lives in the empire of God.

While many of these sayings advocate such a withdrawal, most notably for the itinerant missionaries who in wandering create a self radically dependent upon God, they also advocate love of enemies, not lending money at interest, not expecting to be repaid loans, and many other radically new practices that draw the line between life as usual and the divine empire.

This newness explains the school language here. The breaking of familial bonds inaugurates a school of learning new relationships defined from God's perspective. The social relationships developed in the empire of God may vary from person to person, place to place, and circumstance to circumstance, but withdrawal creates the social laboratory, if that metaphor can be anachronistically used, for transformation.

Saying 70
Q 14:27
Matthew 10:38 and Luke 14:27

Whoever does not seize his cross and follow me is not able to be my student.

The discussion of the affective aspect of participation in the divine empire continues in this saying. The Romans used the cross as a humiliating means of execution across the empire from Spain through the eastern provinces. Crosses, their corpses eaten by animals and their bones exposed to the elements, littered the highways outside cities throughout the empire. Crucifixion was the preferred means of execution for criminals, and it bore great social stigma.

In the spirit of loving the enemy (Saying 6) and not fearing those who can destroy only the body (Saying 49), this saying advocates the embrace of a shameful means of torture as the first step toward entering the divine empire. Precisely as an instrument of death, the cross divides the Roman empire and the empire of God. Only one who has withdrawn from the Roman Empire would embrace its most humiliating instrument of control over the outcasts and criminals of Roman society. Romans fear and avoid crucifixion as an end to life; Jesus' followers seize the cross as the beginning of new life.

Reminiscent of the poor who will enter God's empire, the hungry who will be fed, and the grieving who will be comforted (Saying 4), the pain and suffering of crucifixion functions as an entry point to the divine empire. This saying complements the psychic suffering advocated elsewhere, such as turning the other cheek (Saying 7) and joy at reproach by enemies (Saying 5). It grounds the psychic suffering in the body, in the willing embrace of the possibility (if not the reality) of painful crucifixion. In the end, readers understand a broad spectrum of suffering, reproach, and persecution as preliminary to entrance into real life in the empire of God.

After taking up the cross, one begins to follow Jesus and thereby become his student. Notice that the cross comes before the following. This embrace of crucifixion is not an imitation of Jesus' crucifixion; it precedes becoming part of the communities that formed around Jesus. This crucifixion represents the difference between those who embrace the world as it currently exists and those willing to risk all for something very different. When someone embraces the cross, then study with Jesus becomes possible.

The description of the movements as a school with students again emphasizes the fluidity and malleability of the categories. The saying does not put forward one cross or crucifixion that suits all, but rather posits "seiz[ing] the cross." The cross is essential, but how the crucifixion will happen for each person differs. Participants study themselves, their lives, their commitments, their choices, and their ways of thinking, and embrace the cross in those contexts. Each person intending to enter the divine empire must die to him- or herself in order to begin to construct a new self by associating with Jesus and the divine empire. The school provides the context for understanding the death of the old and the birth of the new.

Saying 71
Q 17:33
Matthew 10:39 and Luke 17:33

Whoever finds his life will destroy it, and the one who destroys his life on my account will find it.

The beauty of this saying resides in its oxymoronic qualities. The words engulf readers in a series of statements literally contradictory, but highly suggestive. The subject of the saying is finding and destroying life. The Greek word *psychē*, here translated "life," may also mean mind, soul, the conscious self or personal identity, and spirit, so the stakes are very high. This saying addresses what makes a person a person, what gives an individual his or her specific identity.

The first statement in the saying argues that whoever finds life, identity, conscious self, will destroy it. On the literal level, that doesn't make sense: one would assume that the person who found him- or herself would be fortunate. The person searched and found, as Saying 35 stipulates. But not so in this saying. The person concludes the search and the result destroys that which is found. Contrarily, the person who destroys his or her life for the sake of Jesus will find it. Here, then, is the key: "on my account."

In these sayings, life refers to the life engaged with the sayings of Jesus. It signifies entrance into the divine empire and intimacy with the one whom God has sent to inaugurate it. In the course of a life lived in worldly empires, a person comes to know and to enter the empire of God. That person has found life and, indeed, the empire of God will destroy life, because the divine empire operates in a manner inverse to worldly empires. The meaning of the word "life" is the key to the saying. In this instance, to find life in God's empire will mean significant changes for the seeker.

Now the saying begins to make sense. A person loses his or her worldly life when he or she engages with Jesus and enters into the empire of God, resulting in the person's finding new, true, and abiding life. The same applies to identity: the seeker who finds his or her new identity in the divine empire destroys the identity that the world provides.

This saying addresses what constitutes true "life," the right mode of thinking, the healthy emotional response, godly consciousness. When the readers understand the wide gap between the life offered in the divine empire and the life offered in every worldly empire, they not only make an important personal and social discovery, they also simultaneously enter the divine empire and destroy their own old identity. This saying calls readers to choose which life they will live, which way of thinking they will adopt, which way of responding will define their lives, which way of consciousness will guide their actions—that of the divine empire or something else. The saying also warns that once readers choose life in the divine empire, their old lives will be destroyed.

Saying 72
Q 14:34–35
Matthew 5:13 and Luke 14:34–35

Salt is good. But if salt becomes tasteless, in what will it serve as seasoning? Neither for the earth nor for the manure [used for fertilizing it] is it ready for use—they throw it out.

Again using common, everyday things to reveal the divine empire, this saying uses salt and seasoning as a way of understanding life in the divine empire. It makes sense at the purely literal level: salt is a fine seasoning, but when it becomes tasteless, it loses its value and cannot even be used for fertilizer.

What might the meaning of this discourse about salt be to the divine empire and to the sayings of Jesus? The sayings do not provide much guidance beyond affirming that meals were important to the various Jesus movements and are a central feature of the divine empire. Can the salt function in relationship to food in the same way that yeast functions in relationship to bread (Saying 62) or the mustard seed in relationship to the garden (Saying 61)? Salt provides something mysterious and beneficial to food: it enhances flavor and makes the whole meal delectable. Analogously, then, salt may represent the participants in the Jesus movements as they live out their daily lives among those living merely in the mundane empires of the world. Or salt may represent the presence of the divine empire in the midst of a Roman empire that without it has no flavor or grace. Or salt may be the person who follows Jesus in a family that does not do so (see Saying 58). The person, participants, or the movement itself adds variety and quality to that which otherwise is bland and tasteless.

In this reading, the saying articulates a further consequence. If the salt, which added variety and quality, should lose its essential features, then it is useless. As a symbol of those who have entered the divine empire, if it loses its flavor (its essence, its reason for being, or its full vigor), the Jesus movements waver and become ineffective. Without fervor and vigor, the divine empire cannot function on the earth. It cannot even serve as a fertilizer. It has no use or value.

This saying argues that participants in the divine empire must maintain their commitment by manifesting their essential difference in relation to those outside the community. To retain their usefulness and flavor, they must maintain their essential goodness in relationship to the deadening life of the worldly empire and remain solidly connected to Jesus, his sayings, and to the divine empire he has inaugurated.

This kind of wisdom saying makes reading Jesus fascinating. The manifold avenues of interpretation take readers from everyday life to the ethos of the divine empire. It means that once readers begin to look at such common things as salting a meal, making bread, gardening, or building a house as manifest events revealing the nature of God, there can be no limit to the way the natural order directs the reader to discover, to search, to find. In this way, readers retain their fervor and their usefulness.

Saying 73
Q 16:13
Matthew 6:24 and Luke 16:13

No one is capable of serving two masters, for either she will hate the one and love the other, or he will cling to one and hold the other in contempt. You are incapable of serving God and Mammon.

The theme of choosing one's allegiances emerges again in this saying. This saying, however, explicitly states that the choice must be made: "No one is capable of serving two masters." These sayings of Jesus have consistently laid out the two choices and called for a decision. This saying moves one step further, providing a rationale for the impossibility of serving two masters and the necessity of choosing one over the other.

Curiously, the rationale involves an emotional response. The words are love and hate, clinging devotion or contempt. Readers and hearers choose because they love or they hate, they adore or they hold in contempt. The choice reaches deep into the well of human relatedness and desire and operates out of that depth. So when combined with the necessity of choosing which master the readers will serve, the saying argues that they will love one and hate the other, be devoted to one and despise the other. The difference and the choice remain affective and clear—a mediating position does not exist.

The introduction of the Aramaic word "Mammon" to the discussion shifts the meaning of the choice significantly. Readers of these sayings by now have become accustomed to the choice between the Roman Empire and the empire of God. That choice is clear. But Mammon refers to wealth and possessions. A participant in the Jesus movements demonstrates his or her love and adoration for the divine empire by his or her social and economic decisions. Jesus says here that participants and readers can choose either to be devoted to the poverty of the divine empire, avoiding all attachments to things that properly belong to the worldly empires (see Sayings 4 and 26), or cling to their wealth and possessions. They must choose one or the other. The appeal of possessions, the strength of power and wealth, lead people away from the radical and complete dependence upon God that these sayings demand (see Sayings 27 and 55).

The choice between the two empires, however, is not necessarily a dramatic switch from one to the other. The smallest attachment to wealth and possessions keeps the emotional and affective part of a person anchored in the empires of the world, blocking him or her from the complete dependence on God necessary to enter into the empire of God. God demands that those who enter the divine empire love only God, depending on God's gracious providence for both physical and emotional needs. There can be no compromise, because one cannot serve both God and Mammon.

Saying 74
Q 16:16
Matthew 11:12–13 and Luke 16:16

The law and the prophets [existed] until John. From that time, the empire of God is overpowered by force and the violent seize it hastily.

God did not create the divine empire out of nothing. The empire had a history. This saying constructs a history in three phases: the time of the law and the prophets that had divine authority until the time of John (see Sayings 1, 2, and 19–22); the time of John's prophetic work; and the period when Jesus inaugurates the empire of God. This history provides an essential orientation for the participants in the Jesus movements and the divine empire, connecting the divine empire not only to the work of John, but also to the Israelite religion. God's intervention in history and God's inauguration of a new empire as an alternative to that of Rome continues a historical process begun long ago and maintained through the time of John.

The recitation of history provides an important part of the construction of a symbolic universe, the system of meanings and connections that explain group identities, social relations, institutions, and cultural patterns. History provides depth to new movements and ways of thinking, while at the same time legitimating the present by connection with noble past events. In this instance, the divine empire's past gathers up the law and prophets as well as the preliminary work of John. They validate the new movements inaugurated by Jesus and they pick up the particular prophetic strain of the history of Israel as the basis of the new divine empire, giving a prophetic slant to the movements.

The sayings have already told us the fate of the prophets: they are killed and stoned (Saying 66), and the legal scholars falsely and perniciously idolize them (Saying 46). Prophets do not fare well with the general public, not even with Jerusalem, the holy city. The sayings also tell us the fate of the prophetic missionaries: they are brought before councils (Saying 53), they embrace the cross (Saying 70), they are reproached and rejected (Saying 5), and they are physically abused (Saying 7) and hated (Saying 6). This saying seems to align the experiences of the prophets of Israel with the experiences of the missionaries of the Jesus movements. Violent people treated them violently.

The saying also explains the current violence against the empire of God. It suggests that in the earlier periods, the law and the prophets and then the mission of John sustained God's rule peacefully or at least without violence. God's rule appeared stable under the law and prophets and throughout John's mission, but afterward it became an object of violent suppression.

That the early Jesus movements suffered internal and external controversy is well established. Paul seems to have consistently gotten himself in trouble with local religious and political authorities (see, for example, 2 Corinthians 11:21–29 for a catalogue of these). But the controversy did not come only from external forces: other apostles followed Paul and disputed his message in an attempt to undermine his authority (the super-apostles of 2 Corinthians 11:5), and Paul even confronted the authority of the pillars of Jerusalem (Galatians 2:1–14). These were heated and violent internal debates, matched by a violent and repressive attempt by the authorities to thwart the various movements and the extension of the empire of God.

This saying puts the violence and opposition of the early Jesus movements into a theological and historical context by identifying them with the experience of religious forebears (the prophets).

Saying 75
Q 16:17
Matthew 5:18 and Luke 16:17

It is easier to disregard heaven and the earth than for one iota or one letter-marking of the law to pass [without notice].

The law theme continues from the previous saying. This saying affirms that the divine empire and the Jesus movements are based on the law. In fact, it seems to argue that the law continues to hold force and have authority within the empire of God. The centrality of the law should not surprise anyone. Paul discusses the contested centrality of the law with the pillars of Jerusalem (Galatians 2:1–14). Here we find a pro-circumcision party arguing that Gentiles must be circumcised; that is, they must become Jews first (Galatians 2:3–5) in order to enter the Jesus movement in Jerusalem, which was apparently aligned with the temple and the law. The conclusion of this

meeting between Paul, James, John, and Peter was the creation of a simpli-
fied law for the Gentiles: "only they would have us remember the poor,
which very thing I was eager to do" (Galatians 2:10 RSV). The law, or some
summary or condensation of the law, continued to apply to participants in
the earliest Jesus movements even for Paul, who did not think that Gentiles
needed to observe the law.

Given that context and the debates within the earliest movements about
the law, this saying makes sense. The law cannot be ignored. The saying
describes a dramatic situation in which someone disregards or overlooks
heaven and earth, yet he or she cannot pass over the smallest detail of the law
written either in Greek (the reference to the iota) or in Hebrew (the reference to the letter-marking).

In reality, it is easy to overlook a small symbol on a written page, but it is
not easy to ignore the physical world. But that is the point. Jesus reverses the
expectation here, announcing that it is easier to ignore the physical world
completely than to overlook the smallest detail of the law. The law has such
force that it cannot be ignored, overlooked, dismissed, or denigrated.

Most people hear the word "law" in relation to Judaism and think rigidity and inflexibility. That characterization, dependent as it is on an ongoing
argument between Protestants (no law) and Catholics (legalists) in the post-
Reformation world, was not the prevailing argument in the ancient world,
which valued the antiquity and nobility of all the laws of ethnic groups,
including the Jews. The law, which included wide-ranging customary and
cultural practices, held great fascination and value. The connection with
ancestral ways of living proved the nobility of a people. Many within the
early Jesus movements valued their ancestral practices as essential to their
identity and to the revealed and expressed will of God. Laws created strong
and cohesive communities; hence, they could not be overlooked.

These sayings, in fact, propose a particular way of living that functioned
as the law, the customary practices, of the early Jesus movements. The values expressed throughout the sayings created an ethos and developed a particular culture for the movement. It is no wonder that Jesus has a saying
supporting the law—even the empire of God depends on it.

In fact, for the hearers and readers of these sayings, new kinds of customs
and laws emerge that hold great importance in the divine empire. New economic customs, new eating patterns, different ways of relating to others are

just a few of these. These new customs and laws become hallmarks of the divine empire. Such embodied customs and laws, in fact, define the empire of God, which has as much physical as spiritual reality for those electing to join it.

Saying 76
Q 16:18
Matthew 5:32 and Luke 16:18

Everyone who puts aside his wife and marries another woman commits adultery, and the one who marries the woman who is put aside [also] commits adultery.

The question of the status of the law continues in this saying. It presents an example of one of the basic laws not to commit adultery, but this saying presents a more vigorous law than that in the Israelite scriptures. This saying aims to protect the community and its members from inadvertently transgressing a law by divorcing or by marrying a divorced woman. The saying functions as an exemplar of the previous saying, which affirms the law.

Clearly, such a saying arose and applied to only one segment of those participating in the Jesus movements. Paul does not present such a position in 1 Corinthians 7, where he deals with various kinds of sexual relationships, including marriage. Paul specifically allows divorce between a believer and an unbelieving partner if the unbelieving partner wishes one (1 Corinthians 7:15). Paul's position emerges as he struggles to make sense of daily living within the ethics of the divine empire. His concern does not reflect any interest in the Jewish law, because he was talking to Gentiles, whom he insisted did not need to observe the law. But for those who did place the law at the center of the Jesus-believing communities, this divorce statement encouraged them to observe the law faithfully. So the same topic can evoke different responses in different circumstances.

These sayings take commitment very seriously. Casual divorce, especially as practiced by emperors and other elites of the Roman Empire, flies in the face of the kind of commitment that is necessary to withdraw from the world and to enter the empire of God. Again, this everyday concern about breaking the marriage bond becomes a way to reveal God and God's empire. If a man can divorce a wife, he can also divorce God, the empire of God, or the community of Jesus' intimates. Likewise, if a woman remarries after divorce, it means that she can move from one husband to another, from one empire to another, and from God to any other who might capture her attention. Such instability is incongruous within the empire of God.

Saying 77
Q 17:1–2
Matthew 18:7, 6 and Luke 17:1–2

It is necessary that the offenses come, but [damn the one] through whom it comes. It is more advantageous for that one if a millstone were placed around his throat and he were hurled into the sea than that he would offend one of these little ones.

In most ascetical systems, seemingly negative things have a positive function. Temptation, for example, becomes an opportunity to resist and test one's mettle; hunger and thirst help in overcoming adversity; sexual hunger obligates supreme self-awareness. Such problems strengthen the ascetic, contributing to his or her personal development and growth as he or she strives to surmount them. The first statement in this saying, "it is necessary that the offenses come," establishes difficulties as positive instruments that test and strengthen the person of faith.

The difficulty in this saying is that it does not define the necessary offenses. At its root, the Greek word translated here "offenses" (*skandala*) refers to traps set for an enemy. In the Roman period, it came to mean offense, stumbling block, or scandal. This saying also employs it as a verb at the end, translated "offend" here.

From within the sayings collection itself, a number of different options emerge. The offense, scandal, or stumbling block may refer to any of the following: the desire for wealth over poverty (Saying 73) and food over hunger (Saying 4); the rejection of reproach as a blessing (Saying 5); the refusal to consider an enemy someone for whom to pray (Saying 6); the inhospitable response to negative demands (Saying 7); the refusal to treat others as one would be treated (Saying 8); the demand to receive interest on loans to others and the expectation of repayment (Saying 9); and many more. In other words, the offenses and stumbling blocks include all the simple but radical patterns of behavior necessitated by one's entrance into the empire of God. And they have the beneficial function of testing the resolve of participants in the divine empire.

The offenses are necessary, but the person who causes them remains responsible: "but [damn the one] through whom it comes." The "it" here is ambiguous: it could refer to the way God has structured the universe or it could refer to one of the offenses in particular. The second part of the saying refers to the latter, but readers must entertain the first possibility as well. Damning God for building in necessary offenses into God's empire makes perfect sense from the perspective of the one who experiences the offense. Granted, it is a radical and potentially dangerous way of relating to God, but honesty about the pain and work that necessary temptations and problems bring forms an essential part of the covenant between God and the participants in God's empire.

Probably readers prefer the second meaning: damning one who causes the specific offenses. In the context of a community, an offense harms others. Refusing to do any of the expected things listed above suggests to others that the requirements of the empire of God do not extend to all. The ethics and practices of the divine community become optional. Such an attitude hinders the progress of others who wish to continue growing and developing in the divine empire. The saying articulates the harmful effect of this bad behavior on others: it would be better to be drowned by tying a millstone around one's neck than to harm one of these little ones. The little ones are those who still wish to mature in the divine empire. They might be children, but more likely they are metaphoric children of the divine empire, those still being formed in the ways of the community. Causing a scandal, putting a stumbling block before others, or giving offense to the mores of the community can be devastating not only to the offending person but also to the entire community. The violence of the manner of drowning indicates the seriousness of such offenses, even though offenses and problems come with the divine imperial territory.

This saying underscores the high price and intense affective cost of entry into the empire of God. The relationships between God and the members of God's empire, as well as among those within the divine empire itself, remain complex, interactive, intense, intimate, and very close to the core of being. This saying does not dodge that complexity in any way and treats difficulties with ultimate importance and significance.

Saying 78
Q 15:4–5a, 7
Matthew 18:12–13 and Luke 15:4–5a, 7

What person among you, having a hundred sheep and losing one from among them, does not leave behind the ninety-nine on the mountains and going forth searches for the lost one? And should it happen that he find it, I say to you that he rejoices over it more than over the ninety-nine who had not wandered away.

This saying shows the illogicality of the ethos of the divine empire and the inversion of common values within it. At the literal level, this narrative makes no sense: a shepherd leaving ninety-nine sheep in order to search on the off chance of finding the lost one. That illogicality of the narrative confronts readers and nudges them to make sense of the narrative.

The first point the saying makes, then, is that the empire of God does not make sense. In relationship to the Roman Empire or to other empires, God's empire operates on a completely different basis, which manifests a radically different ethic and culture. As Paul put it: "For the wisdom of this world is folly with God" (1 Corinthians 3:19 RSV). This narrative illustrates God's folly and the alternative way of thinking inherent in the sayings of Jesus, in the divine empire, and among the various early Jesus movements.

The second point of the saying regards the importance of searching. Other sayings commend the search as essential to engagement with the empire of God: Saying 35 guarantees the success of the search, while Saying 55 requires searching for the divine empire to gain God's providential care. This saying looks at a different aspect, a seemingly foolish search for only one element of a very large group. The saying commends searching after the foolishness of God as a way to understand the divine empire and its subversive and countercultural modalities. The foolishness here relates also to the fact that the narrative does not guarantee success in finding the lost one.

Notice the language: "And should it happen that he find it. . . ." The language attenuates the guarantee given in other sayings, making the prospect of actually finding the lost one chancy. This, too, demonstrates the divine foolishness in God's empire. But the participant in the divine empire feels compelled to search for the lost one despite the slim odds of finding it. Foolishness indeed!

The next point relates to the status of the lost one. The sayings of Jesus often speak of displacement—after all, itinerancy defines the missionary modality in these sayings. The poor, the grieving, the hungry, those without families, those despised and rejected—these are the lost of society whom these sayings elevate to high status and who constitute the majority of those in the divine empire. These lost ones make up those who, as Saying 65 argues, will become the first citizens of God's empire. These whom society has marginalized who have strayed from the security of the community of God's empire become the object of a search, not only by other members of the community, but perhaps even by God's own self. These sayings of Jesus cherish the lost ones to the point that they will be foolishly and illogically pursued until found, even when the possibility defies reason.

Finally, this saying expresses the great joy of the divine empire. The community and God value the many, but the lost one, when found, creates great joy. This saying does not denigrate the many or treat them as worthless. Rather, it elevates the status of the lost, treating them as exalted precisely because they were lost and then returned to the fold. The joy results as much from the finding as from the recognition that the empire of God transforms the world by inverting expectations, subverting the common logic, and bringing unusual and delightful results.

In this story of the lost sheep, if readers quickly identify the shepherd with Jesus, they short-circuit the process. This saying does not make a theological point about Jesus alone, nor just about God, but also about the community and its modes of operation. By engaging with the narrative at multiple levels and from multiple perspectives, readers gain not only an understanding of the divine empire and the early Jesus movements, but also an awareness of the truly subversive and inverted ways of those who have entered the empire of God.

Saying 79
Q 15:[8–10]
Luke 15:8–10

(1) Or what woman having ten drachmas, if she were to lose one drachma, does not light a lamp and sweep the house clean and search until she finds [it]? And finding it, she invites her girlfriends and neighbors, saying, "Be happy with me, because I found the drachma that I had lost."

(2) Thus I say to you, a joy occurs before the angels for one person who fails of his purpose and who then changes course.

The sequence of stories continues with a parallel story about a woman who loses money and then rejoices at finding it (1), followed by a summary theological statement (2). The collections of sayings may deliberately balance a saying about a man (Saying 78) with one about a woman. The ethics and mores of the divine empire demand such equality.

There are numerous connections to other sayings in this story: lighting a lamp invokes Saying 43, sweeping the house suggests Saying 39, the search connects with Saying 35, and the finding complements the previous saying. These intertextual references seem deliberate, and they help us understand that this narrative goes much further than the previous one and moves in different directions. This woman, upon losing her drachma, a Greek coin, does all the things a participant in the divine empire should do: she lights a lamp and does not remain in the darkness, but illuminates the whole space physically (and perhaps even metaphysically); she cleans the house by sweeping it, and thereby prepares herself and her surroundings for the unusual and unexpected to happen; and then she searches until she finds. She prepares the way for God to do the work God has planned.

So the first point that this saying makes is about the preparation necessary to be successful in the divine empire. That preparation does not involve unusual tasks: the preparation, in fact, is simply what seems reasonable under the circumstances. But the woman responds to her loss by engaging in preparatory acts that set the stage for her subsequent finding of the coin. She does not immediately look for the coin, but methodically prepares the way for the coin to be found. And she prepares by doing precisely the things that any member of the Jesus movements and the divine empire should be doing: proclaiming what she knows, cleansing herself and her environment of the debilitating effects of the empires of this world, and searching for what has been lost. The preparation sets the stage for finding the coin.

But her successful search ends in community life. This is the next point of the story. The woman, unlike the shepherd of the previous story, does not simply rejoice alone: she gathers community. She calls in her friends and neighbors and invites them to share in her joy at finding what she has lost. The preparation and the success of the search occasion the affirmation of community and the connectedness of those who live together. The benefit transfers from the individual to the community. The same joy that the shepherd experienced is now the focus of renewed community in the divine empire, a reality that gathers many individuals into communities and many communities into larger communities until God's reign encompasses all things and all people. Section 1 of this saying makes these readings possible.

Section 2, however, lends itself to only one interpretation and it does not follow directly from the first part of the narrative. The saying does not attribute the successful search to the drachma's repentance, to what I have translated as changing course. Nor does it attribute anything sinful or insufficient in the drachma itself. Nor does it even suggest that the woman who lost the coin changed course or needed to repent for anything. Neither the woman nor the coin were in need of repentance. So the connection between the parts is about joy. The woman's joy connects to the joy experienced by the angels.

The scene changes to a heavenly assembly of both humans and angels. The angels, presumably part of the renewed community of section 1 of this saying, rejoice over a person described in two ways: as a person who falls, that is, a sinner; and as a person who changes course, a penitent. The penitent who has lost his or her way and who has returned to the fold brings joy to the angels, the messengers of God. In other words, those who have failed, who for some reason have been unable to live in the divine empire, cause the angels to rejoice when they eventually change course and return. The restoration to the community of one who was lost brings cosmic joy. The joy of the angels replicates the joy of the woman who found the coin and invited her friends to celebrate with her. It represents the joy of a renewed and restored communion.

Two kinds of joy meet in this saying: the joy of finding something lost and the joy of the transformation and restoration of a person. The two joys meet in the divine empire as a place where society's lost enact the renewal of community life and where those who have gone astray find their restoration. The two joys ought not to be collapsed into one; such a reading diminishes meaning rather than expanding it. Rather, the joy that connects the two parts should be read as correlative but unrelated joys that erupt in the divine empire when participants perform properly, first in the preparation of themselves and their households for divine action and second in the repentance of a person who has gone astray.

Saying 80
Q 17:3–4
Matthew 18:15, 21 and Luke 17:3–4

If your brother wrongs you, upbraid him, and if he changes course, forgive him. And if seven times in a day he should wrong you, also seven times you will forgive him.

This saying continues the theme of sinning and repentance from the previous saying. The saying provides the Jesus community with rules for dealing with personal injustices and offenses. The directions are clear: reprove a member of the community who offends or wrongs you; then, if that member of the community changes course, forgive him. This saying requires the direct confrontation of the offender. It expects a level of honesty and intimacy. The admonition to forgive the person who repents reiterates the instruction of Saying 10, on being merciful as God is merciful, only here it is forgiving as God forgives (see also Saying 34).

The subversive nature of the empire of God requires such specific community rules; they replace the laws of the Roman Empire, among others, with policies appropriate to an intimate and varied community where the rule of forgiveness for the repentant takes precedence. So rather than going to court against one another, this saying argues for direct reprimand and forgiveness if the reprimand brings repentance.

The saying goes even further, however, to say that forgiveness should be granted often. Even if the offender wrongs a member of the community seven times in a day, the same procedure should be followed. The offender must still be forgiven. This saying portrays the forbearance that one member of the Jesus community must hold for another: repeated offenses receive repeated forgiveness. There seems no limit to the extent to which members of the community will strive to create harmony out of chaos and community out of failure. It recalls the reciprocal tenet of Saying 8, which stipulates that we should treat others as we expect to be treated.

This saying enjoins readers and hearers to realize that they harm others within the community of the divine empire by holding onto resentments and hurts. The saying guides readers and hearers to release others by direct and honest conversation and by forgiveness in the face of persistent mistreatment. Members of the divine empire must guard against holding grudges, which divide people and destroy the common bonds of community; its participants are enjoined continually to forgive.

Saying 81
Q 17:6
Matthew 17:20b and Luke 17:6

If you have trust just as a mustard seed [has trust], you could say to this mulberry tree, "Be uprooted and be planted in the sea!" And it would obey you.

Readers have already encountered the mustard seed in Saying 61, where the sower deliberately planted a small and intrusive mustard seed so that it would become a haven for many. In that saying, the planter of the mustard seed seemed to have been both foolish in planting what amounts to a weed and expectant in preparing a place that would provide shelter for many birds. This saying personifies the mustard seed, attributing to it the ability to have trust in God, to have faith. Of course, seeds do not really exhibit faith— they merely do what comes naturally to them, given the proper circumstances of soil, water, and sun. So the personification of faith in the mustard seed presents readers with an opportunity to think back over the sayings to discover the meaning of the current saying.

The traditional reading of this saying focuses on the size of the seed: the small mustard seed becomes a tree, and a small level of trust in God becomes sufficient to work miracles by ordering trees to do something unnatural. But if readers reflect on the earlier mustard seed saying, other possibilities emerge. Yes, the small seed can indicate little faith, but there are other possible interpretations. In the earlier saying about the mustard seed, the planter deliberately placed an invasive weed in the garden so it would become a shelter for others. Perhaps the trust of the mustard seed here does not refer to its size but means that someone who is out of place, rejected as superfluous, maybe even one of the lost, can become a haven for others, a protector of the weak, one who reigns in the empire of God. The weed may become a towering tree, while the displaced person may become the agent of provision for many.

Perhaps another meaning of faith in this saying refers to the significance of planting a weed in a garden. The deliberateness of the planting seems to discount the detrimental effect of having a garden choked by mustard weeds. But the sower planted the mustard seed nonetheless, making it available for use by the divine planter for unsuspected and unknown purposes. Who would have thought a mustard seed could become a tree to house many birds? Who would have thought that God would plant a weed that would be used as a haven for many? The mustard seed was available to God and ready for deployment in those unusual circumstances.

Although the saying does not specify what constitutes the mustard seed's faith, the effect is clear. If a participant in the divine empire had such faith, he or she could order a tree to plant itself in the sea and it would obey. This faith makes it possible for the participant in the divine empire to perform wonderful and powerful deeds. These sayings often speak of powerful deeds: Jesus heals the centurion's boy and remarks on the centurion's faith (Saying 18); Jesus identifies the powerful deeds of healing the sick and raising the dead as a sign of his authority and power (Saying 19); Jesus instructs the missionaries to heal the sick wherever they go (Saying 27); and Jesus upbraids cities for ignoring the powerful deeds (Saying 29). The ability to perform miraculous deeds became a hallmark of the early Jesus movements and a dramatic announcement of the power of God's reign and empire (see, for example, 1 Corinthians 2:1–5).

Finding one meaning for this saying is insufficient. Readers should let their imaginations take over. The sheer impossibility of a person commanding a tree to uproot itself and move on its own should show the way. In exploring various possible meanings, interpreters can find their way into the inner workings of the divine empire.

Saying 82
Q 17:[20–21]
Matthew 24:23 and Luke 17:20–21

But being questioned about when the empire of God is coming, he responded to them and said, "The empire of God is not coming with close observation. Nor will someone say, 'Look, here it is!' For the empire of God is within you."

An empire implies both geography and political dominance—things tangible and intangible. One could easily read the divine empire in a number of different ways: as an imperium within the realm of the world that opposes the Roman imperium, as a parallel imperium that exists mostly in heaven where the angels live (see, for example, Saying 79), or as an entirely heavenly imperium that focuses on judgment and the reward of the just (see Sayings 46 and 47). Or the empire of God could be all of these things and more. This saying takes the divine empire into the human person.

The saying recounts how people come to Jesus asking about the time of arrival of the divine empire.: "Where is the empire of which you speak?" The question reflects a legitimate concern. Jesus' answer, however, dismisses geographical and political concepts of the empire of God as being insufficient conceptualizations. He locates the empire of God within the person. The divine empire exists within the person as an orientation to the world, as a divine presence inhabiting the body, as a distinctly different way of understanding oneself and one's relationships, in short, as an interior phenomenon. Paul wrote about the indwelling of Jesus Christ within individuals, all of whom together formed the body of Christ, the church (see, for example, 1 Corinthians 13:27). The concept of a divinized body, one in which the divine presence dwells, formed an important part of early Jesus movements' understanding of themselves. God and God's divine empire were within them. They themselves were part of God and of God's empire.

Does the presence of the empire of God within the person negate other ways of understanding the divine empire? The sayings in this collection work collaboratively to explore various aspects of the divine empire. These explorations take on meaning not only individually but cumulatively, as they resonate with one another. The reader as well adds his or her own nuances and reflections. Gradually, meaning expands. The empire of God, then, is not only what this saying says it is. But this saying, and the fruit of individual and corporate reflection on it, adds yet another dimension to our emerging and evolving understanding of the empire of God, which manifests itself within the individual person and the community: an earthly empire, a parallel empire, and a heavenly empire simultaneously.

For readers and hearers of these sayings, the final statement, "the empire of God is within you," provides strong affirmation. The divine empire does not exist in some ancient time or in some obscure place, it exists within us. The divine empire transcends time and place and yet at the same time instantiates itself in every time and place where seekers hear Jesus' voice and engage with Jesus' words; it is a reality in every generation.

Saying 83
Q 17:23–24
Matthew 24:26–27 and Luke 17:23–24

If they say to you: "See, he is in the deserted places," do not withdraw [there]; "See he is in the storeroom," do not pursue [him there]. For just as lightning exceeds all bounds from east and appears as far as the west, so will the son of humanity be on his day.

This saying does for the elusive "son of humanity" what the previous saying does for the empire of God. The saying, beginning with a vague identification of speakers as "they," contains a series of statements from unidentified people directing the hearer to look for the son of humanity in a variety of places: "See, he is in the deserted places," and "See he is in the storeroom." Seeking is good and the result is guaranteed (Saying 35), so the energy of these anonymous seekers moves in the right direction.

But what about these places? The desert is known in the sayings as the place where Jesus was driven to test himself (Saying 3), as the place where the exorcized demon goes but finds no rest (Saying 39), and as the locus for John's preaching and ministry (Saying 20). The desert should be a good place to look for the son of humanity. But the saying tells the inquirers not to withdraw to the desert to find him. The second place the unidentified people locate the son of humanity is in the household storeroom. This one seems more ridiculous. Why would the heavenly being return to a house or to a room in a house? It does not make sense. The saying directs readers not to pursue him there, either. The desert provides a more plausible venue than the storeroom, but both deceive. They make looking for the son of humanity too literal.

The description of the son of humanity on the day of his coming shatters all presumptions: "For just as lightning exceeds all bounds from east and appears as far as the west, so will the son of humanity be on his day." He will arrive like the lightning in the heavens, stretching from the far east to the far west in brilliant and electrifying light. What an image! It suggests that he will be plainly seen by all, as clearly and dramatically as lightning smashing the boundaries of earth and heaven and east and west. When the final day comes, the son of humanity will appear in a brilliant spectacle that encompasses the heavens and the earth. Seekers will know where to look for him—there will be no avoiding him. Searching in the desert or in the house will not serve them well, or even prepare them for his arrival.

When the empire of God exists within the person (as the previous saying argues), then the coming day of the Lord, the eschatological day, requires another figure to inaugurate the end-time. God, dwelling within the divine empire and located within the individual and corporate bodies of those who have entered the divine empire, must come in some embodied way to inaugurate an end from outside the person, outside the community, and outside the established empire of God on earth. This seems to be the function of the son of humanity, the heavenly figure who breaks in at the end to inaugurate a new day, a new time, and a new era. So this saying, following on the previous one, complements the search for the divine empire within with the search for the one who will instigate the final and dramatic end.

Saying 84
Q 17:37
Matthew 24:28 and Luke 17:37

Wherever the corpse is, there the eagles will gather around.

This saying presents a startling image of raptors surrounding carrion, their putrefying fleshy food. Carrion, the dead flesh, attracts the eagles, vultures, and other raptors for whom rotting flesh is an important source of food. The corpse sustains the lives of other beings. The literal sense is both dramatic and disturbingly familiar.

So what could it mean in the context of these sayings of Jesus? Readers again must fend for themselves. The saying gives no direction. At one level, the saying may be invoking the mode of inversion. The dead corpse, something terrible and offensive, becomes something very positive, food for birds. Something seemingly negative takes on the aura of something very positive, conveying the idea that good will come from evil, good will vindicate bad. So the eagles assembling around the corpse communicates the positive potential that could come out of something very negative. It is a possible interpretation, though not a very satisfying one. Another possible interpretation is that when something so good and delectable is present (now speaking, of course, from the eagle's point of view), it is bound to garner attention and attract people to it, so the corpse is like the empire of God and the eagles are those who find themselves hungry to enter it.

A still more intriguing interpretation is that this saying speaks about rejection and persecution by "devouring" outside sources. Although the divine empire appears to be dead and outsiders seek to devour it, in reality, the divine empire remains unassailable. Paul's "body of Christ" theology, in which the members of the church constitute Jesus' body in the world (Romans 12:4–5; 1 Corinthians 12:12–13), fits this interpretation. The living body of Christ, because it embraces the cross of Jesus (1 Corinthians 1:18), appears as a corpse that will attract persecution, but in fact it is a living being beyond attack from the outside.

More than most, this saying presents a puzzle, a quandary, a mystery to ponder. The dramatic nature of the image draws readers into making connections equally dramatic, helping them to see a reflection of the divine empire in even the most grotesque realities.

Saying 85
Q 17:26–27, ?28–29?, 30
Matthew 24:37–39 and Luke 17:26–30

The day of the son of humanity will be just the same as things that took place in the days of Noah. For in those days, [people] were eating and drinking, marrying and giving in marriage, until the day that Noah entered into the ark and up came the flood and carried them off; so will it also be on the day when the son of humanity is disclosed.

The sayings of Jesus do not often invoke the great epics of the Israelites. In this collection, only Sayings 41, 42, 47, 64, and 66 refer to some part of an Israelite epic. This saying, however, correlates an Israelite epic directly with the experience of the Jesus movements. The first sentence aligns the events and context of the time prior to the flood with the time when God reveals the son of humanity. The saying describes the "day of the son of humanity" as a cataclysm of universal significance, just like the flood.

The description of the time before the flood indicates that people remained unaware of their dire circumstances. They lived what they thought were good lives, eating, drinking, and marrying, but God's flood was coming. God warned Noah, so he built the ark, gathered his family, collected the animals, and safely survived the cataclysm, while the rest of the created world was destroyed. The saying speaks to the early Jesus movements, indicating that many in their times are also unaware of the impending cataclysmic events that God will accomplish when God reveals the son of humanity.

Who correlates to Noah and his family in the time of the early Jesus movements? The saying does not specify, but one obvious reading might be that Jesus is the new Noah who gathers as his family those who have heard his oracles and follow him, who builds the empire of God as an ark into which select people will be gathered. The traditional Christian reading does not inhibit other interpretations. The early Jesus movements may have experienced themselves as a corporate Noah who brings together diverse people into a new family of God, floating on the seas with those few that they have been able to gather into the ark of their community to save them from sure destruction. Or even individual participants in the divine empire might understand themselves as minor Noahs who, within their own social and political circle, have built an ark of salvation for the sick, the lost, and the despised to save them from the cataclysmic effects of the Roman world in which they live.

Other readers may identify themselves with elements in the story. They could see themselves as Noah, or the family, or the ark, or the animals on the ark, or those left behind to be destroyed by the flood waters, helping them to evaluate their own lives.

In this context, the disclosure or revelation of the son of humanity takes on an apocalyptic as well as an eschatological aura. The eschatology simply posits that God will judge the lives and deeds of people on the last day, as has already been described in one form or another in these sayings (for example, Sayings 41 and 42). But this invocation of Noah's flood suggests something far more drastic, an apocalyptic scenario of the end-time in which the judgment includes also the wholesale destruction of people who have resisted or simply ignored God's efforts to gather them into safety. Many participants in the early Jesus movements expected such a cataclysmic and apocalyptic end to the known world, with the return of Jesus to reign on earth in the divine empire. Paul certainly held such a perspective and describes the final catastrophic end in some detail (1 Thessalonians 5:1–11). The apocalyptic expectations probably increased among the early missionaries and participants as they suffered persecution and rejection, but it also added intensity and poignancy to their work. The expectation of Jesus' imminent return impelled the early Jesus movements to work tirelessly on behalf of the empire of God. Paul again stands as an example of this fervor and dedication. So this comparison of Noah's time with the time of the apocalyptic disclosure of the son of humanity is appropriate.

Saying 86
Q 17:34–35
Matthew 24:40–41 and Luke 17:34–35

I tell you: there will be two men in the field; one is taken up and one passed by; two women will be grinding [wheat] in the mill; one is taken up and one passed by.

It is difficult not to read this saying as a correlate to the preceding saying. It presents a scenario where some are selected and some are left behind. The saying does not specify whether it refers to the apocalyptic end-time or to the eschatological day when the elect of God will be gathered together, as Paul envisioned those still alive rising to meet the Lord in the sky (1 Thessalonians 4:13–18).

This saying relates to other sayings that talk about a final judgment and evaluation of people's lives and deeds (Sayings 41 and 42). Unlike those sayings, it tells us that the judgment will result in the election of some to a place in the heavenly divine empire while others will be condemned to remain on earth.

These later sayings seem more and more oriented toward judgment day and its implications, perhaps indicating a gradually more exclusive understanding of what participation in the various Jesus movements meant, of what the impact the presence of the divine empire implied, or of increased opposition to the establishment of an alternative empire in their communities. For whatever reason, the people in the early Jesus movements began to expect an apocalyptic and cataclysmic judgment separating one person from another on the basis of their engagement with the empire of God.

Saying 87
Q 19:12–13, 15–24, 26
Matthew 25:14–15b, 19–29 and Luke 19:12–13, 15–24, 26

(1) A certain person about to travel away summoned ten of his slaves and gave to each one of them ten minas, and said to them, "Engage in business until I return." After a great period of time, the slaves' master returns and makes an accounting with them.

(2) The first one came saying, "Master, your one mina earned ten minas in addition."

And [the master] said to him, "Excellent, good slave, you were trustworthy in little things, I will place you over many [more things]."

(3) And the second [slave] came saying, "Master, your mina made five minas."

[The master] said to him: "Excellent, good slave, you were trustworthy in little things, I will place you over many [more things]."

(4) And the other [slave] came saying, "Master, knowing that you are a harsh person, reaping where you did not sow and gathering from where you did not winnow, and being fearful, I went out and hid your mina in the ground. Here! Take what is yours."

The master said to him, "You good-for-nothing slave! You knew that I reap where I did not sow and gather where I did not winnow! You should have put my silver pieces into the banks, and returning I would acquire what is mine with interest."

(5) So snatch the mina from him and give it to the one who has ten minas, for all things will be given to the one who has, but even what he has will be taken from the one who does not have.

This saying presents a nicely crafted and complex narrative. The rich details provide readers with a plethora of entry points through which to enter the story.

A householder leaves on a trip, entrusting to ten servants ten minas each, an ancient silver coin presumably of reasonable value, with the expectation that they would engage in business. Then the householder returns to settle accounts. At the literal level, the story presents a perfectly plausible scenario. At other levels, however, readers may begin to explore who the master might represent. Again at the literal level and in the context of these sayings, the master may be one of the itinerant missionaries who has been instructed to take nothing along on the mission (Saying 26). It makes complete sense that the missionary would entrust his finances to his servants, and hence the story talks about the responsibilities of those who remain to preserve and maintain the household while the master conducts the mission. The master, by virtue of the mission, does not engage in providing for either himself or his household because God will provide. The responsible agents who remain at home must make the provisions for the household. Or again, the householder may signify God, Jesus, or the son of humanity—all of whom have withdrawn from the scene in order to allow the business of the divine empire to grow. However readers make sense of the first part, it sets the stage for what follows.

The first two servants in sections 2 and 3 have parallel experiences. Since all are given ten minas to begin with, one of these servants increases it by ten, and the other by five. Both of them receive the blessing of the master, who certifies, "you were trustworthy in little things, I will place you over many [more things]." The master used the occasion of his trip to test the ability of the servants, and these two emerged on the good side; their success brings them additional authority. The saying tells us that servants who do what the master expects will be rewarded and find favor in the master's sight. These servants will prosper, even though they did not perform at the same level, one making ten, the other five more minas.

Readers share the satisfaction of the trustworthy slaves. They have performed well and deservedly received a worthy commendation. In a different interpretation of this saying, missionaries successfully conduct the business of the divine empire while their households prosper and grow thanks to faithful servants.

The twist in the narrative occurs in section 4. The attitude shifts dramatically from faithful servants receiving accolades from their master to an accusatory and angry encounter. The third slave criticizes the master as a harsh person who seeks to gain by interest. Now the master is someone who seeks to do what Saying 9 prohibits: to lend money at interest and expect repayment. Readers suddenly change their minds about the master. He even admits that the slave's negative characterization is accurate; he repeats the accusation and then confronts the cowardice and fear of the servant.

The failed slave does three things: he fears, he makes decisions based on the character of the master, and he hides his treasure rather than developing it. The negative turn in the story does not make this slave more appealing to readers, but more problematic. The slave's fear, which caused him to bury the minas instead of putting them in the bank to gain interest, jolts the reader. If the story vindicates the slave's perspective, why should he fear? Readers already know that they should not fear one such as the master, but only God (Saying 49). This slave's response displays the debilitating effect of fear on those who would engage in the business of managing the divine empire. Fear reveals an insufficient faith or level of trust.

The second problem with the slave's response is that he judges the master, accusing the master of gaining from work he had not done. On the one hand, the sayings affirm that laborers should receive a just recompense (Saying 27), but they also affirm that participants in the Jesus movements ought not to create a hierarchy of goodness (Saying 13, regarding students and teachers, for example), nor should they automatically reject anyone before endeavoring to bring them into the divine empire (Saying 28 provides for rejection, but not condemnation). The divine empire embraces all who seek to enter it and who agree to take responsibility. This slave failed by rejecting his master on the basis of his character.

Finally, the slave hides his treasure. The treasure resembles the lamp of Saying 43, hidden rather than employed appropriately to enlighten the mission. The burying of the minas runs counter to the public and enthusiastic proclamation of the empire of God (Saying 48). To bury the gift is tantamount to denying the message of the divine empire.

So the twist in the narrative with this third slave forces readers to consider new questions, new issues, and to construct meaning from a different perspective. But the finale of the story (5) demonstrates the inversion that characterizes the sayings of Jesus: the master orders that the money be taken away from the untrustworthy slave and given to the one who made the most, "for all things will be given to the one who has, but even what he has will be taken from the one who does not have." Here's the clincher! The one who has will gain; the one who has not will lose everything. Those who have entered into the divine empire and done their business well will gain everything, while those who have refused to enter the divine empire will lose everything. Jesus' saying turns the tables on failure. The inversion of this last part sets the stage for a negative reading of the unfaithful slave's thoughts and actions. The story condemns his refusal to invest in the business of the empire, while justifying the actions of those who do. The saying sets up expectations, thwarts them, attempts to shift readers' sympathies toward the fearful slave, but in the end comes back to the inversion that defines the divine empire.

The saying invokes yet another inversion. In the story of the dinner party (Saying 68), business prevented the initial invitees from attending the banquet, and they were condemned. Readers leave that saying thinking that to conduct business interferes with engagement with the divine empire. But here the saying affirms business, using it as an exemplar for the conduct of the divine empire. This saying reverses the earlier seeming condemnation of business. Readers must always be on guard against totalizing the message of any one saying and making it the complete story. Attitudes toward all things in a sayings collection remain fluid and malleable. Ideas shift and change in relationship to one another. The meaning of these sayings is never static. This complex saying about the master and his slaves adequately supports the dynamic view of reading these sayings.

Saying 88
Q 22:28, 30
Matthew 19:28 and Luke 22:28, 30

You who have followed me will sit upon thrones passing sentence upon the twelve tribes of Israel.

The final saying of this collection of Jesus' sayings affirms the status and power of those who have followed him. Again, the saying invokes the scene of final judgment. This scene, however, elevates those who have followed Jesus to the status of judges, sitting on thrones, passing judgment on the Israelites. It is a dramatic end to the collection of sayings.

The tribes of Israel have not been mentioned before in these sayings. The tribes function as a symbol for the historical origins of the Jesus movements and represent the forebears to the Jesus movements. Participants in the movements had varying degrees of connection to the earlier revelation. From the perspective of the Jesus movements, however, the ascendancy belonged to them. Their following Jesus entitled them to a throne and to passing sentence upon others.

The twelve tribes, however, do not necessarily stand outside the divine empire or outside the Jesus movements. Paul envisions that "the saints will judge the world" and that they are also "to judge angels" (1 Corinthians 6:2–3 RSV). Sitting on the throne in judgment does not imply that those being judged remain outside the divine empire (in the case of these sayings) or the body of Christ (for Paul). Judging those in the Jesus movements and of the twelve tribes falls to the saints who have followed Jesus and entered into God's empire.

Readers should read this saying in context. It is spoken to the hungry, the poor, the grieving, the rejected, the scorned, the belittled, the humiliated ones. The affirmation and exaltation of this saying addresses people whose lives in no way would position them for such status and authority except in the empire of God, where all the patterns are reversed and where God has replaced the Roman Empire with God's own empire. This saying represents the final exaltation of those who were the lowest (Saying 65), giving them thrones in the divine empire worthy of their faithfulness and trust in God. This saying enacts the reversals and the blessings affirmed throughout the sayings.

Scripture Index

MATTHEW *(continued)*		10:24–25a	19 (Saying 13)
5:1–4	17 (Saying 4)	10:26–27	29–30 (Saying 48)
5:6	17 (Saying 4)	10:28	30 (Saying 49)
5:11–12	17 (Saying 5)	10:29–31	30 (Saying 50)
5:13	37 (Saying 72)	10:32–33	30 (Saying 51)
5:15	28 (Saying 43)	10:34–35	33 (Saying 58)
5:44–45	17 (Saying 6)	10:37	36 (Saying 69)
5:18	37 (Saying 75)	10:38	36 (Saying 70)
5:25–26	33 (Saying 60)	10:39	36 (Saying 71)
5:32	38 (Saying 76)	10:40	24 (Saying 30)
5:39b–42	17 (Saying 7)	11:2–6	20–21 (Saying 19)
5:46–47	18 (Saying 9)	11:7–11	21 (Saying 20)
5:48	18 (Saying 10)	11:12–13	37 (Saying 74)
6:9–13a	25 (Saying 34)	11:16–19	21–22 (Saying 22)
6:19–21	31 (Saying 54)	11:21–24	24 (Saying 29)
6:22–23	28 (Saying 44)	11:25–26	24 (Saying 31)
6:24	37 (Saying 73)	11:27	24 (Saying 32)
6:25–33	31–32 (Saying 55)	11:29	26 (Saying 37)
7:1–2	18 (Saying 11)	12:25–28	26 (Saying 36)
7:3–5	19 (Saying 14)	12:30	26 (Saying 38)
7:7–11	25 (Saying 35)	12:32a–b	31 (Saying 52)
7:12	18 (Saying 8)	12:33–35	19 (Saying 15)
7:13–14	34 (Saying 63)	12:38–40	27 (Saying 41)
7:16b	19 (Saying 15)	12:41–42	27–28 (Saying 42)
7:18	19 (Saying 15)	12:43–45	27 (Saying 39)
7:21	19 (Saying 16)	13:16–17	25 (Saying 33)
7:22–23	34 (Saying 63)	13:31–32	34 (Saying 61)
7:24–27	20 (Saying 17)	13:33	34 (Saying 62)
7:28a	20 (Saying 18)	15:14	18 (Saying 12)
8:5–10	20 (Saying 18)	16:2–3	33 (Saying 59)
8:11–12	35 (Saying 64)	17:20b	39 (Saying 81)
8:13	20 (Saying 18)	18:6–7	38 (Saying 77)
8:19–22	22 (Saying 23)	18:12–13	38 (Saying 78)
9:32–34	26 (Saying 36)	18:15	39 (Saying 80)
9:37–38	22 (Saying 24)	18:21	39 (Saying 80)
10:7–8	23 (Saying 27)	19:28	41 (Saying 88)
10:9–10a	23 (Saying 26)	20:16	35 (Saying 65)
10:10b–13	23 (Saying 27)	21:32	21 (Saying 21)
10:14–15	23 (Saying 28)	22:2–10	36 (Saying 68)
10:16	23 (Saying 25)	23:1–2a	28–29 (Saying 45)
10:19	31 (Saying 53)	23:4	29 (Saying 46)

Subject Index